Memory Thinking for Rust

Slides with Descriptions and Source Code Illustrations

Second Editon

Dmitry Vostokov
Software Diagnostics Services

OpenTask

Memory Thinking for Rust: Slides with Descriptions and Source Code Illustrations, Second Editon

Published by OpenTask, Republic of Ireland

OpenTask books are available through booksellers and distributors worldwide. For further information or comments, send requests to press@opentask.com.

Product and company names mentioned in this book may be trademarks of their owners.

A CIP catalog record for this book is available from the British Library.

ISBN-13: 978-1912636488 (Paperback)

Revision 2.02 (May 2025)

Table of Contents

4

8

Preface

This reference book is a part of the Memory Thinking for Rust training course organized by Software Diagnostics Services[1]. The text contains slides, brief notes highlighting particular points, and related source code with execution output. The book's detailed Table of Contents makes the usual Index redundant. We hope this reference is helpful for the following audiences:

- Rust developers who want to deepen their knowledge;
- Non-C and C++ developers (for example, Java, Scala, Python) who want to learn more about pointer and reference internals;
- C and C++ developers who want to port their memory thinking to Rust quickly.

The new edition updates and extends the existing topics, adding some missing in the first edition.

If you encounter any error, please use the contact form on the Software Diagnostics Services web site or, alternatively, via Twitter @DumpAnalysis.

Facebook group:

http://www.facebook.com/groups/dumpanalysis

LinkedIn page and group:

https://www.linkedin.com/company/software-diagnostics-institute/
https://www.linkedin.com/groups/8473045/

---

[1] www.patterndiagnostics.com

About the Author

Dmitry Vostokov is an internationally recognized expert, speaker, educator, scientist, inventor, and author. He founded the pattern-oriented software diagnostics, forensics, and prognostics discipline (Systematic Software Diagnostics) and Software Diagnostics Institute (DA+TA: DumpAnalysis.org + TraceAnalysis.org). Vostokov has also authored over 50 books on software diagnostics, anomaly detection and analysis, software and memory forensics, root cause analysis and problem solving, memory dump analysis, debugging, software trace and log analysis, reverse engineering, and malware analysis. He has over 30 years of experience in software architecture, design, development, and maintenance in various industries, including leadership, technical, and people management roles. Dmitry founded OpenTask Iterative and Incremental Publishing (OpenTask.com) and Software Diagnostics Technology and Services (former Memory Dump Analysis Services) PatternDiagnostics.com. In his spare time, he explores Software Narratology and Quantum Software Diagnostics. His interest areas are theoretical software diagnostics and its mathematical and computer science foundations, application of formal logic, semiotics, artificial intelligence, machine learning, and data mining to diagnostics and anomaly detection, software diagnostics engineering and diagnostics-driven development, diagnostics workflow and interaction. Recent interest areas also include functional programming, cloud native computing, monitoring, observability, visualization, security, automation, applications of category theory to software diagnostics, development and big data, and diagnostics of artificial intelligence.

Introduction

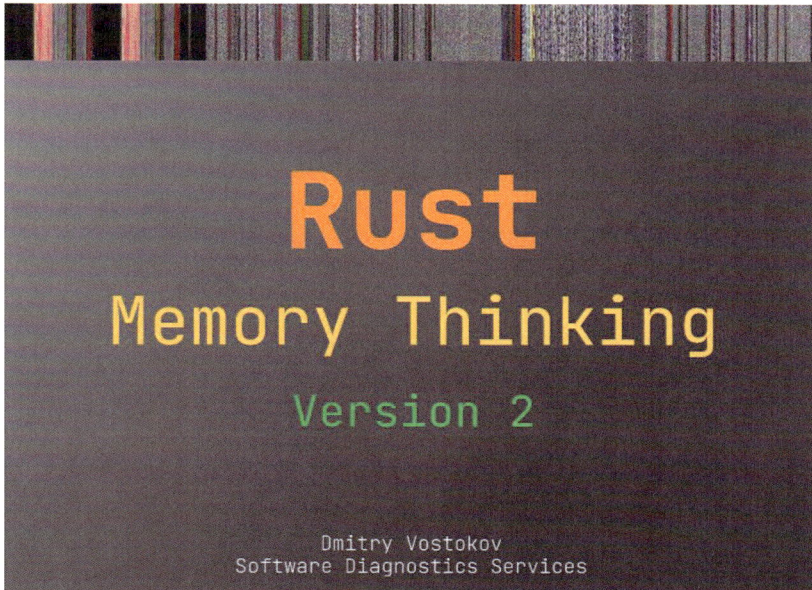

Prerequisites

To get most of this training, you are expected to have basic development experience in Rust, C, or C++ and optional basic memory dump analysis experience. I also included the necessary x64 and A64 disassembly reviews for some topics. If you don't have memory dump analysis experience, you will also learn some basics too, because we use the Microsoft debugger, WinDbg from Debugging Tools for Windows, or the WinDbg app for some exercises, and GDB for Linux exercise variants.

Training Goals

Training Goals

- Review fundamentals of Rust

- Review Rust specifics from a memory analysis perspective

- Use WinDbg and GDB for learning Rust internals

© 2025 Software Diagnostics Services

Our primary goal is to review Rust from a memory analysis perspective. First, we review the fundamentals of Rust. Then, we learn various Rust features, focusing on memory and internals. Throughout our course, we use WinDbg and GDB for exploration.

Warning

Warning

This is not a Rust course for C or C++ developers. But knowledge of C and C++ helps.

© 2025 Software Diagnostics Services

Here is just a warning if you assume this course presupposes the knowledge of C or C++. This course assumes that you don't know C and C++. However, such knowledge may help.

Training Principles

Training Principles

- ◉ Talk only about what I can show

- ◉ Lots of pictures

- ◉ Lots of examples

- ◉ Original content and examples

© 2025 Software Diagnostics Services

There were many training formats to consider, and I decided that the best approach was to concentrate on slides, code examples, and hands-on demonstrations that could be verified.

Schedule

Schedule

```
◉ let sessions: Vec<Session> =
      vec![Session::default(); 10];

◉ assert_eq!(sessions.len(), 10);

◉ assert!(sessions.capacity() >= 10);
```

© 2025 Software Diagnostics Services

Originally, I planned the training to have only 5 one-hour sessions, but I gradually extended it to 10 sessions to fit all necessary material in sufficient detail.

Training Idea

Training Idea

- Similar C and C++ courses for Windows and Linux
- System programming language role
- Memory dump analysis training courses
- Debugging training courses

© 2025 Software Diagnostics Services

After I created similar Windows-based and Linux-based training for C and C++, it was natural to port it to Rust since it conceptually shares some memory semantics with C and C++ and has a system programming language role. Also, attendees of debugging, memory dump, and core dump analysis training courses may benefit from Rust memory thinking training since Rust is now a somewhat "official" language in both Windows and Linux.

General Rust Aspects

General Rust Aspects

- Philosophy of unsafe pointers
- Philosophy of values
- Rust: a Copernican revolution
- Rust philosophy of values
- Ownership
- Lifetime
- Rust philosophy of pointers
- References
- Static, stack, and heap memory
- Memory and pointers
- Basic types
- Size and alignment
- Conversion
- Tuples and tuple-like structs
- Structs
- Source code and symbols
- Free functions
- Function pointers and references
- Associated functions
- Type-associated functions
- Trait functions and objects
- Trait object memory layout
- Dynamic dispatch
- Constructors and destructors
- Clone and Copy
- Parameters by value
- Parameters by reference/pointer
- Closures and captures
- Pinning
- Smart pointers
- Return values
- Trait object parameters
- Enums
- Const values

© 2025 Software Diagnostics Services

The general Rust aspects that we discuss in this course:

- Philosophy of unsafe pointers
- Philosophy of values
- Rust: a Copernican revolution
- Rust philosophy of values
- Ownership
- Lifetime
- Rust philosophy of pointers
- References
- Static, stack, and heap memory
- Memory and pointers
- Basic types
- Size and alignment
- Conversion
- Tuples and tuple-like structs

- Structs
- Source code and symbols
- Free functions
- Function pointers and references
- Associated functions
- Type-associated functions
- Trait functions and objects
- Trait object memory layout
- Dynamic dispatch
- Constructors and destructors
- Clone and Copy
- Parameters by value
- Parameters by reference/pointer
- Closures and captures
- Pinning
- Smart pointers
- Return values
- Trait object parameters
- Enums
- Const values

What We Do Not Cover

What We Do Not Cover

We promise to include these topics in the third edition

© 2025 Software Diagnostics Services

Of course, there are Rust topics that we did not include. I promise to include them in the third edition.

Linux Rust Aspects

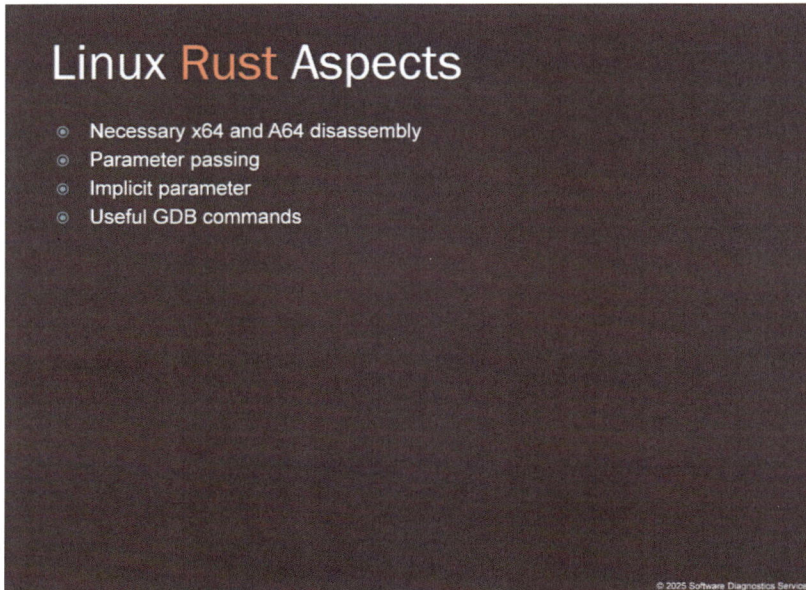

In addition, we also discuss related Linux aspects, including:

- Necessary x64 and A64 disassembly
- Parameter passing
- Implicit parameter
- Useful GDB commands

Windows Rust Aspects

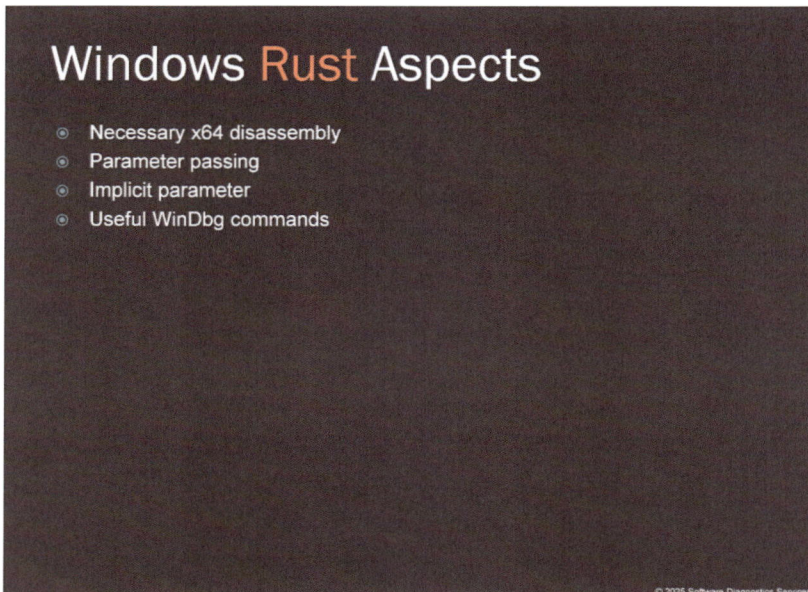

We also discuss related Windows aspects, including:

- Necessary x64 disassembly
- Parameter passing
- Implicit parameter
- Useful WinDbg commands

Why Rust?

First, why did we create this course? If you develop in Rust, memory thinking will help you become a better developer and maintainer of Rust projects, especially if you use a lot of unsafe code in your projects. Even if you don't develop in Rust, knowledge of Rust memory internals is necessary for many post-construction activities, such as memory dump analysis, since it becomes a part of an operating system. Imagine Rust displaces C and C++ by 2049, but all listed activities on this slide remain:

- Interfacing
- Malware analysis
- Vulnerability analysis and exploitation
- Reversing
- Diagnostics
- Low-level debugging
- OS Monitoring
- Memory forensics
- Crash and hang analysis
- Secure coding
- Static code analysis
- Trace and log analysis

My Genealogy of Rust

This history slide is only about Rust and the genealogy of my knowledge through C, C++, and Scala languages. As you see, my main programming languages are C and C++, and I also worked for a static C++ analysis company specializing in C++ and C++ Standard Library semantics. I first heard about Rust and its fat pointers in 2015 when delivering a WinDbg debugging presentation. In 2020, I moved to functional programming in Scala, which also influenced my C++ coding for new projects and eased my transition to idiomatic Rust. I paid attention to Rust again since it is actively promoted by Microsoft, and, in addition to a few Rust exercises in the latest revisions of training courses, I wrote the whole Rust Windows memory dump analysis book last year.

Old CV

https://opentask.com/Vostokov/CV.htm

Rust Mastery Process

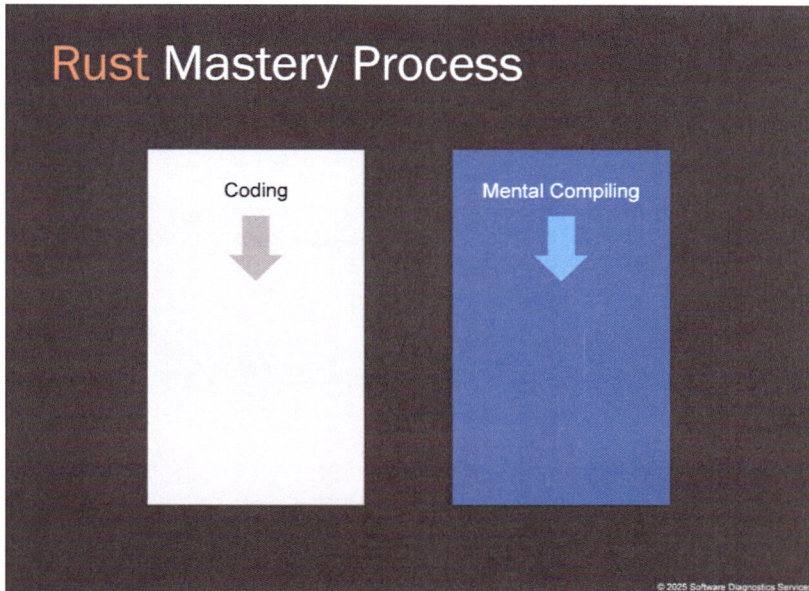

Despite high-level features in Rust, there's still much low-level overlap with how compilers work with memory, and when I program in Rust, I mentally compile to memory. This helps when I have a doubt about whether this or that construct. I also believe that looking at how Rust constructs are implemented in memory greatly helps in learning this language and also in interfacing with OS, C, and C++.

Thought Process

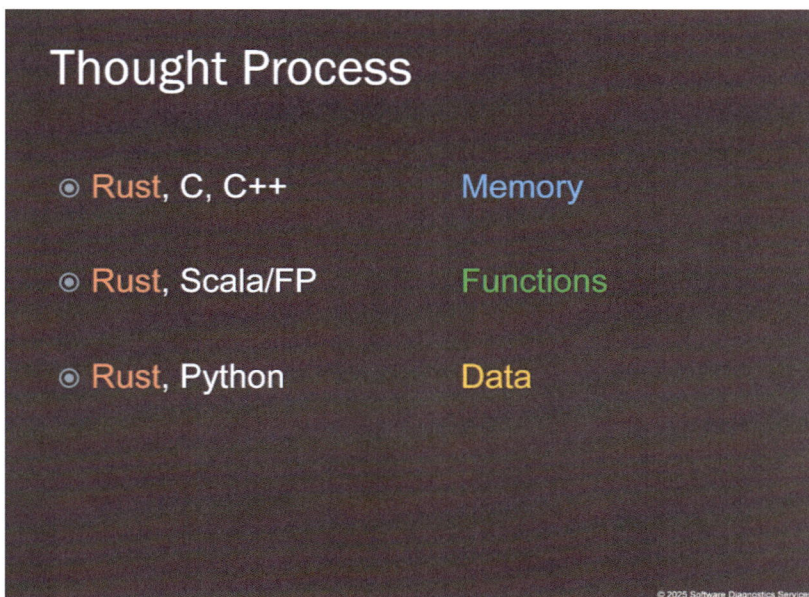

This slide about a thought process when using a programming language is perhaps controversial. With C and C++, we think about memory; with Scala/FP, we think about functions; and with Python, we think about data. But with Rust, we think about everything.

Philosophy of Unsafe Pointers

© 2025 Software Diagnostics Services

We start with pointers, the most important concept in languages like C and C++. Pointers, or more correctly, pointer types, are also used extensively in Rust, although with restrictions in safe code. Pointer usage in unsafe Rust code is conceptually like C and C++. I originally created this approach in 2015 but now extended it for this training.

A General Pointer Concept

A General Pointer Concept

Includes common features of:

⊙ Pointers, smart pointers, references, and function pointers in C and C++

⊙ References, raw pointers, smart pointers, and function pointers in Rust (safe and unsafe)

© 2025 Software Diagnostics Services

Pointer

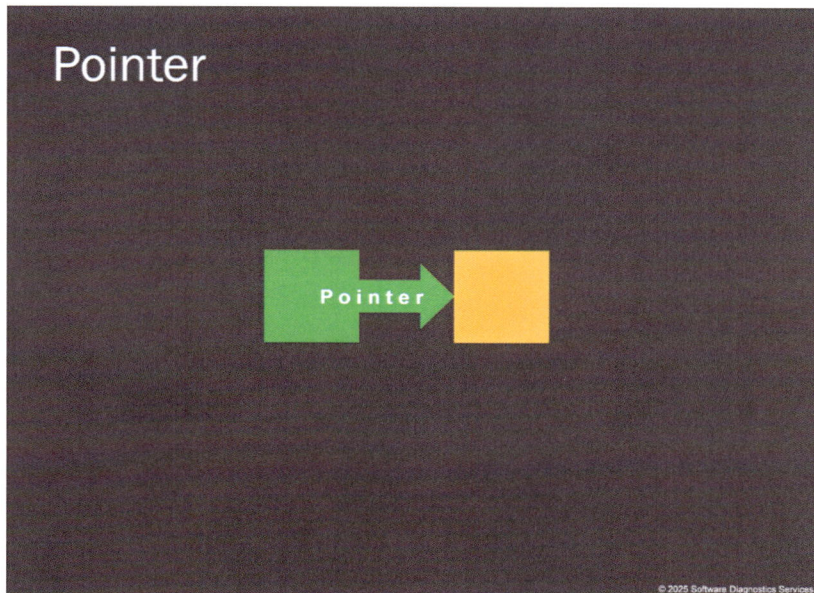

Conceptually, a pointer is an entity that refers (or points) to some other entity. We say entity, not an object, so as not to confuse it with objects in object-oriented programming. This can be my finger, for example, pointing to an apple.

Pointer Dereference

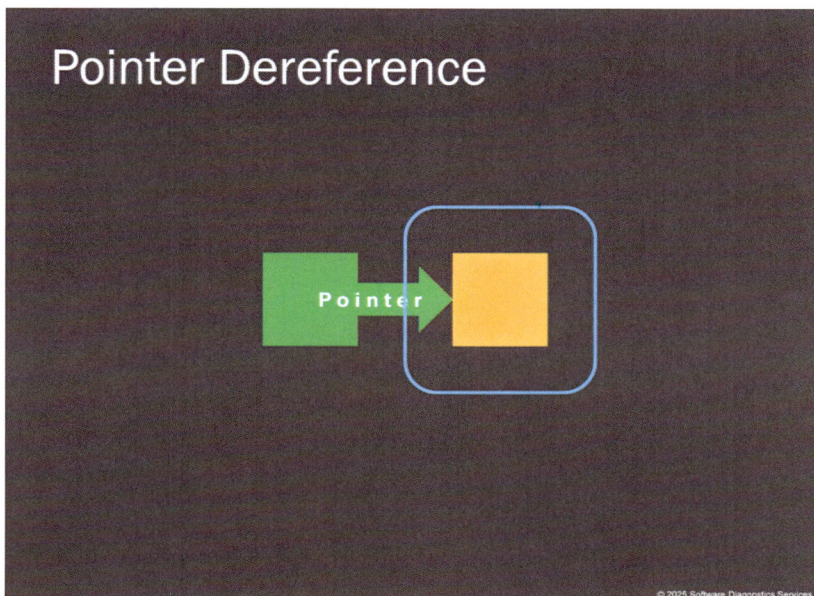

A pointer dereference is an act of getting the entity it references for further inspection or usage. Imagine I point to an apple, and you grab it to eat.

One to Many

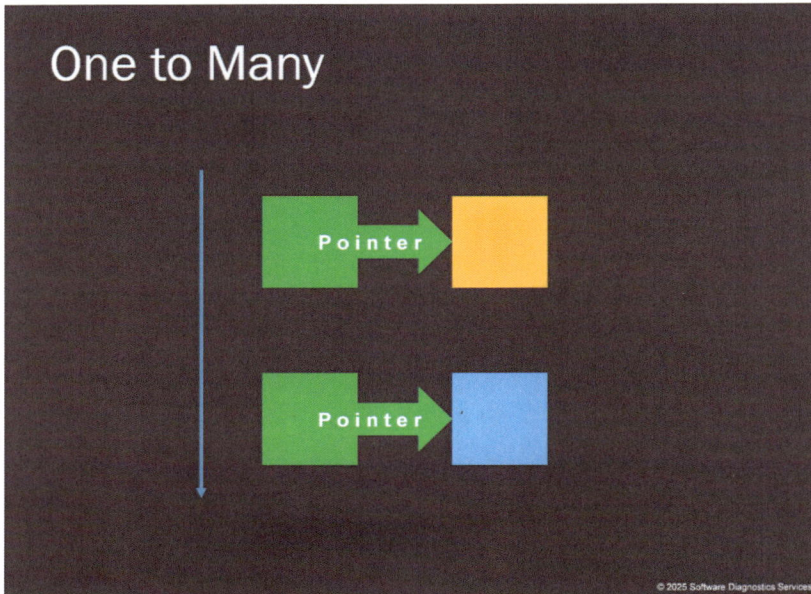

During its lifetime, a pointer may point to different entities. If no pointer points to an entity, it may become lost in certain execution scenarios, the so-called memory leak.

Many to One

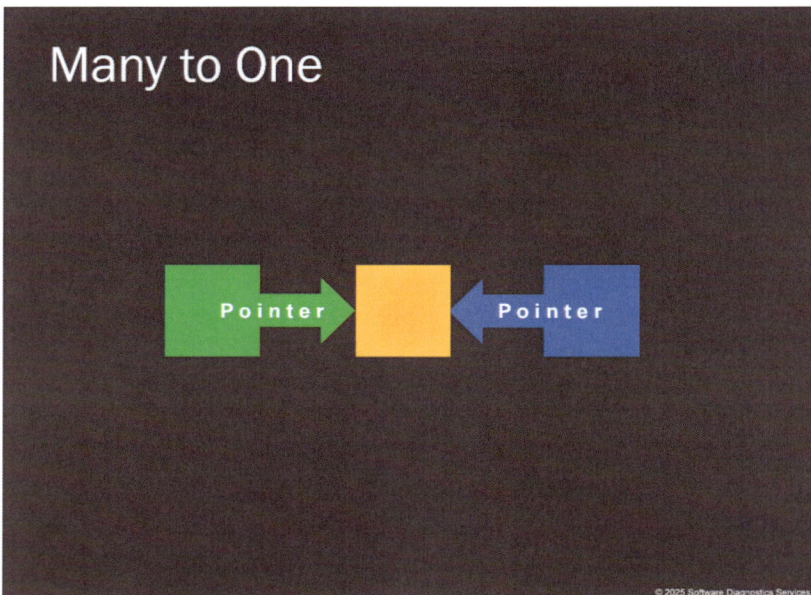

Several pointers can refer (or point) to the same entity. For example, two people are pointing to the same apple. So, conceptually, pointers are distinct from entities they point to. Should we call the latter pointees?

Many to One Dereference

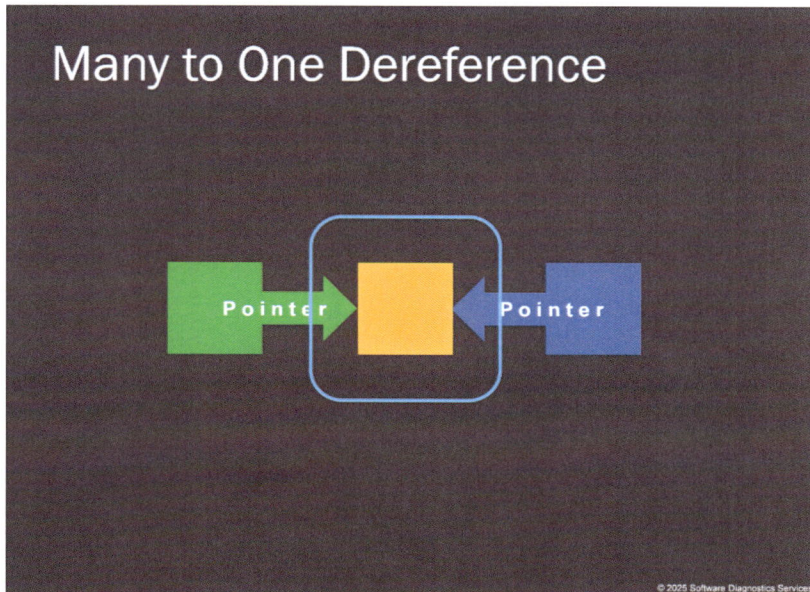

Of course, if you dereference a pointer pointing to the same object, you get the same object. If you grab an apple, I point to, at the same time as you do, we both get the same apple.

Invalid Pointer

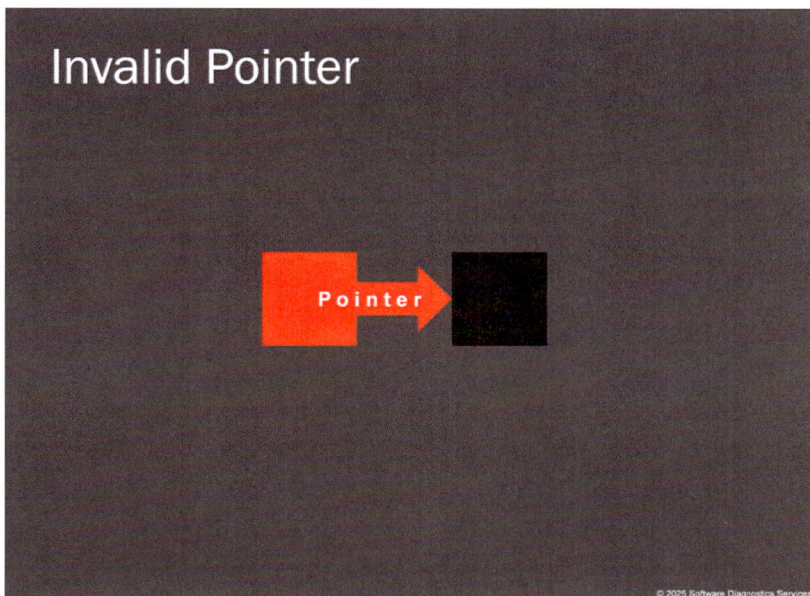

Some pointers may be invalid; for example, I may point to an imaginary apple.

Invalid Pointer Dereference

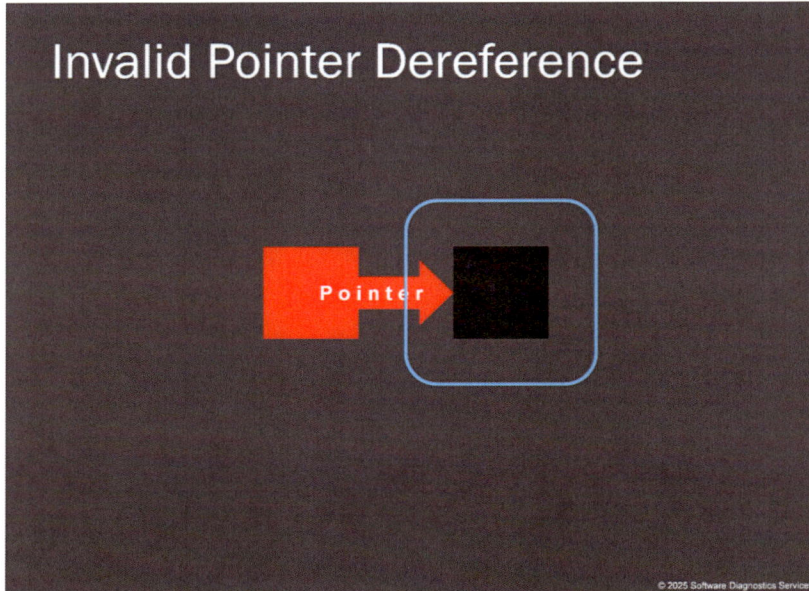

When you dereference an invalid pointer, you get a problem; for example, you fail to get an imaginary apple I point to.

Wild (Dangling) Pointer

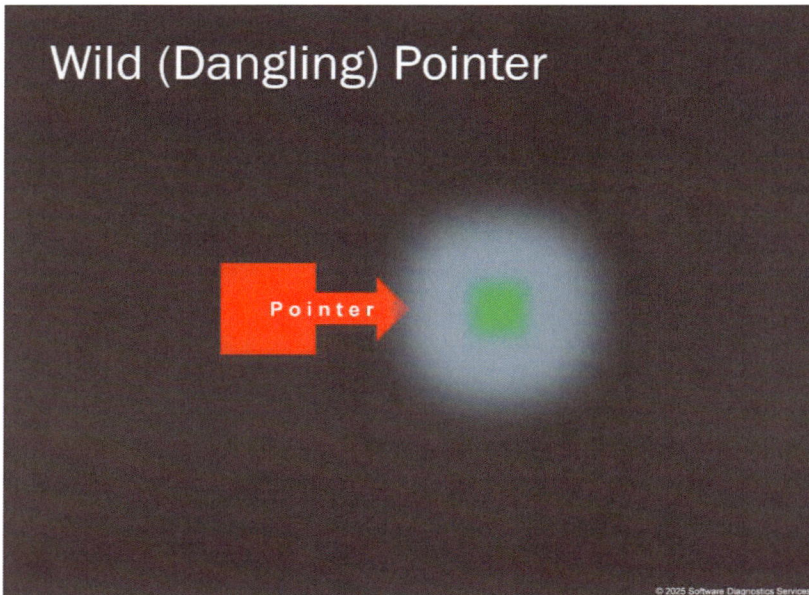

Some pointers are called dangling – they used to point to valid entities some time ago but not anymore, so a dereference fails. You're reaching for an apple that I point to, but someone snatches it a split second ago.

Pointer to Pointer

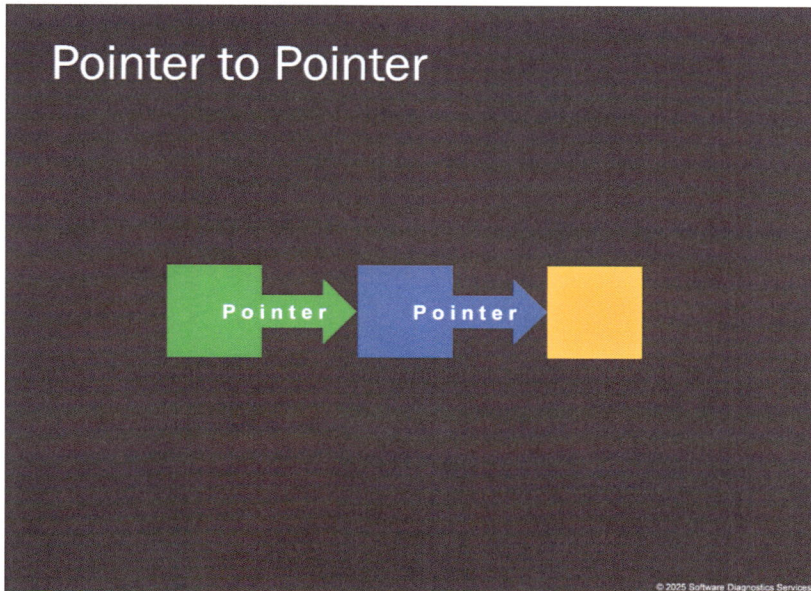

Since a pointer is also an entity that can be pointed to, there can be a chain of pointers. You point to me; I point to an apple.

Pointer to Pointer Dereference

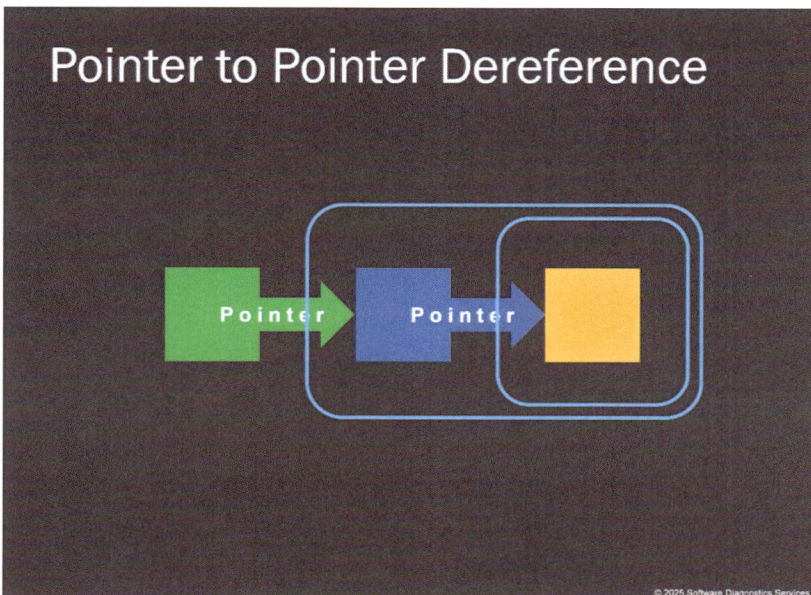

When we dereference the first pointer, we get an entity, another pointer, which we can also dereference to get the underlying entity. You point to me, but an alien snatches me with an apple I point to. Inside a ship, another alien takes an apple for analysis.

Naming Pointers and Entities

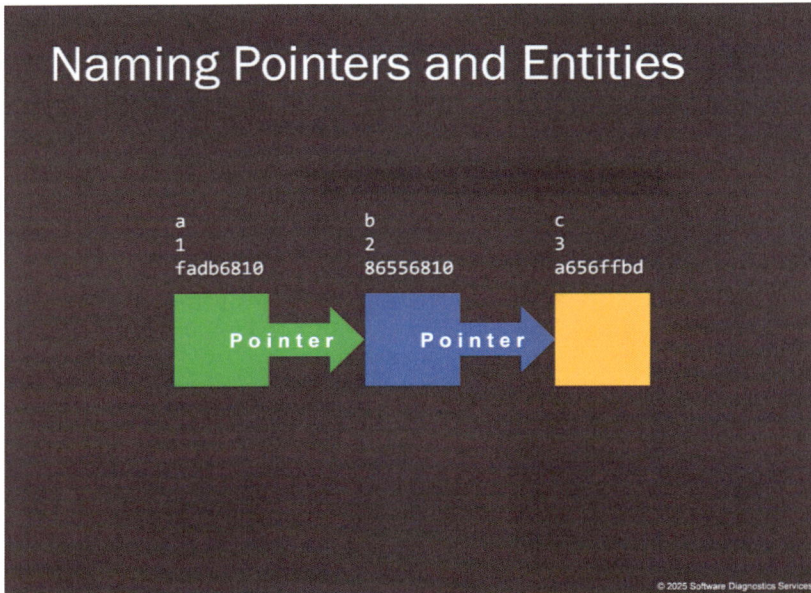

Names are distinct from entities. Names can be programming language identifiers or just unique numbers or IDs.

Names as Pointer Content

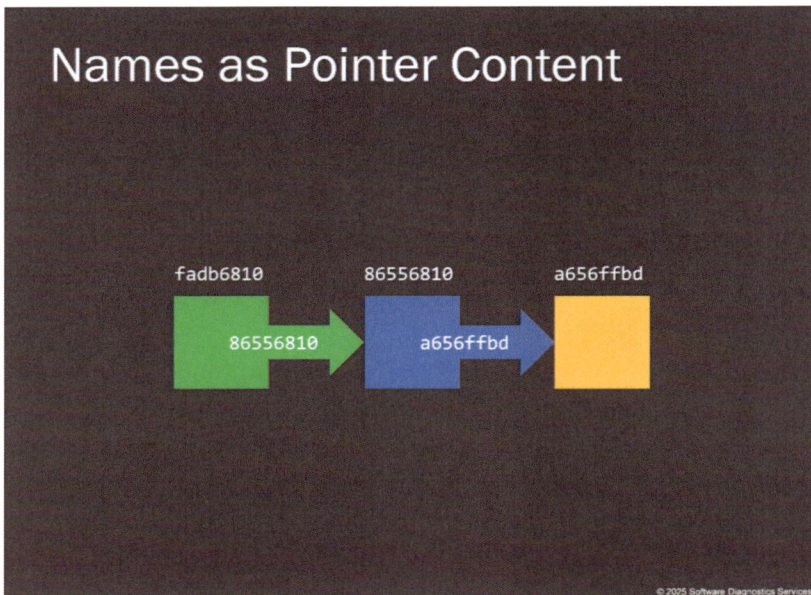

Pointers, as entities, may contain names, and these names may be names of pointers, too. If a pointer contains only a name, we say the pointer value is the name. So, the pointer value can be another pointer name, and the latter pointer value is the name of some other entity.

Pointers as Entities

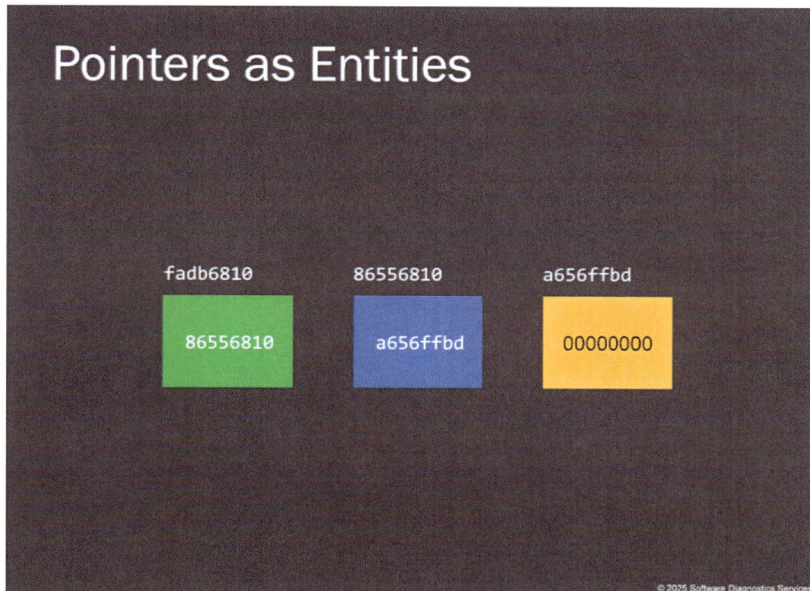

Pointer dereference is an act. If we put acts aside, pointers are just entities with some content that can be interpreted as a name if necessary. All these dereferences happen only at runtime. The pointer content (its value) may be invalid for all time without any problem until we use it.

Unsafe Rust Code Examples

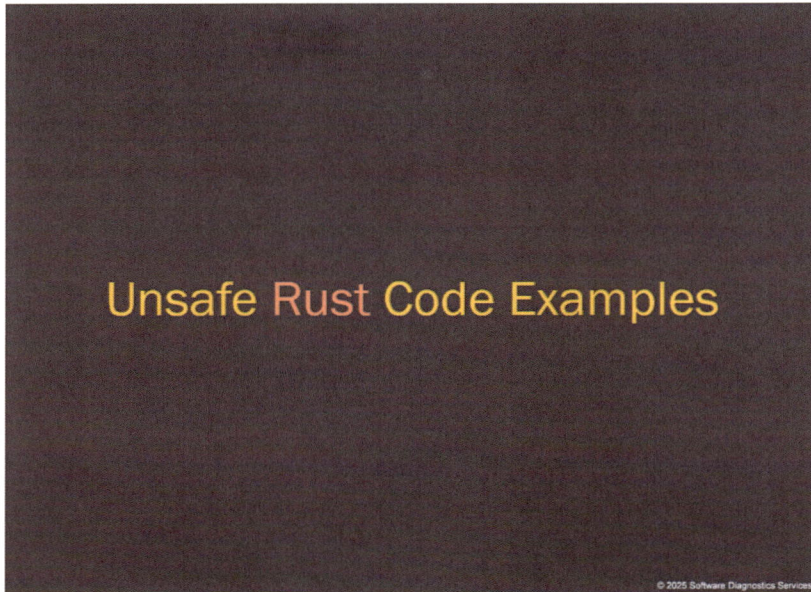

The `unsafe-pointers` project can be found in the archive[2]. In the following slide descriptions, we only show relevant code snippets and their output on various platforms.

[2] https://www.patterndiagnostics.com/Training/MTRust/MTRust.zip

Pointer

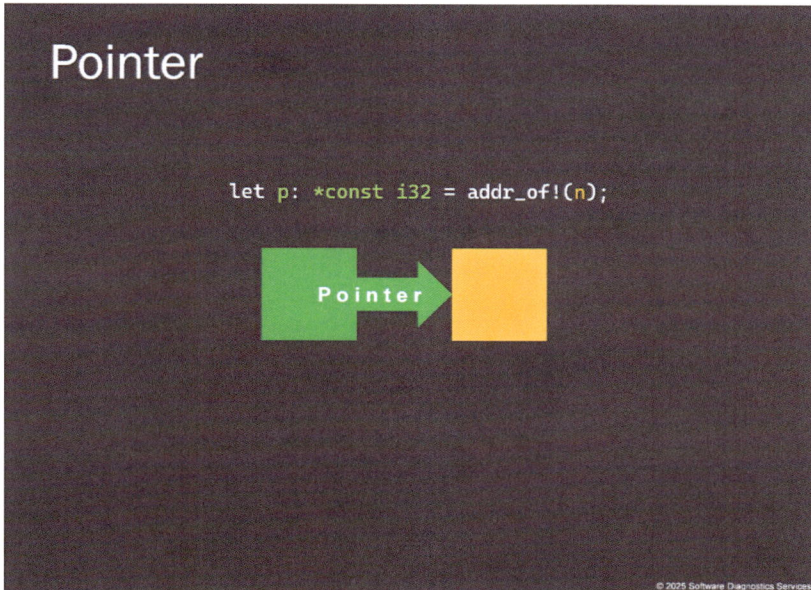

```rust
println!("--- Pointer ---");
// #[allow(unused_unsafe)]
// unsafe
{
    let n: i32 = 0;
    let p: *const i32 = addr_of!(n);

    println!("n value: {:?} address of n: {:?} \n\
        p value: {:?} address of p: {:?}", n, addr_of!(n), p, addr_of!(p));
}
```

Windows output:

```
--- Pointer ---
n value: 0 address of n: 0xb7a42fe44c
p value: 0xb7a42fe44c address of p: 0xb7a42fe450
```

x64 Linux output:

```
--- Pointer ---
n value: 0 address of n: 0x7ffda37659e4
p value: 0x7ffda37659e4 address of p: 0x7ffda37659e8
```

A64 Linux output:

```
--- Pointer ---
n value: 0 address of n: 0xffffff507a1c
p value: 0xffffff507a1c address of p: 0xffffff507a20
```

Unsafe Pointer Dereference

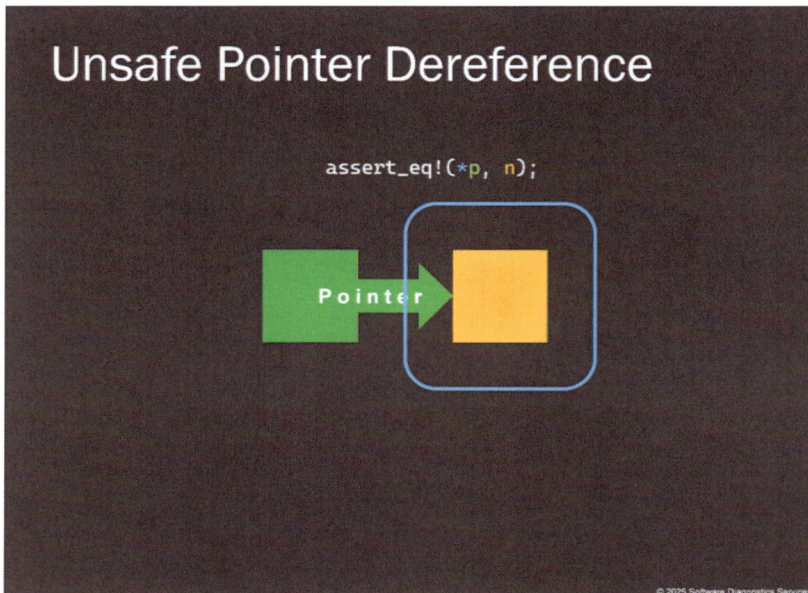

```
println!("--- Unsafe Pointer Dereference ---");
unsafe {
    let n: i32 = 0;
    let p: *const i32 = addr_of!(n);
    assert_eq!(*p, n);

    println!("n value: {:?} address of n: {:?} \n\
        p value: {:?} dereference of p: {:?} address of p: {:?}",
        n, addr_of!(n), p, *p, addr_of!(p));
}
```

Windows output:

```
--- Unsafe Pointer Dereference ---
n value: 0 address of n: 0xb7a42fe50c
p value: 0xb7a42fe50c dereference of p: 0 address of p: 0xb7a42fe510
```

x64 Linux output:

```
--- Unsafe Pointer Dereference ---
n value: 0 address of n: 0x7ffda3765aa4
p value: 0x7ffda3765aa4 dereference of p: 0 address of p: 0x7ffda3765aa8
```

A64 Linux output:

```
--- Unsafe Pointer Dereference ---
n value: 0 address of n: 0xffffff507adc
p value: 0xffffff507adc dereference of p: 0 address of p: 0xffffff507ae0
```

One to Many

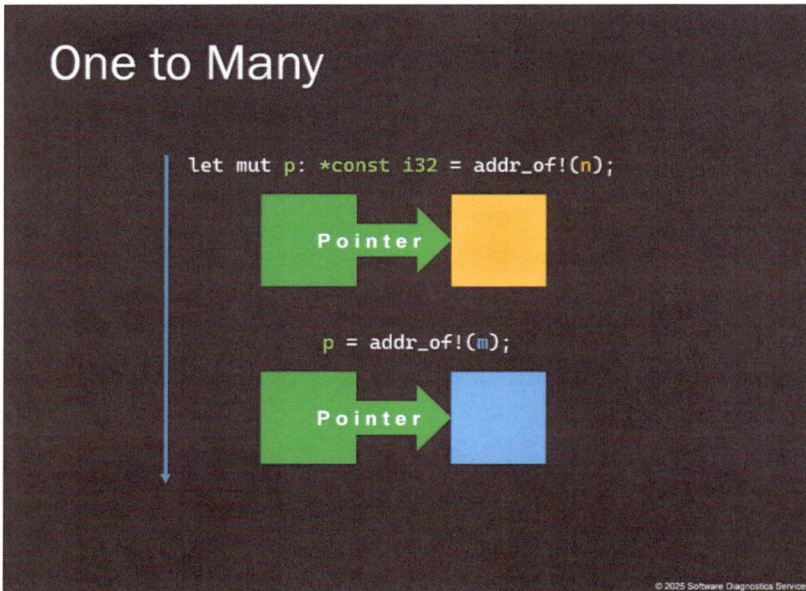

```
println!("--- One to Many ---");
// #[allow(unused_unsafe)]
// unsafe
{
    let n: i32 = 0;
    let mut p: *const i32 = addr_of!(n);

    println!("n value: {:?} address of n: {:?} \n\
        p value: {:?} address of p: {:?}",
        n, addr_of!(n), p, addr_of!(p));

    let m: i32 = 1;
    p = addr_of!(m);

    println!("m value: {:?} address of m: {:?} \n\
        p value: {:?} address of p: {:?}",
        m, adcr_of!(m), p, addr_of!(p));
}
```

Windows output:

```
--- One to Many ---
n value: 0 address of n: 0xeeae5de264
p value: 0xeeae5de264 address of p: 0xeeae5de268
m value: 1 address of m: 0xeeae5de334
p value: 0xeeae5de334 address of p: 0xeeae5de268
```

x64 Linux output:

```
--- One to Many ---
n value: 0 address of n: 0x7ffd6791a9c4
p value: 0x7ffd6791a9c4 address of p: 0x7ffd6791a9c8
m value: 1 address of m: 0x7ffd6791aa54
p value: 0x7ffd6791aa54 address of p: 0x7ffd6791a9c8
```

A64 Linux output:

```
--- One to Many ---
n value: 0 address of n: 0xffffc16f0314
p value: 0xffffc16f0314 address of p: 0xffffc16f0318
m value: 1 address of m: 0xffffc16f03ec
p value: 0xffffc16f03ec address of p: 0xffffc16f0318
```

Memory Leak

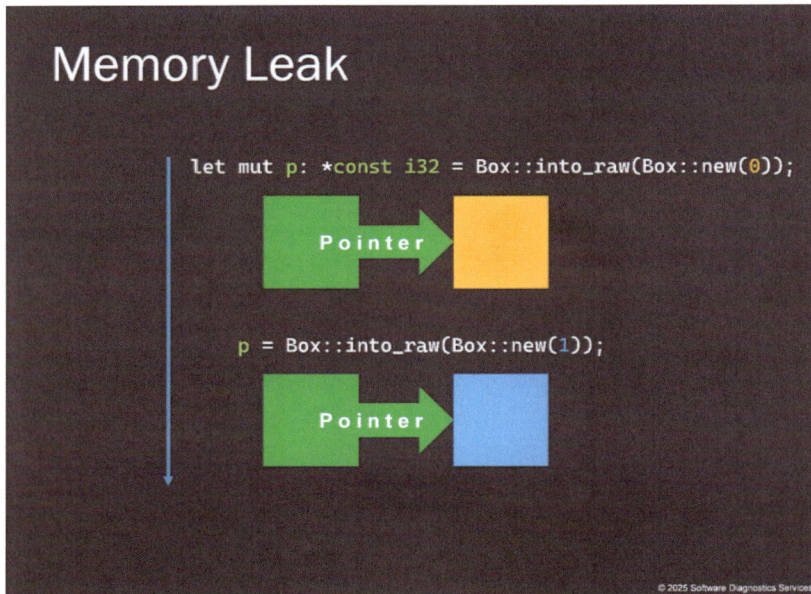

```rust
println!("--- Memory Leak ---");
unsafe {
    let mut p: *const i32 = Box::into_raw(Box::new(0));

    println!("p value: {:?} dereference of p: {:?} address of p: {:?}",
        p, *p, addr_of!(p));

    //loop {
        p = Box::into_raw(Box::new(1));

        println!("p value: {:?} dereference of p: {:?} address of p: {:?}",
            p, *p, addr_of!(p));
    //}
}
```

Windows output:

```
--- Memory Leak ---
p value: 0x1c8c7d0ade0 dereference of p: 0 address of p: 0x64a015e508
p value: 0x1c8c7d10a70 dereference of p: 1 address of p: 0x64a015e508
```

x64 Linux output:

```
--- Memory Leak ---
p value: 0x5557e04d9a50 dereference of p: 0 address of p: 0x7ffd90a5ad38
p value: 0x5557e04d9a70 dereference of p: 1 address of p: 0x7ffd90a5ad38
```

A64 Linux output:

```
--- Memory Leak ---
p value: 0xc06dac03fb10 dereference of p: 0 address of p: 0xffffd4101788
p value: 0xc06dac03fb30 dereference of p: 1 address of p: 0xffffd4101788
```

Many to One

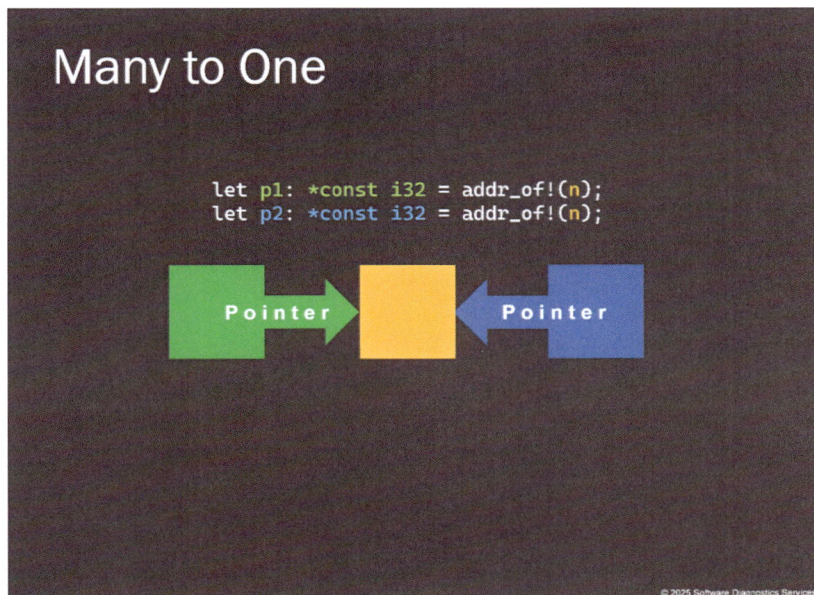

```
println!("--- Many to One ---");
// #[allow(unused_unsafe)]
// unsafe
{
    let n: i32 = 0;
    let mut p: *const i32 = addr_of!(n);

    println!("n value: {:?} address of n: {:?} \n\
        p value: {:?} address of p: {:?}",
        n, addr_of!(n), p, addr_of!(p));

    let m: i32 = 1;
    p = addr_of!(m);

    println!("m value: {:?} address of m: {:?} \n\
        p value: {:?} address of p: {:?}",
        m, addr_of!(m), p, addr_of!(p));
}
```

Windows output:

```
--- Many to One ---
n value: 0 address of n: 0xb7a42fe624
p1 value: 0xb7a42fe624 address of p1: 0xb7a42fe628
p2 value: 0xb7a42fe624 address of p2: 0xb7a42fe630
```

x64 Linux output:

```
--- Many to One ---
n value: 0 address of n: 0x7ffda3765bbc
p1 value: 0x7ffda3765bbc address of p1: 0x7ffda3765bc0
p2 value: 0x7ffda3765bbc address of p2: 0x7ffda3765bc8
```

A64 Linux output:

```
--- Many to One ---
n value: 0 address of n: 0xffffff507bf4
p1 value: 0xffffff507bf4 address of p1: 0xffffff507bf8
p2 value: 0xffffff507bf4 address of p2: 0xffffff507c00
```

Unsafe Many to One Dereference

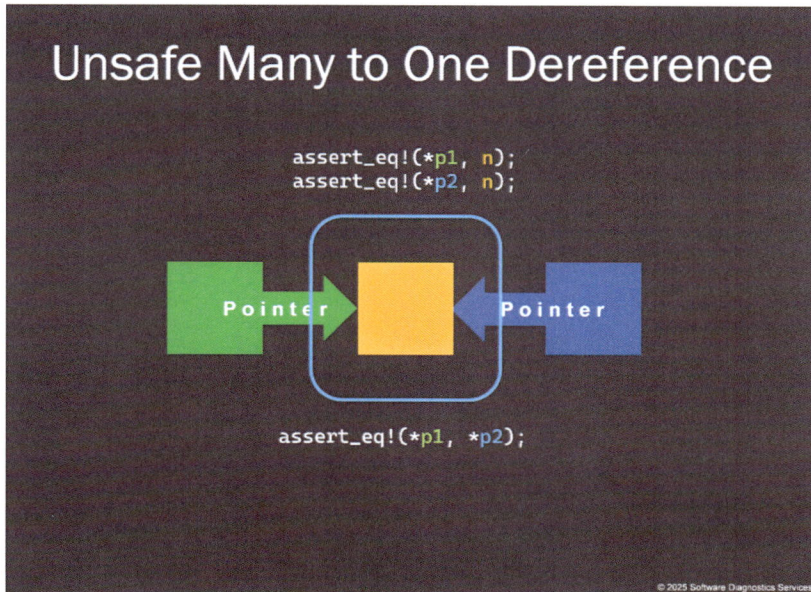

```rust
println!("--- Unsafe Many to One Dereference ---");
unsafe {
    let n: i32 = 0;
    let p1: *const i32 = addr_of!(n);
    let p2: *const i32 = addr_of!(n);
    assert_eq!(*p1, *p2);

    println!("n value: {:?} address of n: {:?} \n\
        p1 value: {:?} dereference of p1: {:?} address of p1: {:?} \n\
        p2 value: {:?} dereference of p2: {:?} address of p2: {:?}",
        n, addr_of!(n), p1, *p1, addr_of!(p1), p2, *p2,
        addr_of!(p2));
}
```

Windows output:

```
--- Unsafe Many to One Dereference ---
n value: 0 address of n: 0xb7a42fe75c
p1 value: 0xb7a42fe75c dereference of p1: 0 address of p1: 0xb7a42fe760
p2 value: 0xb7a42fe75c dereference of p2: 0 address of p2: 0xb7a42fe768
```

x64 Linux output:

```
--- Unsafe Many to One Dereference ---
n value: 0 address of n: 0x7ffda3765cf4
p1 value: 0x7ffda3765cf4 dereference of p1: 0 address of p1: 0x7ffda3765cf8
p2 value: 0x7ffda3765cf4 dereference of p2: 0 address of p2: 0x7ffda3765d00
```

A64 Linux output:

```
--- Unsafe Many to One Dereference ---
n value: 0 address of n: 0xffffff507d2c
p1 value: 0xffffff507d2c dereference of p1: 0 address of p1: 0xffffff507d30
p2 value: 0xffffff507d2c dereference of p2: 0 address of p2: 0xffffff507d38
```

Invalid Pointer

```rust
println!("--- Invalid Pointer ---");
// #[allow(unused_unsafe)]
// unsafe
{
    let p: *const i32 = 0xffff_ffff_0000_0000 as *const i32;

    println!("p value: {:?} address of p: {:?}", p, addr_of!(p));
}
```

Windows output:

```
--- Invalid Pointer ---
p value: 0xffffffff00000000 address of p: 0xb7a42fe8b0
```

x64 Linux output:

```
--- Invalid Pointer ---
p value: 0xffffffff00000000 address of p: 0x7ffda3765e48
```

A64 Linux output:

```
--- Invalid Pointer ---
p value: 0xffffffff00000000 address of p: 0xffffff507e80
```

Unsafe Invalid Pointer Dereference (Alignment)

```rust
println!("--- Unsafe Invalid Pointer Dereference (alignment) ---");
unsafe {
    let p: *mut i32 = 1_usize as *mut i32;

    println!("p value: {:?} address of p: {:?}", p,
        addr_of!(p));

    // *p = 0;
}
```

Windows output:

```
--- Unsafe Invalid Pointer Dereference (alignment) ---
p value: 0x1 address of p: 0xb7a42fe940
```

x64 Linux output:

```
--- Unsafe Invalid Pointer Dereference (alignment) ---
p value: 0x1 address of p: 0x7ffda3765ed8
```

A64 Linux output:

```
--- Unsafe Invalid Pointer Dereference (alignment) ---
p value: 0x1 address of p: 0xffffff507f10
```

Unsafe Invalid Pointer Dereference (Access Violation)

```
println!("--- Unsafe Invalid Pointer Dereference (access violation) ---");
unsafe {
    let p: *mut i32 = 4_usize as *mut i32;

    println!("p value: {:?} address of p: {:?}", p,
        addr_of!(p));

    // *p = 0;
}
```

Windows output:

```
--- Unsafe Invalid Pointer Dereference (access violation) ---
p value: 0x4 address of p: 0xb7a42fe9d0
```

x64 Linux output:

```
--- Unsafe Invalid Pointer Dereference (access violation) ---
p value: 0x4 address of p: 0x7ffda3765f68
```

A64 Linux output:

```
--- Unsafe Invalid Pointer Dereference (access violation) ---
p value: 0x4 address of p: 0xffffff507fa0
```

Unsafe Wild (Dangling) Pointer

```rust
println!("--- Unsafe Wild (Dangling) Pointer ---");
unsafe {
    let pn: Box<i32> = Box::new(0);
    let p: *mut i32 = Box::into_raw(pn);

    println!("p value: {:?} dereference of p: {:?} address of p: {:?}",
        p, *p, addr_of!(p));

    // drop(Box::from_raw(p));
    assert_eq!(*p, 0);

    println!("p value: {:?} dereference of p: {:?} address of p: {:?}",
        p, *p, addr_of!(p));
}
```

Windows output:

```
--- Unsafe Wild (Dangling) Pointer ---
p value: 0x2232ba6f760 dereference of p: 0 address of p: 0xb7a42fea60
p value: 0x2232ba6f760 dereference of p: 0 address of p: 0xb7a42fea60
```

x64 Linux output:

```
--- Unsafe Wild (Dangling) Pointer ---
p value: 0x5564b7dc7ae0 dereference of p: 0 address of p: 0x7ffda3765ff8
p value: 0x5564b7dc7ae0 dereference of p: 0 address of p: 0x7ffda3765ff8
```

A64 Linux output:

```
--- Unsafe Wild (Dangling) Pointer ---
p value: 0xaaab1ac38ad0 dereference of p: 0 address of p: 0xffffff508030
p value: 0xaaab1ac38ad0 dereference of p: 0 address of p: 0xffffff508030
```

Pointer to Pointer

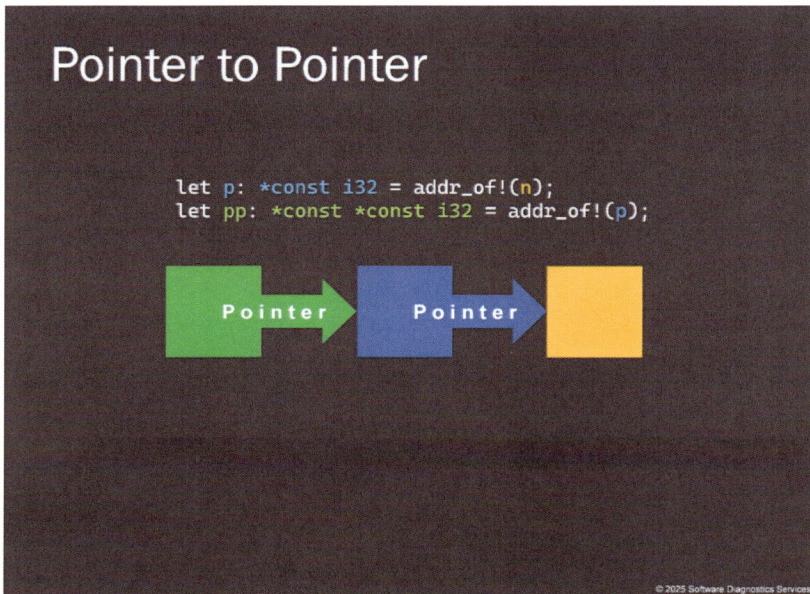

```
println!("--- Pointer to Pointer ---");
// #[allow(unused_unsafe)]
// unsafe
{
    let n: i32 = 0;
    let p: *const i32 = addr_of!(n);
    let pp: *const *const i32 = addr_of!(p);

    println!("n value: {:?} address of n: {:?} \n\
        p value: {:?} address of p: {:?} \n\
        pp value: {:?} address of pp: {:?}",
        n, addr_of!(n), p, addr_of!(p), pp, addr_of!(pp));
}
```

Windows output:

```
--- Pointer to Pointer ---
n value: 0 address of n: 0xb7a42febb4
p value: 0xb7a42febb4 address of p: 0xb7a42febb8
pp value: 0xb7a42febb8 address of pp: 0xb7a42febc0
```

x64 Linux output:

```
--- Pointer to Pointer ---
n value: 0 address of n: 0x7ffda376614c
p value: 0x7ffda376614c address of p: 0x7ffda3766150
pp value: 0x7ffda3766150 address of pp: 0x7ffda3766158
```

A64 Linux output:

```
--- Pointer to Pointer ---
n value: 0 address of n: 0x7ffda376614c
p value: 0x7ffda376614c address of p: 0x7ffda3766150
pp value: 0x7ffda3766150 address of pp: 0x7ffda3766158
```

Unsafe Pointer to Pointer Dereference

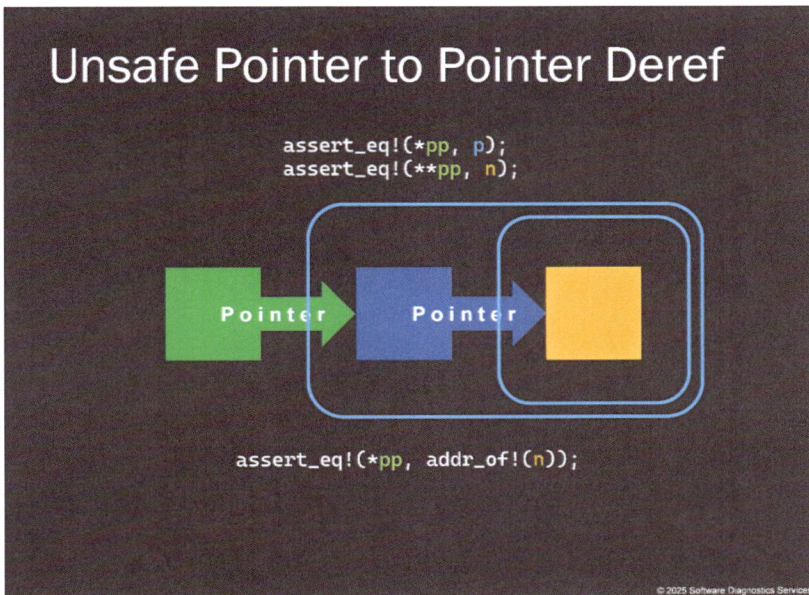

```rust
println!("--- Unsafe Pointer to Pointer Dereference ---");
unsafe {
    let n: i32 = 0;
    let p: *const i32 = addr_of!(n);
    let pp: *const *const i32 = addr_of!(p);
    assert_eq!(*pp, p);
    assert_eq!(*pp, addr_of!(n));
    assert_eq!(**pp, n);

    println!("n value: {:?} address of n: {:?} \n\
        p value: {:?} address of p: {:?} \n\
        pp value: {:?} address of pp: {:?} \n\
        dereference of pp: {:?} double dereference of pp: {:?}",
        n, addr_of!(n), p, addr_of!(p), pp,
        addr_of!(pp), *pp, **pp);
}
```

Windows output:

```
--- Unsafe Pointer to Pointer Dereference ---
n value: 0 address of n: 0xb7a42feca4
p value: 0xb7a42feca4 address of p: 0xb7a42feca8
pp value: 0xb7a42feca8 address of pp: 0xb7a42fecb0
dereference of pp: 0xb7a42feca4 double dereference of pp: 0
```

x64 Linux output:

```
--- Unsafe Pointer to Pointer Dereference ---
n value: 0 address of n: 0x7ffda376623c
p value: 0x7ffda376623c address of p: 0x7ffda3766240
pp value: 0x7ffda3766240 address of pp: 0x7ffda3766248
dereference of pp: 0x7ffda376623c double dereference of pp: 0
```

A64 Linux output:

```
--- Unsafe Pointer to Pointer Dereference ---
n value: 0 address of n: 0xffffff508274
p value: 0xffffff508274 address of p: 0xffffff508278
pp value: 0xffffff508278 address of pp: 0xffffff508280
dereference of pp: 0xffffff508274 double dereference of pp: 0
```

Philosophy of Values

In the previous unsafe philosophy of pointers section, we saw that pointers are first-class and can point to anything. What they point to are values. There is a different philosophy where values are first-class, and pointers are second-class.

The values project can be found in the archive[3]. In the following slide descriptions, we only show relevant code snippets and their output on various platforms.

---

[3] https://www.patterndiagnostics.com/Training/MTRust/MTRust.zip

Values and Owners

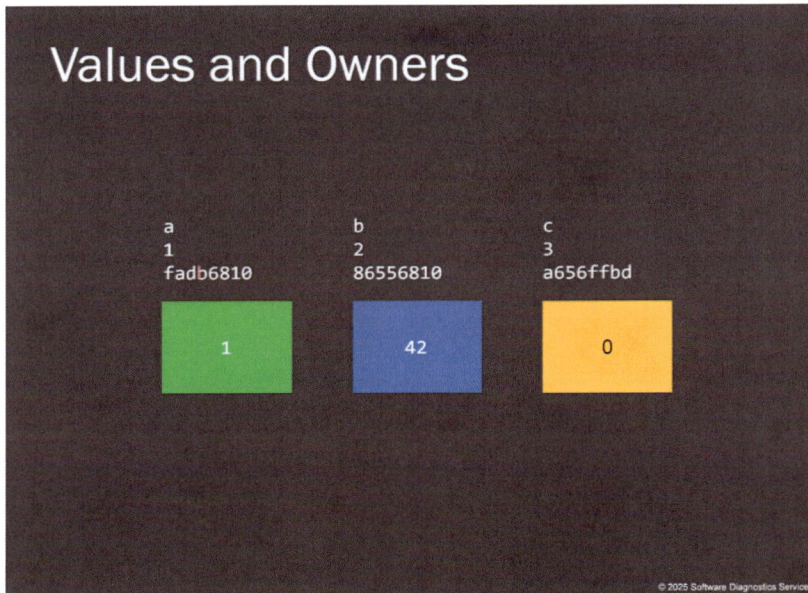

Values have owners. These can be named variables that have associated memory addresses.

```
println!("--- Values and Owners ---");
{
    let a: i32 = 1;
    let b: i32 = 42;
    let c: i32 = 0;

    println!("a({:?}): {:?} b({:?}): {:?} c({:?}): {:?}",
        addr_of!(a), a, addr_of!(b), b, addr_of!(c),
        c);
}
```

Windows output:

```
--- Values and Owners ---
a(0x70d99e71c): 1 b(0x70d99e720): 42 c(0x70d99e724): 0
```

x64 Linux output:

```
--- Values and Owners ---
a(0x7fff22fce5ec): 1 b(0x7fff22fce5f0): 42 c(0x7fff22fce5f4): 0
```

A64 Linux output:

```
--- Values and Owners ---
a(0xffffff761a34): 1 b(0xffffff761a38): 42 c(0xffffff761a3c): 0
```

Moving Values

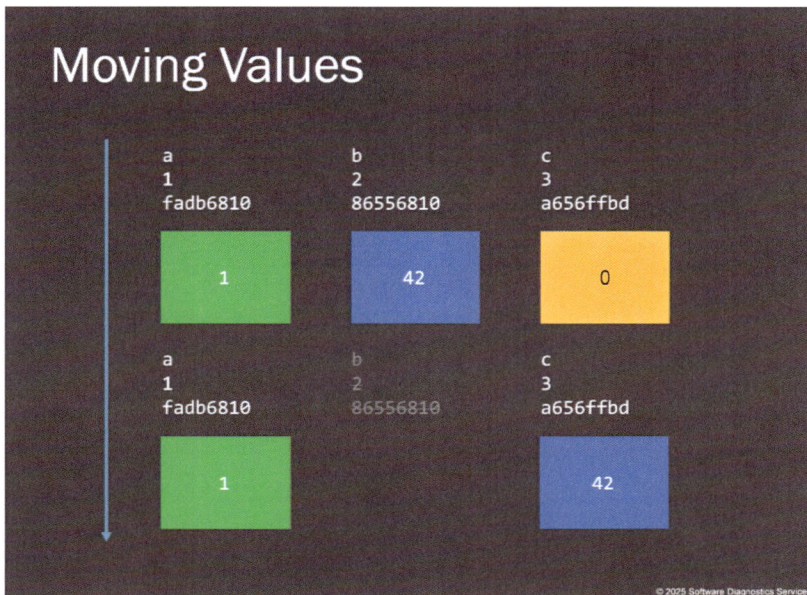

We can change owners of values by moving them. The previous owners and their values become invalid.

```rust
println!("--- Moving Values ---");
{
    #[derive(Debug)]
    struct Val(i32);

    let a: Val = Val(1);
    let b: Val = Val(42);
    let mut c: Val  = Val(0);

    println!("a({:?}): {:?} b({:?}): {:?} c({:?}): {:?}",
        addr_of!(a), a, addr_of!(b), b, addr_of!(c),
        c);

    c = b;

    println!("a({:?}): {:?} b(...): ... c({:?}): {:?}",
        addr_of!(a), a, /*addr_of!(b), b,*/
        addr_of!(c), c);
}
```

Windows output:

```
--- Moving Values ---
a(0x70d99e804): Val(1) b(0x70d99e808): Val(42) c(0x70d99e80c): Val(0)
a(0x70d99e804): Val(1) b(...): ... c(0x70d99e80c): Val(42)
```

x64 Linux output:

```
--- Moving Values ---
a(0x7fff22fce6d4): Val(1) b(0x7fff22fce6d8): Val(42) c(0x7fff22fce6dc): Val(0)
a(0x7fff22fce6d4): Val(1) b(...): ... c(0x7fff22fce6dc): Val(42)
```

A64 Linux output:

```
--- Moving Values ---
a(0xffffff761b1c): Val(1) b(0xffffff761b20): Val(42) c(0xffffff761b24): Val(0)
a(0xffffff761b1c): Val(1) b(...): ... c(0xffffff761b24): Val(42)
```

Copying Values

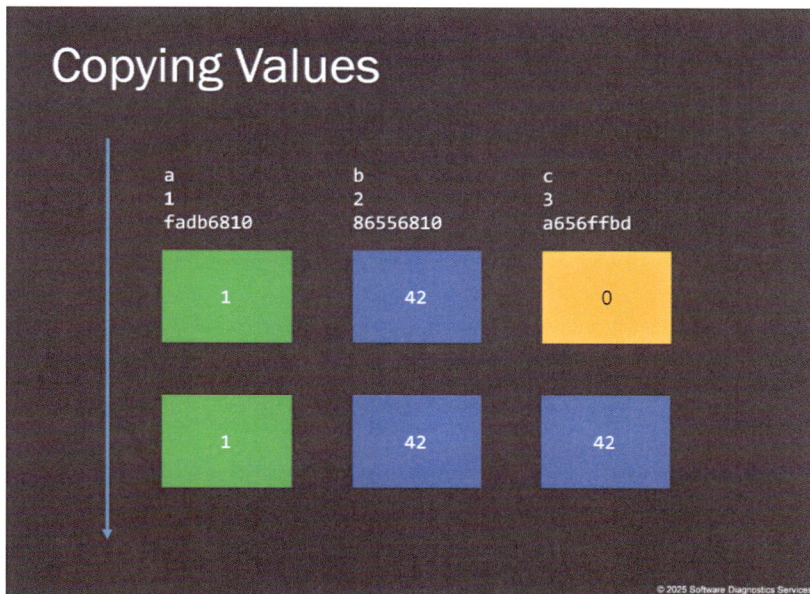

If values can be copied, for example, basic types such as integers, then their contents are simply copied, not moved, and the previous owner still owns the value.

```
println!("--- Copying Values ---");
{
    #[derive(Debug, Clone, Copy)]
    struct Val(i32);

    let a: Val = Val(1);
    let b: Val = Val(42);
    let mut c: Val  = Val(0);

    println!("a({:?}): {:?} b({:?}): {:?} c({:?}): {:?}",
        addr_of!(a), a, addr_of!(b), b, addr_of!(c),
        c);

    c = b;

    println!("a({:?}): {:?} b({:?}): {:?} c({:?}): {:?}",
        addr_of!(a), a, addr_of!(b), b, addr_of!(c),
        c);
}
```

Windows output:

```
--- Copying Values ---
a(0x70d99e96c): Val(1) b(0x70d99e970): Val(42) c(0x70d99e974): Val(0)
a(0x70d99e96c): Val(1) b(0x70d99e970): Val(42) c(0x70d99e974): Val(42)
```

x64 Linux output:

```
--- Copying Values ---
a(0x7fff22fce83c): Val(1) b(0x7fff22fce840): Val(42) c(0x7fff22fce844): Val(0)
a(0x7fff22fce83c): Val(1) b(0x7fff22fce840): Val(42) c(0x7fff22fce844): Val(42)
```

A64 Linux output:

```
--- Copying Values ---
a(0xffffff761c84): Val(1) b(0xffffff761c88): Val(42) c(0xffffff761c8c): Val(0)
a(0xffffff761c84): Val(1) b(0xffffff761c88): Val(42) c(0xffffff761c8c): Val(42)
```

Dropping Values

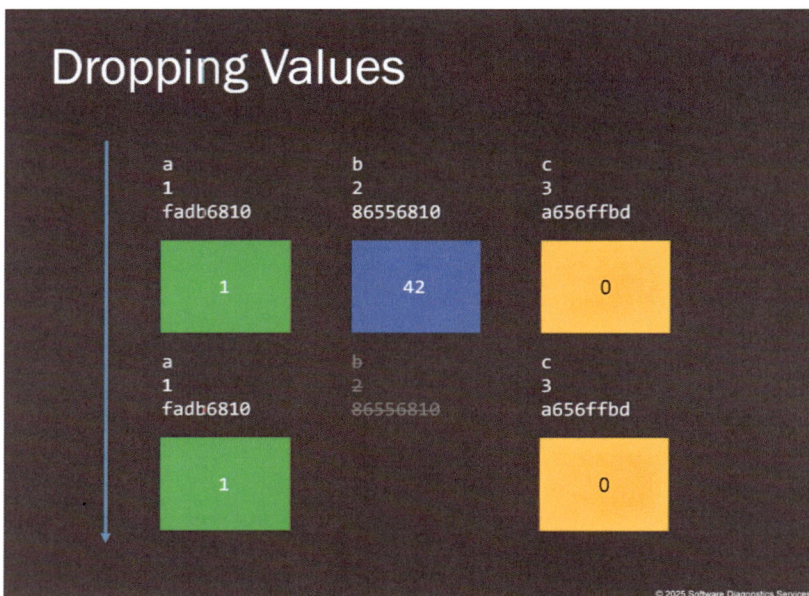

It is also possible to drop values – they cease to exist together with their owner.

```rust
println!("--- Dropping Values ---");
{
    #[derive(Debug)]
    struct Val(i32);

    let a: Val = Val(1);
    let b: Val = Val(42);
    let c: Val = Val(0);

    println!("a({:?}): {:?} b({:?}): {:?} c({:?}): {:?}",
        addr_of!(a), a, addr_of!(b), b, addr_of!(c),
        c);

    drop(b);

    println!("a({:?}): {:?} b(...): ... c({:?}): {:?}",
        addr_of!(a), a, /*addr_of!(b), b,*/
        addr_of!(c), c);
}
```

Windows output:

```
--- Dropping Values ---
a(0x70d99eafc): Val(1) b(0x70d99eb00): Val(42) c(0x70d99eb04): Val(0)
a(0x70d99eafc): Val(1) b(...): ... c(0x70d99eb04): Val(0)
```

x64 Linux output:

```
--- Dropping Values ---
a(0x7fff22fce9cc): Val(1) b(0x7fff22fce9d0): Val(42) c(0x7fff22fce9d4): Val(0)
a(0x7fff22fce9cc): Val(1) b(...): ... c(0x7fff22fce9d4): Val(0)
```

A64 Linux output:

```
--- Dropping Values ---
a(0xffffff761e14): Val(1) b(0xffffff761e18): Val(42) c(0xffffff761e1c): Val(0)
a(0xffffff761e14): Val(1) b(...): ... c(0xffffff761e1c): Val(0)
```

Ownership Tree

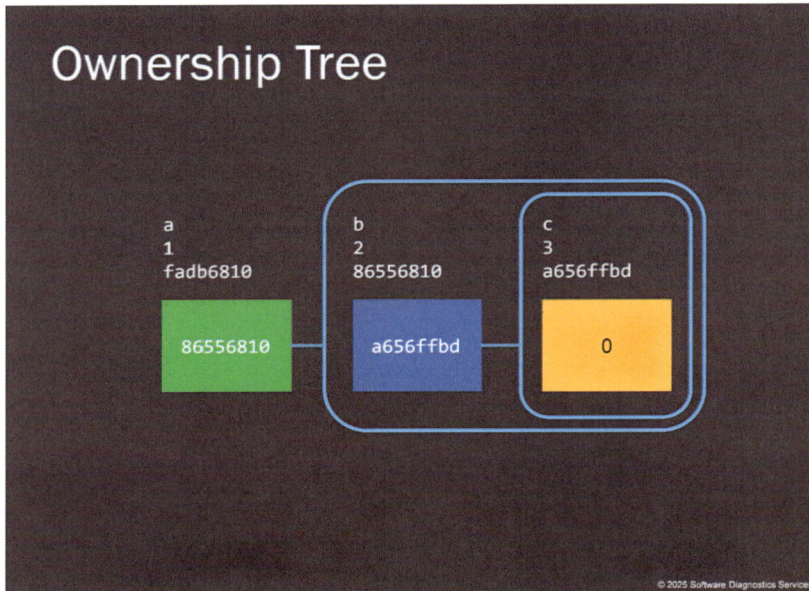

Owners may own owners via the so-called ownership tree. The value can be the owner of another value as well. The slide shows a linear structure, but when we look at Rust tuples, structs, arrays, and collections later, we see that they can contain several values, and each one may be an owner.

```rust
println!("--- Ownership Tree ---");
{
    #[derive(Debug)]
    struct ValOwnerOwner(Box<ValOwner>);
    #[derive(Debug)]
    struct ValOwner(Box<Val>);
    #[derive(Debug)]
    struct Val(i32);

    let a: ValOwnerOwner = ValOwnerOwner(Box::new(ValOwner(Box::new(Val(0)))));

    println!("a({:?}): {:?} b({:?}): {:?} c({:?}): {:?}",
        addr_of!(a), a, a.0.as_ref() as *const ValOwner,
        a.0, a.0.0.as_ref() as *const Val, a.0.0);
}
```

Windows output:

```
--- Ownership Tree ---
a(0x70d99ec60): ValOwnerOwner(ValOwner(Val(0))) b(0x130c10705b0): ValOwner(Val(0))
c(0x130c1070590): Val(0)
```

x64 Linux output:

```
--- Ownership Tree ---
a(0x7fff22fceb30): ValOwnerOwner(ValOwner(Val(0))) b(0x556c880c8a00):
ValOwner(Val(0)) c(0x556c880c89e0): Val(0)
```

A64 Linux output:

```
--- Ownership Tree ---
a(0xffffff761f78): ValOwnerOwner(ValOwner(Val(0))) b(0xaaaaefc0eaf0):
ValOwner(Val(0)) c(0xaaaaefc0ead0): Val(0)
```

Ownership Tree and Drops

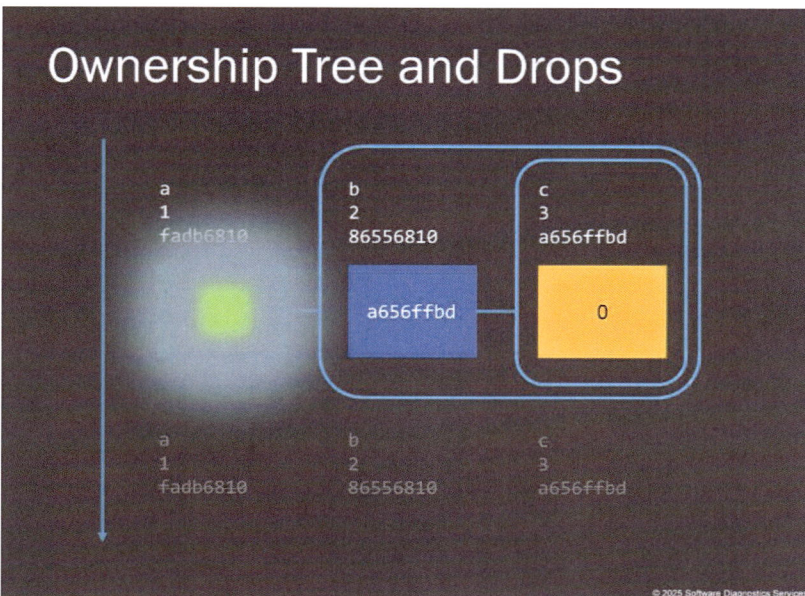

If you drop the root owner value, all other values are dropped, too, and the root owner becomes invalid.

Partial Drops

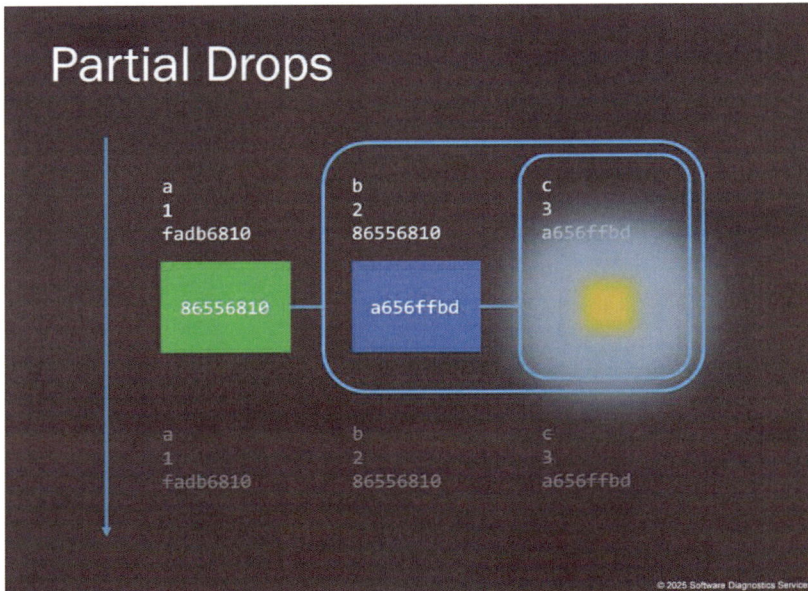

Partial drops invalidate the whole ownership tree.

```
println!("--- Partial Drops ---");
{
    #[derive(Debug)]
    struct ValOwnerOwner(Box<ValOwner>);
    #[derive(Debug)]
    struct ValOwner(Box<Val>);
    #[derive(Debug)]
    struct Val(i32);

    let a: ValOwnerOwner = ValOwnerOwner(Box::new(ValOwner(Box::new(Val(0)))));

    println!("a({:?}): {:?} b({:?}): {:?} c({:?}): {:?}",
        addr_of!(a), a, a.0.as_ref() as *const ValOwner,
        a.0, a.0.0.as_ref() as *const Val, a.0.0);

    drop(a.0.0);

    // println!("a({:?}): {:?} b({:?}): {:?} c(...): ...",
    //     addr_of!(a), a, a.0.as_ref() as *const ValOwner, a.0, /*a.0.0.as_ref() as
*const Val, a.0.0*/);

    // drop(a.0);
```

```
    // println!("a({:?}): {:?} b(...): ... c(...): ...",
    //    addr_of!(a), a, /*a.0.as_ref() as *const ValOwner, a.0, a.0.0.as_ref() as
*const Val, a.0.0*/);

    // drop(a);

    println!("a(...): ... b(...): ... c(...): ...",
            /*addr_of!(a), a, a.0.as_ref() as *const ValOwner, a.0, a.0.0.as_ref() as
*const Val, a.0.0*/);
}
```

Windows output:

```
--- Partial Drops ---
a(0x70d99ed50): ValOwnerOwner(ValOwner(Val(0))) b(0x130c10705b0): ValOwner(Val(0))
c(0x130c1070590): Val(0)
a(...): ... b(...): ... c(...): ...
```

x64 Linux output:

```
--- Partial Drops ---
a(0x7fff22fcec20): ValOwnerOwner(ValOwner(Val(0))) b(0x556c880c89e0):
ValOwner(Val(0)) c(0x556c880c8a00): Val(0)
a(...): ... b(...): ... c(...): ...
```

A64 Linux output:

```
--- Partial Drops ---
a(0xffffff762068): ValOwnerOwner(ValOwner(Val(0))) b(0xaaaaefc0ead0):
ValOwner(Val(0)) c(0xaaaaefc0eaf0): Val(0)
a(...): ... b(...): ... c(...): ...
```

Ownership Tree and Moves

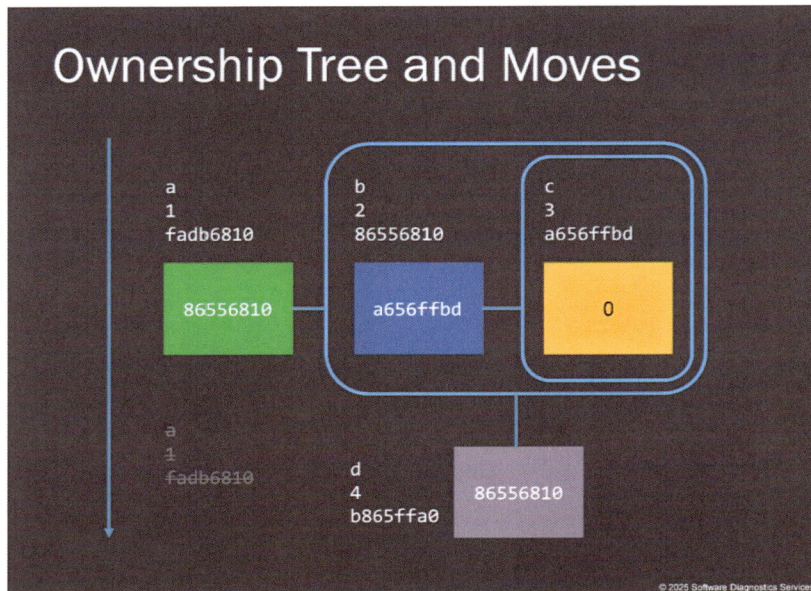

```rust
println!("--- Ownership Tree and Moves ---");
{
    #[derive(Debug)]
    struct ValOwner(Box<Val>);
    #[derive(Debug)]
    struct Val(i32);

    let a: ValOwner = ValOwner(Box::new(Val(0)));
    let c: ValOwner;

    println!("a({:?}): {:?} b({:?}): {:?} c(...): ...",
        addr_of!(a), a, a.0.as_ref() as *const Val,
        a.0, /*addr_of!(c) as *const ValOwner, c*/);

    c = a;

    println!("a(...): ... b({:?}): {:?} c({:?}): {:?}",
        /*addr_of!(a), a,*/ c.0.as_ref() as *const Val,
        c.0, addr_of!(c) as *const ValOwner, c);
}
```

Windows output:

```
--- Ownership Tree and Moves ---
a(0x70d99ee70): ValOwner(Val(0)) b(0x130c1070590): Val(0) c(...): ...
a(...): ... b(0x130c1070590): Val(0) c(0x70d99ee80): ValOwner(Val(0))
```

x64 Linux output:

```
--- Ownership Tree and Moves ---
a(0x7fff22fced40): ValOwner(Val(0)) b(0x556c880c89e0): Val(0) c(...): ...
a(...): ... b(0x556c880c89e0): Val(0) c(0x7fff22fced50): ValOwner(Val(0))
```

A64 Linux output:

```
--- Ownership Tree and Moves ---
a(0xffffff762188): ValOwner(Val(0)) b(0xaaaaefc0ead0): Val(0) c(...): ...
a(...): ... b(0xaaaaefc0ead0): Val(0) c(0xffffff762198): ValOwner(Val(0))
```

Multiple Owners (not in Rust)

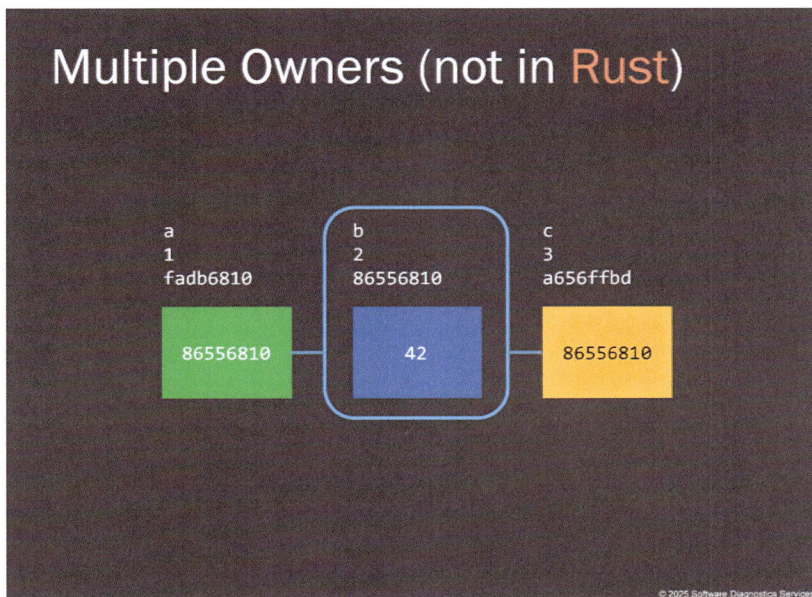

Although in this philosophy of values, we allow multiple owners of the same value – this is not allowed in Rust.

Multiple Owners and Drops

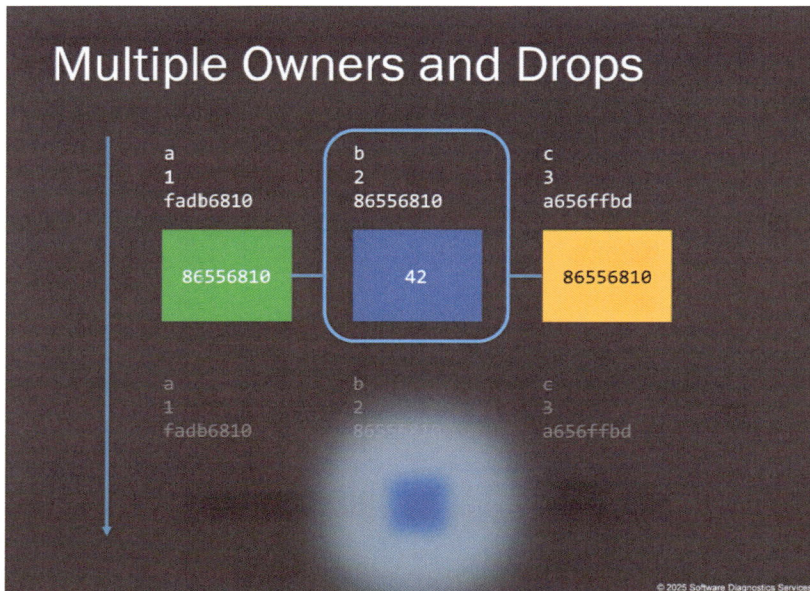

If, however, multiple ownership is allowed, dropping a value should invalidate all its owners.

Owners vs. Pointers

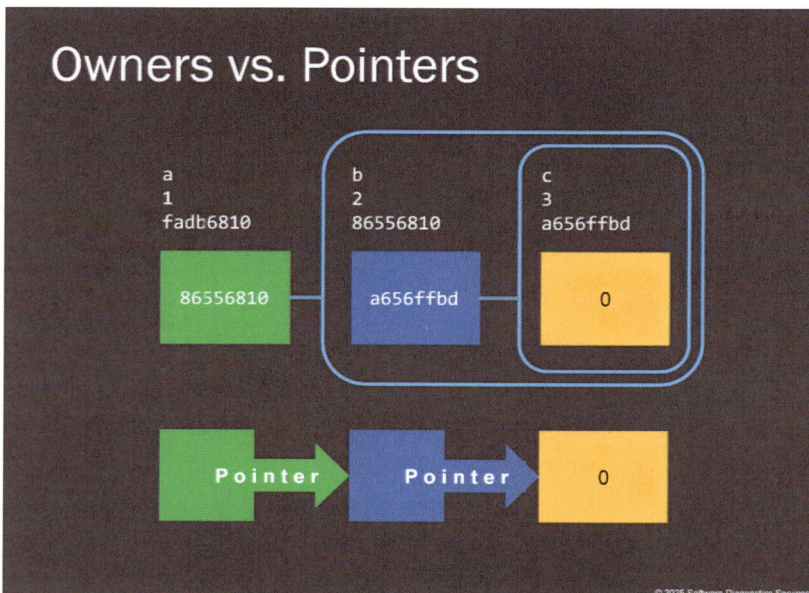

Ownership can be implemented as a pointer (variable). But just a memory address (name) can be an owner.

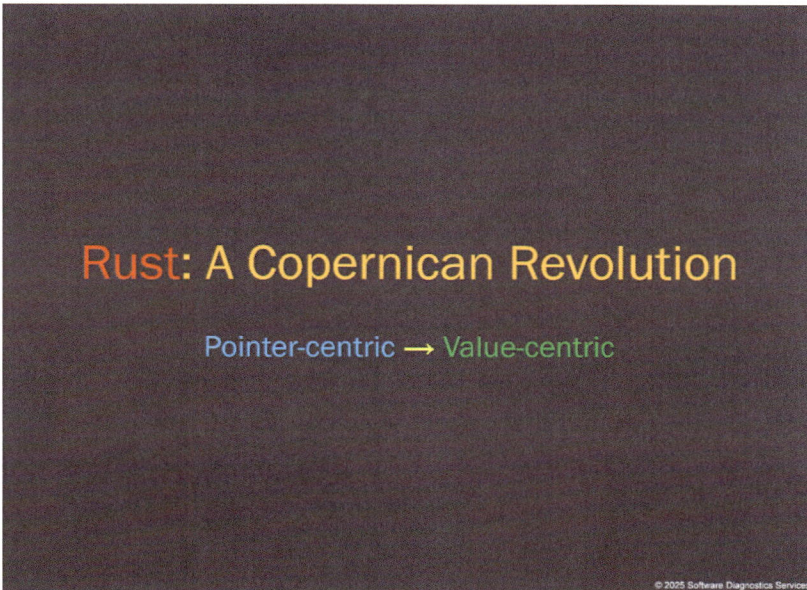

Based on the comparison of the two philosophies, we can say that Rust introduced a Copernican revolution: from pointer-centric to value-centric. Let's see why.

Values Revolve Around Pointers

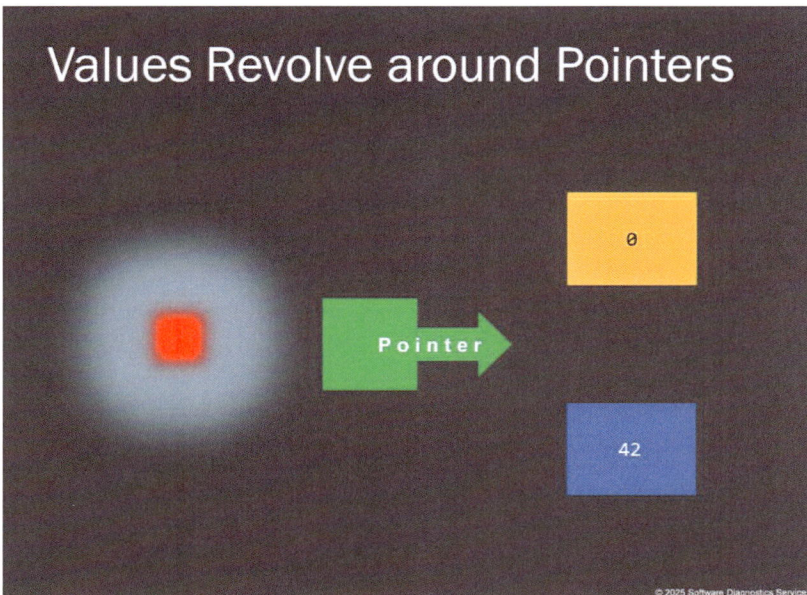

Previous languages like C and C++ allowed a pointer to point to any value, including invalid ones. This is a pointer-centric view where a pointer is at the center.

Owners Revolve Around Values

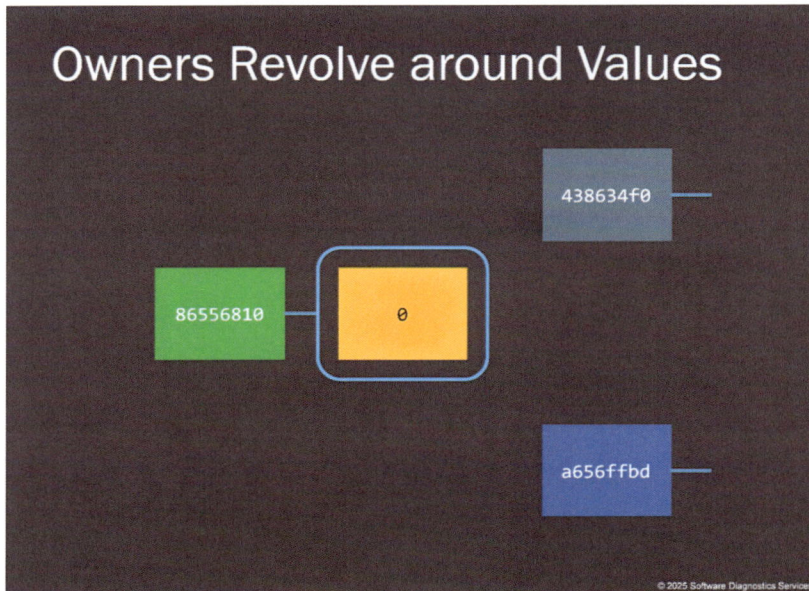

Rust inverts the view with a value at the center, and owners (including pointer owners) can be changed (a value is moved between them).

Rust Philosophy of Values

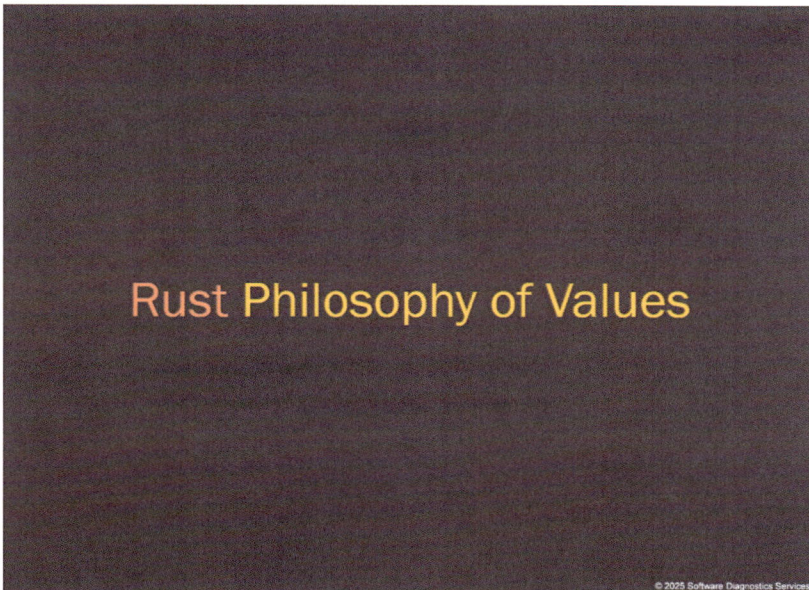

Rust extends the philosophy of values even further.

The `values` project can be found in the archive[4]. In the following slide descriptions, we only show relevant code snippets and their output on various platforms.

---

[4] https://www.patterndiagnostics.com/Training/MTRust/MTRust.zip

Restricted Ownership

A value has only a single owner. It is possible to define an uninitialized owner in code, but it is forbidden to use it (even to get an address), and it will be caught at compile time.

```
println!("--- Restricted Ownership ---");
{
    let a: i32;

    // println!("{:?}", addr_of!(a));

    a = 0;

    println!("{:?}", addr_of!(a));
}
```

Windows output:

```
--- Restricted Ownership ---
0x70d99efbc
```

x64 Linux output:

```
--- Restricted Ownership ---
0x7fff22fcee8c
```

A64 Linux output:

```
--- Restricted Ownership ---
0xffffff7622d4
```

Value Lifetime

Value Lifetime

- Tied to its owner's lifetime

- If moved, its lifetime continues with the new owner, and the previous owner's lifetime ends

- Out-of-scope ends value lifetime

- Drop of a non-Copy value ends its lifetime

© 2025 Software Diagnostics Services

The lifetime of a value is tied to its owner's lifetime. If you want the value to outlive its owner, you must move it to another owner. If a value is moved, its lifetime continues with the new owner's lifetime, but the previous owner's lifetime ends. A value lifetime ends when its owner goes out of scope or, if a value is non-Copy, it was dropped.

```rust
println!("--- Value Lifetime ---");
{
    {
        let a: i32 = 0;
    }

    // println!("{:?}", a);

    let a: i32 = 0;

    drop(a);

    println!("{:?}", a);

    #[derive(Debug)]
    struct Val(i32);

    let b: Val = Val(0);

    drop(b);

    // println!("{:?}", b);

    let mut c: Val = Val(0);

    {
        let d: Val = c;
    }

    // println!("{:?}", c);

    {
        let d: Val = Val(1);

        c = d;
    }

    println!("{:?}", c);
}
```

Windows output:

```
--- Value Lifetime ---
0
Val(1)
```

x64 Linux output:

```
--- Value Lifetime ---
0
Val(1)
```

A64 Linux output:

```
--- Value Lifetime ---
0
Val(1)
```

Owner Lifetime

Owner Lifetime

- Out-of-scope ends its owner's lifetime
- Drop of a non-Copy value ends its owner's lifetime
- If a value is moved, its owner's lifetime ends
- Owner names can be reintroduced (name-to-value binding)

© 2025 Software Diagnostics Services

If an owner goes out of scope, its value goes out of scope too if not moved, and the lifetime of both ends. If a value is moved, its owner becomes invalid; therefore, its lifetime ends. A drop of a non-Copy value ends its owner's lifetime. Compared to other languages such as C and C++, you can reintroduce the same name either in the same or inner scope and the new name will shadow the original one (but it continues its invisible lifetime unless it goes out of scope).

```rust
println!("--- Owner Lifetime ---");
{
    #[derive(Debug)]
    struct Val(i32);

    let a: Val = Val(0);

    drop(a);

    let a: Val = Val(0);

    let pa1: *const Val = addr_of!(a);

    println!("a: {:?}", a);

    let a: Val = Val(1);

    let pa2: *const Val = addr_of!(a);

    println!("a: {:?}", a);

    unsafe {
        println!("pa1: {pa1:p} *pa1: {:?} pa2: {pa2:p} *pa2: {:?}", *pa1, *pa2);
    }
}
```

Windows output:

```
--- Owner Lifetime ---
Val(0)
Val(1)
pa1: 0xe93b8febac *pa1: Val(0) pa2: 0xe93b8fec0c *pa2: Val(1)
```

x64 Linux output:

```
--- Owner Lifetime ---
Val(0)
Val(1)
pa1: 0x7fff7f445bb4 *pa1: Val(0) pa2: 0x7fff7f445c14 *pa2: Val(1)
```

A64 Linux output:

```
--- Owner Lifetime ---
Val(0)
Val(1)
pa1: 0xffffecde4b44 *pa1: Val(0) pa2: 0xffffecde4ba4 *pa2: Val(1)
```

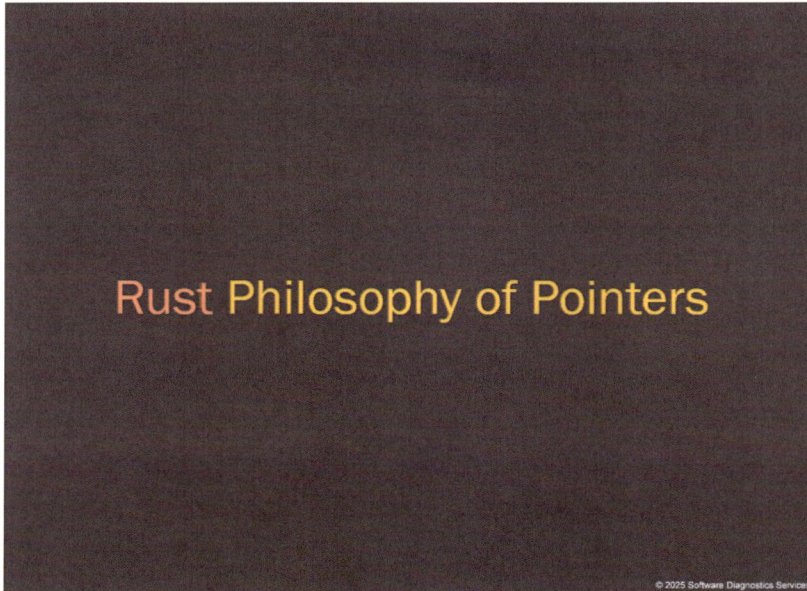

Rust Philosophy of Pointers

© 2025 Software Diagnostics Services

However, using only values with single owners is too constraining and makes common programming idioms, such as sharing values, impossible. Pointers are still needed, but Rust reinterprets them and restricts their use.

The references project can be found in the archive[5]. In the following slide descriptions, we only show relevant code snippets and their output on various platforms.

---

[5] https://www.patterndiagnostics.com/Training/MTRust/MTRust.zip

Types of Pointers

Rust includes several types of pointers. In this section, I cover only safe references. We previously looked at unsafe raw pointers. Some of the remaining pointer types will be covered later.

Mut Pointers vs. Pointers to Mut

```rust
println!("--- Mut Pointers vs. Pointers to Mut ---");
{
    let n: i32 = 0;
    let pn: *const i32 = addr_of!(n);

    #[allow(unused_mut)]
    let mut m: i32 = 0;
    let pm: *mut i32 = addr_of_mut!(m);

    #[allow(unused_mut)]
    let mut mpn: *const i32 = addr_of!(n);

    #[allow(unused_mut)]
    let mut mpm: *mut i32 = addr_of_mut!(m);
}
```

References as Pointer Types

Instead of unsafe raw pointers to refer to values in various code places instead of copying and moving values, Rust offers shared read-only references and mutable readable and writable references. We can define a reference variable without initializing it. But to use it you need to initialize it referring to some value. This prevents referring to garbage. References and pointers are of different types.

```rust
println!("--- References as Pointer Types ---");
{
    let n: i32 = 0;
    let r: &i32;

    r = &n;

    let r2: &i32 = r;

    println!("r: {r:p} r2: {r2:p}");

    let mut m: i32 = 0;
    let r: &i32 = &m;

    let mr: &mut i32 = &mut m;
}
```

Windows output:

```
--- References as Pointer Types ---
r: 0xca83cfee4c r2: 0xca83cfee4c
```

x64 Linux output:

```
--- References as Pointer Types ---
r: 0x7ffca5900384 r2: 0x7ffca5900384
```

A64 Linux output:

```
--- References as Pointer Types ---
r: 0xfffff9ce569c r2: 0xfffff9ce569c
```

Mut Refs vs. Refs to Mut

```
println!("--- Mut Refs vs. Refs to Mut ---");
{
    let n: i32 = 0;
    let rn: &i32 = &n;

    let mut m: i32 = 0;
    let rm: &mut i32 = &mut m;

    #[allow(unused_mut)]
    let mut mrn: &i32 = &n;

    #[allow(unused_mut)]
    let mut mrm: &mut i32 = &mut m;
}
```

References as Addresses

However, reference values are conceptually memory addresses. So, we can assign reference values to pointers. Here, we mean a reference value, not the value it points to.

```
println!("--- References as Addresses ---");
{
    let n: i32 = 0;
    let r: &i32 = &n;
    let p1: *const i32 = addr_of!(n);
    let p2: *const i32 = &n;

    assert_eq!(addr_of!(n), &n);
    assert_eq!(addr_of!(n), r);
    assert_eq!(*r, n);
    assert_eq!(r as *const i32, p1);
    assert_eq!(r as *const i32, p2);
    assert_eq!(&n as *const i32, p1);
    assert_eq!(&n as *const i32, p2);

    println!("&n: {:p} r: {r:p} *r: {r} p1: {p1:?} p2: {p2:?}", &n);

    unsafe {
        println!("&r: {:?} value of r: 0x{:x}", addr_of!(r),
            *(addr_of!(r) as *const usize));
    }
}
```

```
    let mut m: i32 = 0;

    println!("&mut m {:p}", &mut m);

    let mr: &mut i32 = &mut m;

    println!("mr: {mr:p} *mr: {mr}");

    let mp1: *mut i32 = &mut m;

    println!("mp1: {mp1:?}");

    let mp2: *mut i32 = addr_of_mut!(m);

    println!("mp2: {mp2:?}");
}
```

Windows output:

```
--- References as Addresses ---
&n: 0xcf64b6eb9c r: 0xcf64b6eb9c *r: 0 p1: 0xcf64b6eb9c p2: 0xcf64b6eb9c
&r: 0xcf64b6eba0 value of r: 0xcf64b6eb9c
&mut m 0xcf64b6eefc
mr: 0xcf64b6eefc *mr: 0
mp1: 0xcf64b6eefc
mp2: 0xcf64b6eefc
```

x64 Linux output:

```
--- References as Addresses ---
&n: 0x7ffff612e6ac r: 0x7ffff612e6ac *r: 0 p1: 0x7ffff612e6ac p2: 0x7ffff612e6ac
&r: 0x7ffff612e6b0 value of r: 0x7ffff612e6ac
&mut m 0x7ffff612ea0c
mr: 0x7ffff612ea0c *mr: 0
mp1: 0x7ffff612ea0c
mp2: 0x7ffff612ea0c
```

A64 Linux output:

```
--- References as Addresses ---
&n: 0xfffff18b8d24 r: 0xfffff18b8d24 *r: 0 p1: 0xfffff18b8d24 p2: 0xfffff18b8d24
&r: 0xfffff18b8d28 value of r: 0xfffff18b8d24
&mut m 0xfffff18b909c
mr: 0xfffff18b909c *mr: 0
mp1: 0xfffff18b909c
mp2: 0xfffff18b909c
```

Borrowing References

Taking a reference of value is called borrowing a reference to it. We can borrow as many shared references to the same value as needed or only one mutable reference. But as soon as we borrow a shared reference, the previously borrowed mutable reference (if it exists) becomes invalid. The same is the other way around; if we borrow a mutable reference, all previously borrowed shared references become invalid. This prevents all sorts of unintended value overwrites.

```rust
println!("--- Borrowing References ---");
{
    let mut n: i32 = 0;

    let mr1: &mut i32 = &mut n;
    let r1: &i32 = &n;
    let r2: &i32 = &n;
    //let mr2: &mut i32 = &mut n;

    //println!("mr1: {mr1:p}");
    println!("r1: {r1:p} r2: {r2:p}");
    //println!("mr2: {mr2:p}");
    //println!("mr1: {mr1:p} mr2: {mr2:p}");
}
```

Windows output:

```
--- Borrowing References ---
r1: 0xca83cff364 r2: 0xca83cff364
```

x64 Linux output:

```
--- Borrowing References ---
r1: 0x7ffca590089c r2: 0x7ffca590089c
```

A64 Linux output:

```
--- Borrowing References ---
r1: 0x7ffca590089c r2: 0x7ffca590089c
```

Reference Lifetime

A lifetime of a reference must be less or equal to the lifetime of a value it refers to. This prevents dangling references to values that are no longer available. It is possible to have static lifetime references (local or static) referring to static variables. Static values and static references to static values must also be initialized.

```
println!("--- Reference Lifetime ---");
{
    struct Val(i32);

    let v: Val = Val(0);
    let r: &Val = &v;

    //drop(v);

    println!("r: {r:p}");

    let n: i32 = 0;
    //let rs: &'static i32 = &n;

    let r: &i32 = &NS;
    let rs: &'static i32 = &NS;
    println!("rs: {rs:p}");
    unsafe {
        RS = rs;
    }
}
```

```
static NS: i32 = 0;
static mut RS: &i32 = &NS;
```

Windows output:

```
--- Reference Lifetime ---
r: 0xca83cff3fc
rs: 0x7ff78743c700
```

x64 Linux output:

```
--- Reference Lifetime ---
r: 0x7ffca5900934
rs: 0x5615fcf540cc
```

A64 Linux output:

```
--- Reference Lifetime ---
r: 0xfffff9ce5c4c
rs: 0xaaaad0c5e128
```

x64 Disassembly Review

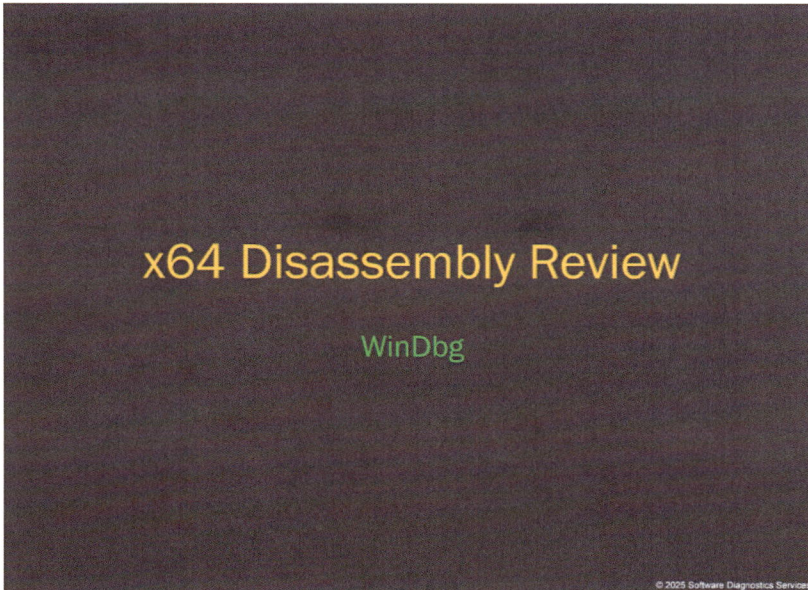

WinDbg

© 2025 Software Diagnostics Services

x64 CPU Registers

x64 CPU Registers

- **RAX** ⊃ **EAX** ⊃ **AX** ⊇ {**AH, AL**} | RAX 64-bit | EAX 32-bit |
- ALU: **RAX**, **RDX**
- Counter: **RCX**
- Memory copy: **RSI** (src), **RDI** (dst)
- Stack: **RSP**
- Frame Pointer: **RSP**, **RBP**
- Next instruction: **RIP**
- New: **R8 – R15**, **Rx(D|W|B)**

© 2025 Software Diagnostics Services

There are familiar 32-bit CPU register names, such as **EAX,** that are extended to 64-bit names, such as **RAX**. Most of them are traditionally specialized, such as ALU, counter, and memory copy registers. Although, now they all can be used as general-purpose registers. There is, of course, a stack pointer, **RSP**, and it also takes the role of a frame pointer, which is also used to address local variables and saved parameters. It can be used for stack reconstruction. In Microsoft compiler code generation implementations, **RBP** is also used as a general-purpose register. An instruction pointer **RIP** is saved in the stack memory region with every function call, then restored on return from the called function. In addition, the x64 platform features another eight general-purpose registers, from **R8** to **R15**.

Instructions and Registers

Instructions and Registers

⊙ Opcode DST, SRC

⊙ Examples:

```
mov   rax, 10h        ; RAX ← 0x10
mov   r13, rdx        ; R13 ← RDX
add   r10, 10h        ; R10 ← R10 + 0x10
imul  edx, ecx        ; EDX ← EDX * ECX
call  rdx             ; RDX already contains
                      ;    the address of func (&func)
                      ; PUSH RIP; RIP ← &func
sub   rsp, 30h        ; RSP ← RSP-0x30
                      ; make room for local variables
```

© 2025 Software Diagnostics Services

This slide shows a few examples of CPU instructions involving operations with registers, such as moving a value and doing arithmetic. The direction of operands is opposite to the AT&T x64 disassembly flavor if you are accustomed to default GDB disassembly on Linux.

Memory and Stack Addressing

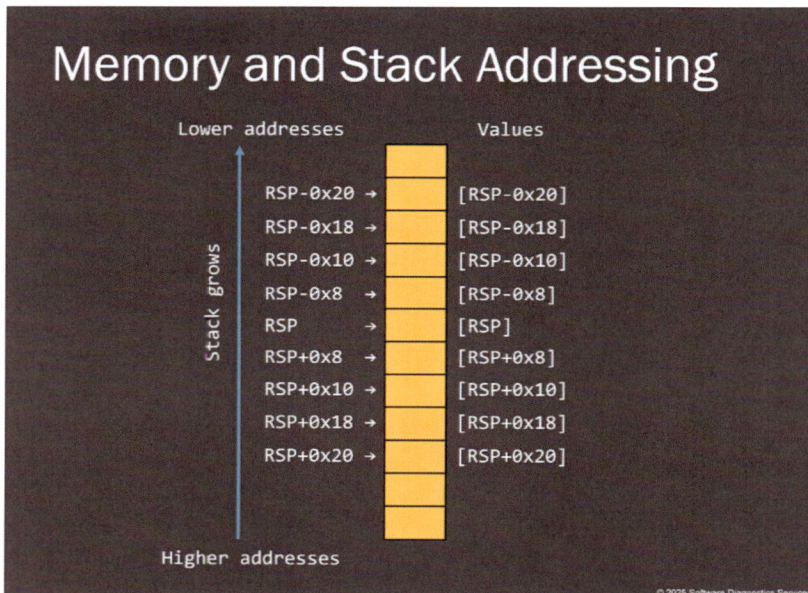

Memory and Stack Addressing

Lower addresses		Values
RSP-0x20 →		[RSP-0x20]
RSP-0x18 →		[RSP-0x18]
RSP-0x10 →		[RSP-0x10]
RSP-0x8 →		[RSP-0x8]
RSP →		[RSP]
RSP+0x8 →		[RSP+0x8]
RSP+0x10 →		[RSP+0x10]
RSP+0x18 →		[RSP+0x18]
RSP+0x20 →		[RSP+0x20]

Stack grows

Higher addresses

© 2025 Software Diagnostics Services

Before we look at operations with memory, let's look at a graphical representation of memory addressing where, for simplicity, I use 64-bit (or 8-byte) memory cells. A thread stack is just any other memory region, so instead of **RSP**, any other register can be used. Please note that the stack grows towards lower addresses, so to access the previously pushed values, you need to use positive offsets from **RSP**. The Rust compiler sometimes chooses **RBP** to address stack values.

Memory Cell Sizes

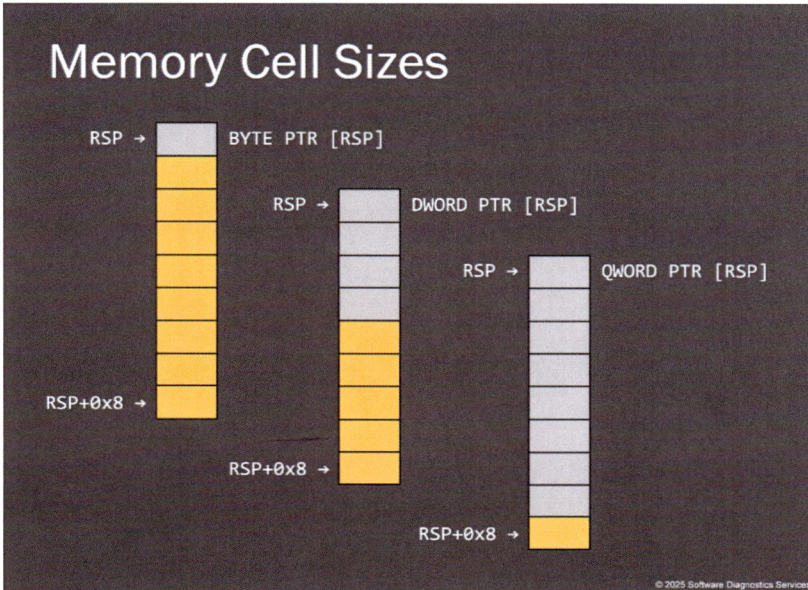

Here, each memory cell is 8-bit (or one byte). When we have a register pointing to memory, and we want to work with the value at that address, we need to specify the size of memory cells to work with, for example, **BYTE PTR** if we want to work with a byte, **DWORD PTR** if we want to work with 32-bit double words, and **QWORD PTR** if we want to work with 64-bit quad words. There's also **WORD PTR** for 16-bit values. This notation is different from Linux GDB, where we have bytes, half-words, words, and double words.

Memory Load Instructions

Constants are encoded in instructions, but if we need arbitrary values, we must get them from memory. Square brackets show memory access relative to an address stored in some register.

Memory Store Instructions

```
Memory Store Instructions

⊙ Opcode PTR [DST+Offset], SRC

⊙ Opcode DST|SRC

⊙ Examples:

mov   qword ptr [rbp-20h], rcx ; 64-bit value at address RBP-0x20
                               ;   ← RCX
mov   byte ptr [0], 1          ; 8-bit value at address 0 ← 1
push  rsi                      ; RSP ← RSP - 8
                               ; value at address RSP ← RSI
inc   dword ptr [rcx]          ; 32-bit value at address RCX ←
                               ;   1 + 32-bit value at address RCX

© 2025 Software Diagnostics Services
```

Storing is similar to loading.

Flow Instructions

```
Flow Instructions

⊙ Opcode DST

⊙ Opcode PTR [DST]

⊙ Examples:

jmp   00007ff6`9ef2f008   ; RIP ← 0x7ff69ef2f008
                          ; ("goto" 0x7ff69ef2f008)
jmp   qword ptr [rax+10h] ; RIP ← value at address RAX+0x10
call  00007ff5`9ef21400   ; RSP ← RSP – 8
00007ff6`9ef21057:        ; value at address RSP ← 0x7ff69ef21057
                          ; RIP ← 0x7ff69ef21400
                          ; ("goto" 0x7ff69ef21400)

© 2025 Software Diagnostics Services
```

Goto (an unconditional jump) is implemented via the **JMP** instruction. Function calls are implemented via **CALL** instruction. For conditional branches, please look at the official Intel documentation. We don't use these instructions in our exercises.

Function Parameters

On the x64 platform, the first 4 Rust function parameters from left to right are moved to CPU registers, and the rest are passed via stack locations.

Struct Function Parameters

When a struct function is called, the first parameter is implicit. It is an object address to help functions differentiate between objects of the same struct type and reference correct fields' memory. The rest of the parameters are passed as usual.

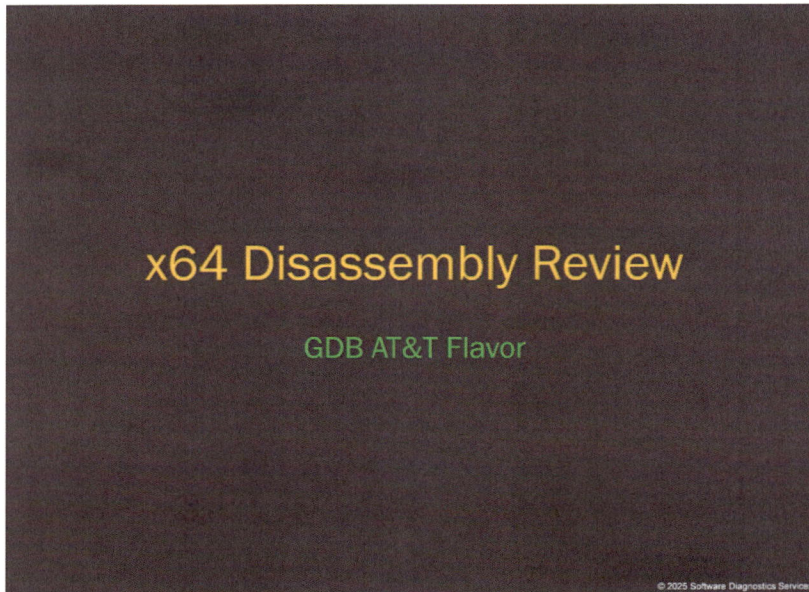

x64 CPU Registers

There are familiar 32-bit CPU register names, such as **EAX,** that are extended to 64-bit names, such as **RAX**. Most of them are traditionally specialized, such as ALU, counter, and memory copy registers. Although, now they all can be used as general-purpose registers. There is, of course, a stack pointer, **RSP**, and, additionally, a frame pointer, **RBP**, that is used to address local variables and saved parameters. It can be used for backtrace reconstruction. In some compiler code generation implementations, **RBP** is also used as a general-purpose register, with **RSP** taking the role of a frame pointer. An instruction pointer RIP is saved in the stack memory region with every function call, then restored on return from the called function. In addition, the x64 platform features another eight general-purpose registers, from **R8** to **R15**.

x64 Instructions and Registers

x64 Instructions and Registers

- Opcode SRC, DST # default AT&T flavour

- Examples:

```
mov    $0x10, %rax        # 0x10 → RAX
mov    %rsp, %rbp         # RSP → RBP
add    $0x10, %r10        # R10 + 0x10 → R10
imul   %ecx, %edx         # ECX * EDX → EDX
callq  *%rdx              # RDX already contains
                          #    the address of func (&func)
                          # PUSH RIP; &func → RIP
sub    $0x30, %rsp        # RSP-0x30 → RSP
                          # make room for local variables
```

© 2025 Software Diagnostics Services

This slide shows a few examples of CPU instructions involving operations with registers, such as moving a value and doing arithmetic. The direction of operands is opposite to the Intel x64 disassembly flavor if you are accustomed to WinDbg on Windows. It is possible to use the Intel disassembly flavor in GDB, but we opted for the default AT&T flavor in line with our **Accelerated Linux Core Dump Analysis** and **Accelerated Linux Disassembly, Reconstruction, and Reversing** books.

Memory and Stack Addressing

Memory and Stack Addressing

Lower addresses

```
RSP-0x20 →        ← RBP-0x20
RSP-0x18 →        ← RBP-0x18
RSP-0x10 →        ← RBP-0x10
RSP-0x8  →        ← RBP-0x8
RSP      →        ← RBP
RSP+0x8  →        ← RBP+0x8
RSP+0x10 →        ← RBP+0x10
RSP+0x18 →        ← RBP+0x18
RSP+0x20 →        ← RBP+0x20
```

Stack grows

Higher addresses

© 2025 Software Diagnostics Services

Before we look at operations with memory, let's look at a graphical representation of memory addressing. A thread stack is just any other memory region, so instead of **RSP** and **RBP,** any other register can be used. Please note that the stack grows towards lower addresses, so to access the previously pushed values, you need to use positive offsets from **RSP**.

x64 Memory Load Instructions

```
x64 Memory Load Instructions

  ⊙ Opcode Offset(SRC), DST

  ⊙ Opcode DST

  ⊙ Examples:

mov   0x10(%rsp), %rax      # value at address RSP+0x10 → RAX
mov   -0x10(%rbp), %rcx     # value at address RBP-0x10 → RCX
add   (%rax), %rdx          # RDX + value at address RAX → RDX
pop   %rdi                  # value at address RSP → RDI
                            # RSP + 8 → RSP
lea   0x20(%rbp), %r8       # address RBP+0x20 → R8

© 2025 Software Diagnostics Services
```

Constants are encoded in instructions, but if we need arbitrary values, we must get them from memory. Round brackets show memory access relative to an address stored in some register.

x64 Memory Store Instructions

```
x64 Memory Store Instructions

  ⊙ Opcode SRC, Offset(DST)

  ⊙ Opcode SRC|DST

  ⊙ Examples:

mov   %rcx, -0x20(%rbp)     # RCX → value at address RBP-0x20
addl  $1, (%rax)            # 1 + 32-bit value at address RAX →
                            #     32-bit value at address RAX
push  %rsi                  # RSP - 8 → RSP
                            # RSI → value at address RSP
inc   (%rcx)                # 1 + value at address RCX →
                            #     value at address RCX

© 2025 Software Diagnostics Services
```

Storing is similar to loading.

x64 Flow Instructions

x64 Flow Instructions

- ⊙ Opcode DST

- ⊙ Examples:

```
jmpq    0x10493fc1c        # 0x10493fc1c → RIP
                           # ("goto" 0x10493fc1c)

jmpq    *0x100(%rip)       # value at address RIP+0x100 → RIP

callq   0x10493ff74        # RSP - 8 → RSP
0x10493fc14:               # 0x10493fc14 → value at address RSP
                           # 0x10493ff74 → RIP
                           # ("goto" 0x10493ff74)
```

© 2025 Software Diagnostics Services

Goto (an unconditional jump) is implemented via the **JMP** instruction. Function calls are implemented via **CALL** instruction. For conditional branches, please look at the official Intel documentation.

x64 Function Parameters

x64 Function Parameters

- ⊙ fn func(...);

- ⊙ Left to right via RDI, RSI, RDX, RCX, R8, R9, stack

- ⊙ stack: (%RSP), 0x8(%RSP), 0x10(%RSP), ...

© 2025 Software Diagnostics Services

On the x64 Linux platform, the first six Rust function parameters from left to right are moved to CPU registers, and the rest are passed via stack locations.

x64 Struct Function Parameters

x64 Struct Function Parameters

- ◉ RDI

  Implicit struct object memory address (&myStruct)

  ```
  let myStruct: Struct = ...;
  myStruct.func(...);
  ```

- ◉ RSI, RDX, RCX, R8, R9, stack

  The rest of the struct function parameters

  ```
  impl Struct {
    fn func(&self, ...);
  }
  ```

© 2025 Software Diagnostics Services

When a struct function is called, the first parameter is implicit and, on the x64 Linux platform, is passed via **RDI**. It is an object address to help struct function differentiate between objects of the same struct type and reference correct fields' memory. The rest of the parameters are passed as usual.

ARM64 Disassembly Review

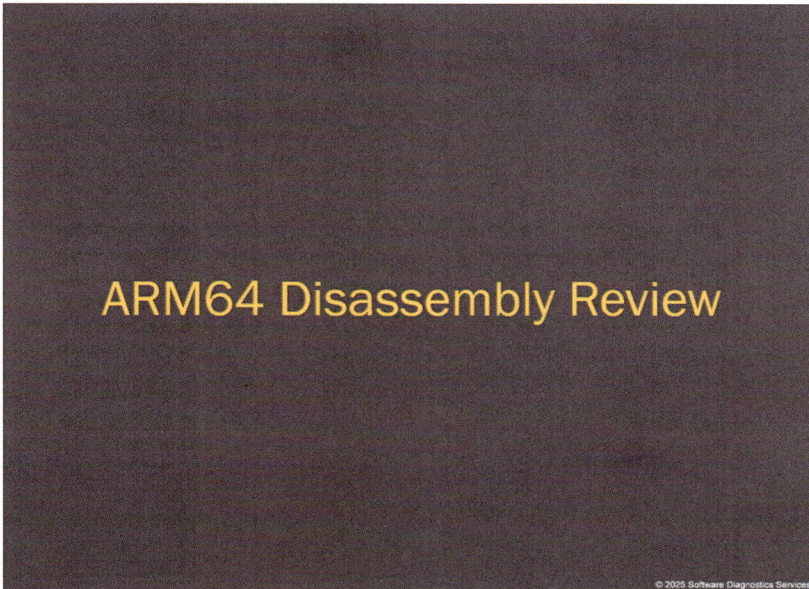

© 2025 Software Diagnostics Services

A64 CPU Registers

A64 CPU Registers

- **X0 – X28**, **W0 – W28**
- **X16** (**XIP0**), **X17** (**XIP1**)
- Stack: **SP**, **X29** (**FP**)
- Next instruction: **PC**
- Link register: **X30** (**LR**)
- Zero register: **XZR**, **WZR**

| X 64-bit | W 32-bit |

© 2025 Software Diagnostics Services

There are 31 general registers from **X0** and **X30**, with some delegated to specific tasks such as intra-procedure calls (**X16**, **XIP0**, and **X17**, **XIP1**), addressing stack frames (Frame Pointer, **FP**, **X29**) and return addresses, the so-called Link Register (**LR**, **X30**). When you call a function, the return address of a caller is saved in **LR**, not on the stack as in Intel/AMD x64. The return instruction in a callee uses the address in **LR** to assign it to **PC** and resume execution. But if a callee calls other functions, the current **LR** needs to be manually saved somewhere, usually on the stack. There's Stack Pointer, **SP**, of course. To get zero values, there's the so-called Zero Register, **XZR**. All **X** registers are 64-bit, and 32-bit lower parts are addressed via the **W** prefix. Next, we briefly look at some aspects.

A64 Instructions and Registers

This slide shows a few examples of CPU instructions that involve operations with registers, for example, moving a value and doing arithmetic. The direction of operands is the same as in the Intel x64 disassembly flavor if you are accustomed to WinDbg on Windows. It is equivalent to an assignment. **BLR** is a call of some function whose address is in the register. **BL** means Branch and Link.

Memory and Stack Addressing

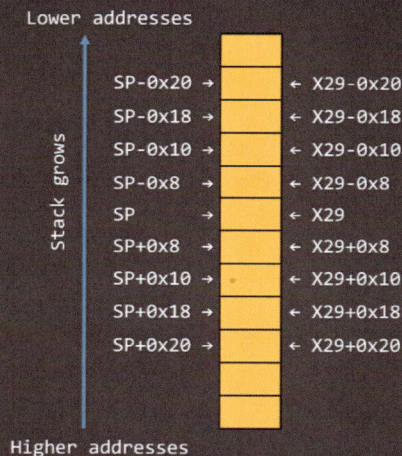

Before we look at operations with memory, let's look at a graphical representation of memory addressing. A thread stack is just any other memory region, so instead of **SP** and **X29 (FP)**, any other register can be used. Please note that the stack grows towards lower addresses, so to access the previously pushed values, you need to use positive offsets from **SP**.

A64 Memory Load Instructions

```
A64 Memory Load Instructions

⊙ Opcode DST, DST₂, [SRC, Offset]

⊙ Opcode DST, DST₂, [SRC], Offset // Postincrement

⊙ Examples:

ldr   x0, [sp]              // X0 ← value at address SP+0
ldr   x0, [x29, #-8]        // X0 ← value at address X29-0x8
ldp   x29, x30, [sp, #32]   // X29 ← value at address SP+32 (0x20)
                           // X30 ← value at address SP+40 (0x28)
ldp   x29, x30, [sp], #16   // X29 ← value at address SP+0
                           // X30 ← value at address SP+8
                           // SP ← SP+16 (0x10)

© 2025 Software Diagnostics Services
```

Constants are encoded in instructions, but if we need arbitrary values, we must get them from memory. Square brackets show memory access relative to an address stored in some register. There's also an option to adjust the value of the register after load, the so-called **Postincrement**, which can be negative.

A64 Memory Store Instructions

```
A64 Memory Store Instructions

⊙ Opcode SRC, SRC₂, [DST, Offset]

⊙ Opcode SRC, SRC₂, [DST, Offset]! // Preincrement

⊙ Examples:

str   x0, [sp, #16]        // x0 → value at address SP+16 (0x10)
str   x0, [x29, #-8]       // x0 → value at address X29-8
stp   x29, x30, [sp, #32]  // x29 → value at address SP+32 (0x20)
                          // x30 → value at address SP+40 (0x28)
stp   x29, x30, [sp, #-16]! // SP ← SP-16 (-0x10)
                          // x29 → set value at address SP
                          // x30 → set value at address SP+8

© 2025 Software Diagnostics Services
```

Storing operand order goes in the other direction compared to other instructions. There's a possibility to **Preincrement** the destination register before storing values.

A64 Flow Instructions

```
A64 Flow Instructions

  ⊙ Opcode DST

  ⊙ Examples:

  adrp  x0, 0x420000      // x0 ← 0x420000

  b     0x401000          // PC ← 0x401000
                          // ("goto" 0x401000)
  br    x17               // PC ← the value of X17

  0x401020:               // PC == 0x401020
  bl    0x401080          // LR ← PC+4 (0x401024)
                          // PC ← 0x401080
                          // ("goto" 0x401080)

                                    © 2025 Software Diagnostics Services
```

Because the size of every instruction is 4 bytes (32 bits), it is only possible to encode a part of a large 4GB address range, either as a relative offset to the current **PC** or via **ADRP** instruction. Goto (an unconditional branch) is implemented via the **B** instruction. Function calls are implemented via the **BL** (Branch and Link) instruction.

A64 Function Parameters

```
A64 Function Parameters

  ⊙ fn func(...);

  ⊙ Left to right via X0 – X7, [SP], [SP+8], [SP+16], ...

                                    © 2025 Software Diagnostics Services
```

On the ARM64 Linux platform, the first eight parameters are passed via registers from left to right and the rest – via the stack locations.

A64 Struct Function Parameters

A64 Struct Function Parameters

- **X0**

  Implicit struct object memory address (&myStruct)

  ```
  let myStruct: Struct = ...;
  myStruct.func(...);
  ```

- **X1 – X7, [SP], [SP+8], [SP+16], ...**

  The rest of the struct function parameters

  ```
  impl Struct {
    fn func(&self, ...);
  }
  ```

© 2025 Software Diagnostics Services

When a struct function is called, the first parameter is implicit and, on the ARM64 Linux platform, is passed via **X0**. It is an object address to help struct functions differentiate between objects of the same struct type and reference correct fields' memory. The rest of the parameters are passed as usual.

Memory Storage

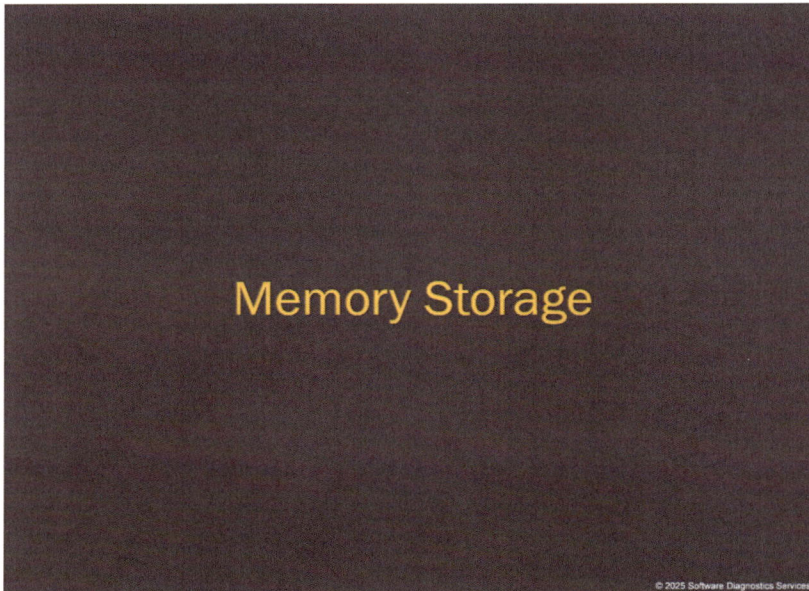

Memory Storage

© 2025 Software Diagnostics Services

What memory storage is used to store values ultimately has an influence on program behavior.

The memory-storage project can be found in the archive[6]. In the following slide descriptions, we only show relevant code snippets and their output on various platforms.

[6] https://www.patterndiagnostics.com/Training/MTRust/MTRust.zip

Memory Regions

All computer memory is physical memory. However, unless you write specific hardware-related kernel-mode drivers or modules, you don't really work with physical memory in your applications and services. You work with the so-called virtual memory, an abstraction that allows you to think that your process works linearly ordered computer memory cells, each with its own memory address. Processes allocate memory in pages of virtual memory. But they can dedicate some of the virtual memory regions for specialized purposes. SSH abbreviation is a good mnemonic for static, stack, and heap types of memory regions. We now look at these three region types separately.

Dynamic Virtual Memory

Virtual memory is dynamic — we have terabytes of virtual memory for an x64 process. But it is not really a memory you can write or read to. It needs to be committed — physical memory pages associated with virtual memory regions. All these committed virtual memory regions are used as underlying memory pages for static data, stack, and heap regions. Even large heap blocks are allocated using this mechanism. In Rust, you can use FFI OS API to allocate large chunks of virtual memory for your own usage.

Static Memory

Static memory is per process and usually contains program data, such as string literals. It can be read-only memory pages. Static memory is shared between all process threads, so caution is needed for multithreaded access. It is "always there", having a static lifetime, so any pointers or references to it are valid for the duration of the process.

Rust Static Memory Values

We can consider the static value address as the owner of the value. Rust also requires the static value to be initialized by a constant value (although the value can be changed later for mutable values, which is considered unsafe. Static values persist and are still accessible after their variables are out of scope (if we have pointers or references to them). Old unsafe idiom of persisting mutable static value changes across function calls is also possible.

Global vs. Local Static

Global vs. Local Static

- ⦿ Local static values are visible only in the current scope

- ⦿ Global static values are visible from different scopes

© 2025 Software Diagnostics Services

Rust Static Memory References

Rust Static Memory References

- ⦿ Static reference can only reference a static variable

- ⦿ Shared (mutable) reference to a mutable static value is discouraged

© 2025 Software Diagnostics Services

```rust
static GSV: i32 = 1;

fn main() {

println!("--- Static Memory ---");
{
    {
        let _v: i32 = 0;
        // static SV: i32 = _v;
    }

    static SV: i32 = 0;
    static mut SMR: &i32 = &SV;

    #[allow(static_mut_refs)]
    unsafe {
        println!("address of SV: {:?} address of SMR: {:?} value of SMR: {SMR:p}",
addr_of!(SV), addr_of!(SMR));

        static SV2: i32 = 0;
        SMR = &SV2;

        println!("address of SV2: {:?} address of SMR: {:?} value of SMR: {SMR:p}",
addr_of!(SV2), addr_of!(SMR));

        static STR: &str = "Hello, Static Memory!";
        println!("address of STR: {:?} value of STR: {STR:p} ", addr_of!(STR));
    }

    #[allow(static_mut_refs)]
    unsafe {
        // println!("address of SV2: {:?}", addr_of!(SV2));
        println!("address of SMR: {:?} value of SMR: {SMR:p}", addr_of!(SMR));

        static STR: &str = "Hello, Static Memory!";
        println!("address of STR: {:?} value of STR: {STR:p} ", addr_of!(STR));
    }

    {
        #[allow(dead_code)]
        struct Val(i32);
```

```rust
        let v: Val = Val(0);
        let _v2: Val = v;

        static _SV: Val = Val(0);
        // static SV2: Val = _SV;
    }


    {
        let _v: i32 = 0;
        // static SVR: &i32 = &_v;

        static SV: i32 = 0;
        let _svr: &i32 = &SV;
    }

    #[allow(static_mut_refs)]
    unsafe {
        unsafe fn foo() {
            static mut SMV: i32 = 0;
            println!("value of SMV: {SMV}");
            SMV += 1;
        }

        for _ in 0..10 {
            foo();
        }
    }

    println!("address of GSV: {:?} value of GSV: {GSV:?}", addr_of!(GSV));
}


}
```

Windows output:

```
--- Static Memory ---
address of SV: 0x7ff77466c858 address of SMR: 0x7ff774676000 value of SMR:
0x7ff77466c858
address of SV2: 0x7ff77466c85c address of SMR: 0x7ff774676000 value of SMR:
0x7ff77466c85c
address of STR: 0x7ff77466c860 value of STR: 0x7ff77466c638
address of SMR: 0x7ff774676000 value of SMR: 0x7ff77466c85c
address of STR: 0x7ff77466c870 value of STR: 0x7ff77466c638
value of SMV: 0
value of SMV: 1
value of SMV: 2
value of SMV: 3
value of SMV: 4
value of SMV: 5
value of SMV: 6
value of SMV: 7
value of SMV: 8
value of SMV: 9
address of GSV: 0x7ff77466c360 value of GSV: 1
```

x64 Linux output:

```
--- Static Memory ---
address of SV: 0x564d073b41c8 address of SMR: 0x564d073c6008 value of SMR:
0x564d073b41c8
address of SV2: 0x564d073b41cc address of SMR: 0x564d073c6008 value of SMR:
0x564d073b41cc
address of STR: 0x564d073c2e18 value of STR: 0x564d073b40f6
address of SMR: 0x564d073c6008 value of SMR: 0x564d073b41cc
address of STR: 0x564d073c2e28 value of STR: 0x564d073b40f6
value of SMV: 0
value of SMV: 1
value of SMV: 2
value of SMV: 3
value of SMV: 4
value of SMV: 5
value of SMV: 6
value of SMV: 7
value of SMV: 8
value of SMV: 9
```

```
address of GSV: 0x564d073b4000 value of GSV: 1
```

A64 Linux output:

```
--- Static Memory ---
address of SV: 0xc632f43913bc address of SMR: 0xc632f43b3010 value of SMR:
0xc632f43913bc
address of SV2: 0xc632f43913c0 address of SMR: 0xc632f43b3010 value of SMR:
0xc632f43913c0
address of STR: 0xc632f43b03a0 value of STR: 0xc632f43912ea
address of SMR: 0xc632f43b3010 value of SMR: 0xc632f43913c0
address of STR: 0xc632f43b03b0 value of STR: 0xc632f43912ea
value of SMV: 0
value of SMV: 1
value of SMV: 2
value of SMV: 3
value of SMV: 4
value of SMV: 5
value of SMV: 6
value of SMV: 7
value of SMV: 8
value of SMV: 9
address of GSV: 0xc632f43911f4 value of GSV: 1
```

Stack Memory

Stack memory regions are separate for each process thread and provide some degree of isolation. The purpose of stack memory is to have some space for function frame data such as parameters and local values. Such frames are temporary: once a function returns to its caller frame, frame memory can be reused by subsequent function calls so we should treat memory values before and after each call as undefined, containing garbage. However, for the duration of a function call, frame memory values can point to (contain addresses of) static, stack, and heap memory.

Thread Stack Frames

What are thread stack frames? This diagram illustrates the concept.

Local Value Lifecycle

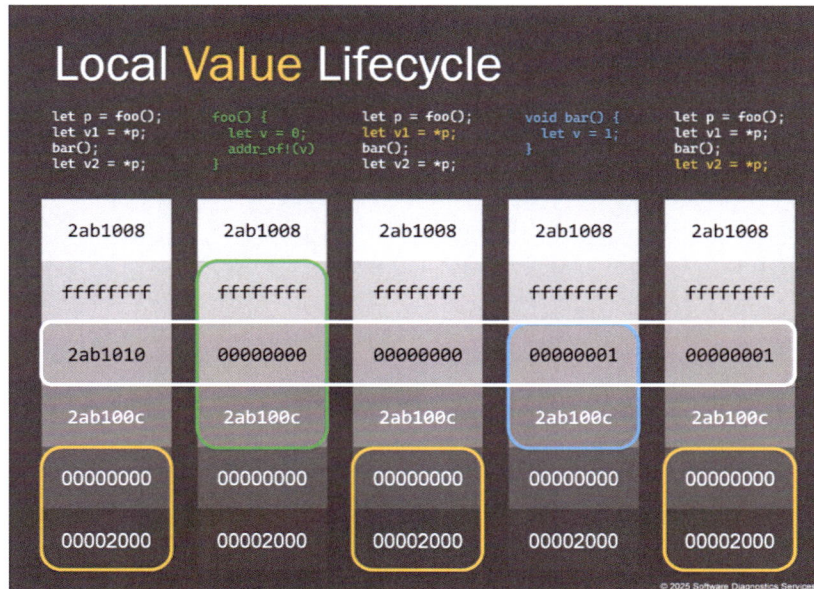

Local variable values are only valid during the duration of a function call. Unsafe code that doesn't respect value lifetimes can be dangerous. This sequence illustrates that. Suppose we call the function foo. Inside, a stack frame is created that contains the value of the local variable v. The function returns the address of that value. In the caller, we save the value that the address points to and call another function that overwrites the previous stack frame with new values. Upon the return, we dereference the pointer again and get a different value.

Scope

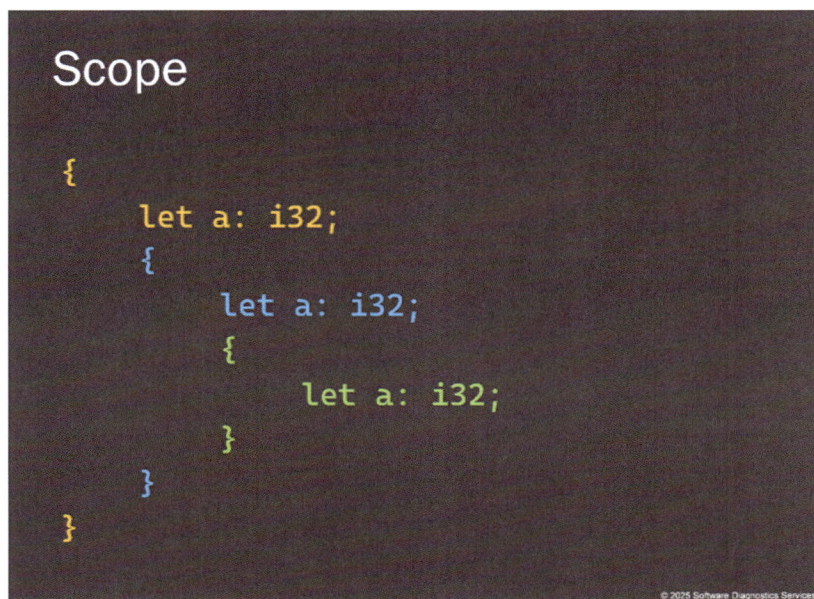

We already mentioned scopes a few times before. Scopes of variables can be nested with variable names in the nested scope, hiding variables with the same name in the enclosing scope. Usually, the stack space for all variables inside a function's scopes is allocated at once when the function is entered.

Rust Stack Memory Values

As you see from the previous slides, stack values are temporary and additionally bound to the owner's scope, be it a function body or some nested block of code.

Rust Stack Memory References

Stack memory values may contain addresses of static and heap values. Rust automatically drops (deallocates) a heap value when its reference owner goes out of scope.

```
println!("--- Stack Memory ---");
{
    unsafe {
        unsafe fn foo() -> *const i32 {
            let v: i32 = 0;
            println!("foo:: address of v: {:?} value of v: {v}", addr_of!(v));
            addr_of!(v)
        }

        fn bar() {
            let v: i32 = 1;
            println!("bar:: address of v: {:?} value of v: {v}", addr_of!(v));
        }

        let p: *const i32 = foo();
        let v: i32 = *p;
        println!("value of p: {p:?} value of v: {v}");
        bar();
        let v: i32 = *p;
        println!("value of p: {p:?} value of v: {v}");
        println!("value of p: {p:?} dereference of p: {:?}", *p);
    }

    {
        let string: &str = "Hello, Static Memory!";
        println!("address of string: {:?} value of string: {string:p} ",
addr_of!(string));
    }

    {
        let hv: Box<i32> = Box::new(0);

        println!("address of hv: {:?}", addr_of!(hv));

        // drop(hv);
    }

    {
        let a: i32 = 1;
        {
            let a: i32 = 2;
            {
```

```
        let a: i32 =3;

            println!("value of a: {a}");
        }

        println!("value of a: {a}");
        }

        println!("value of a: {a}");
    }

}
```

Windows output:

```
--- Stack Memory ---
foo:: address of v: 0x17977bee1c value of v: 0
value of p: 0x17977bee1c value of v: 0
bar:: address of v: 0x17977bee1c value of v: 1
value of p: 0x17977bee1c value of v: 1
value of p: 0x17977bee1c dereference of p: 23
address of string: 0x17977bf310 value of string: 0x7ff7b420d690
address of hv: 0x17977bf378
value of a: 3
value of a: 2
value of a: 1
```

x64 Linux output:

```
--- Stack Memory ---
foo:: address of v: 0x7ffcb84dc78c value of v: 0
value of p: 0x7ffcb84dc78c value of v: 0
bar:: address of v: 0x7ffcb84dc78c value of v: 1
value of p: 0x7ffcb84dc78c value of v: 1
value of p: 0x7ffcb84dc78c dereference of p: 0
address of string: 0x7ffcb84dcdd0 value of string: 0x55b1ea30d12b
address of hv: 0x7ffcb84dce38
value of a: 3
value of a: 2
value of a: 1
```

A64 Linux output:

```
--- Stack Memory ---
foo:: address of v: 0xffffc3f4c704 value of v: 0
value of p: 0xffffc3f4c704 value of v: 0
bar:: address of v: 0xffffc3f4c704 value of v: 1
value of p: 0xffffc3f4c704 value of v: 1
value of p: 0xffffc3f4c704 dereference of p: 43690
address of string: 0xffffc3f4cd20 value of string: 0xaaaac218f0fe
address of hv: 0xffffc3f4cd88
value of a: 3
value of a: 2
value of a: 1
```

Heap Memory

Like static memory, heap memory is also accessible to and shared between all process threads. It is also dynamic, with the total amount of allocated memory changing over time. After heap-allocated memory is freed or released, its contents become undefined due to subsequent allocations or heap compactification. Values allocated from the heap may contain pointers to static and other heap memory. Generally, if heap memory contains pointers to stack memory, it may be a red flag since stack memory is defined only for the duration of the function call unless heap memory is also released before the return of the function call.

Rust Heap Memory Values

In Rust, heap memory values are temporary and accessible until explicitly dropped or their owners become out of scope. Also, heap value can contain references to stack values of the same or greater lifetime.

```rust
println!("--- Heap Memory ---");
{
    let hv: Box<i32> = Box::new(0);

    println!("address of hv: {:?}, address of heap allocation: {hv:p} value of heap allocation: {hv}", addr_of!(hv));

    let sv: i32 = 0;
    println!("address of sv: {:?}", addr_of!(sv));
    {
        #[derive(Debug)]
        struct Val<'a>(&'a i32);

        let hval: Box<Val> = Box::new(Val(&sv));

        println!("address of hval: {:?}, address of heap allocation: {hval:p} value of heap allocation: {:p}", addr_of!(hval), hval.0);
    }

    unsafe {
        use std::alloc::{alloc, dealloc, Layout};
```

```
        let l: Layout = Layout::from_size_align_unchecked(512, 1);
        let p: *mut u8 = alloc(l);

        println!("address of p: {:?} value of p: {:p}", addr_of!(p), p);

        dealloc(p, l);
    }
}
```

Windows output:

```
--- Heap Memory ---
address of hv: 0x17977bf3f8, address of heap allocation: 0x1c158c5bf10 value of heap
allocation: 0
address of sv: 0x17977bf47c
address of hval: 0x17977bf4c8, address of heap allocation: 0x1c158c5bf30 value of
heap allocation: 0x17977bf47c
address of p: 0x17977bf558 value of p: 0x1c158c65d30
```

x64 Linux output:

```
--- Heap Memory ---
address of hv: 0x7ffcb84dceb8, address of heap allocation: 0x55b1eb845ae0 value of
heap allocation: 0
address of sv: 0x7ffcb84dcf3c
address of hval: 0x7ffcb84dcf88, address of heap allocation: 0x55b1eb845b00 value of
heap allocation: 0x7ffcb84dcf3c
address of p: 0x7ffcb84dd018 value of p: 0x55b1eb845b20
```

A64 Linux output:

```
--- Heap Memory ---
address of hv: 0xffffc3f4ce08, address of heap allocation: 0xaaaade85cad0 value of
heap allocation: 0
address of sv: 0xffffc3f4ce8c
address of hval: 0xffffc3f4ced8, address of heap allocation: 0xaaaade85caf0 value of
heap allocation: 0xffffc3f4ce8c
address of p: 0xffffc3f4cf68 value of p: 0xaaaade85cb10
```

Rust Const Values

```rust
println!("--- Rust Const Values ---");
{
    const CV: i32 = 1;
    #[allow(non_snake_case)]
    let rCV: &i32 = &CV;

    // println!("address of CV: {:?}", addr_of!(CV));
    println!("value of CV: {CV}");

    println!("value of rCV: {rCV:p} value of *rCV {:?}", *rCV);

    unsafe {
        #[allow(non_snake_case)]
        let pCV: *const i32 = rCV as *const i32;

        println!("value of pCV: {pCV:p} value of *pCV {:?}", *pCV);
    }

    // let n: i32 = 2;
    // const rCV: &i32 = &n;
}
```

Windows output:

```
--- Rust Const Values ---
value of CV: 1
value of rCV: 0x7ff7929bc888 value of *rCV 1
value of pCV: 0x7ff7929bc888 value of *pCV 1
```

x64 Linux output:

```
--- Rust Const Values ---
value of CV: 1
value of rCV: 0x5606d755e1e4 value of *rCV 1
value of pCV: 0x5606d755e1e4 value of *pCV 1
```

A64 Linux output:

```
--- Rust Const Values ---
value of CV: 1
value of rCV: 0xc36a2f9216a8 value of *rCV 1
value of pCV: 0xc36a2f9216a8 value of *pCV 1
```

Useful WinDbg Commands

Useful WinDbg Commands

- `!address [<address>]`
- `bp memory_storage::main / g`
- `uf memory_storage::main`
- `x memory_storage!memory_storage::*`
- `dt memory_storage!<type> / dx`
- `dps <address> / db / dd`
- `~<thread>k`
- `dv /i /V`

© 2025 Software Diagnostics Services

Useful GDB Commands

Useful GDB Commands

- `break memory_storage::main`
- `run / continue / next`
- `info proc mappings`
- `disassemble memory_storage::main`
- `info types / locals / variables / ptype`
- `x/gx <address>`
- `x/s <address>`
- `thread apply <thread> <command>`

© 2025 Software Diagnostics Services

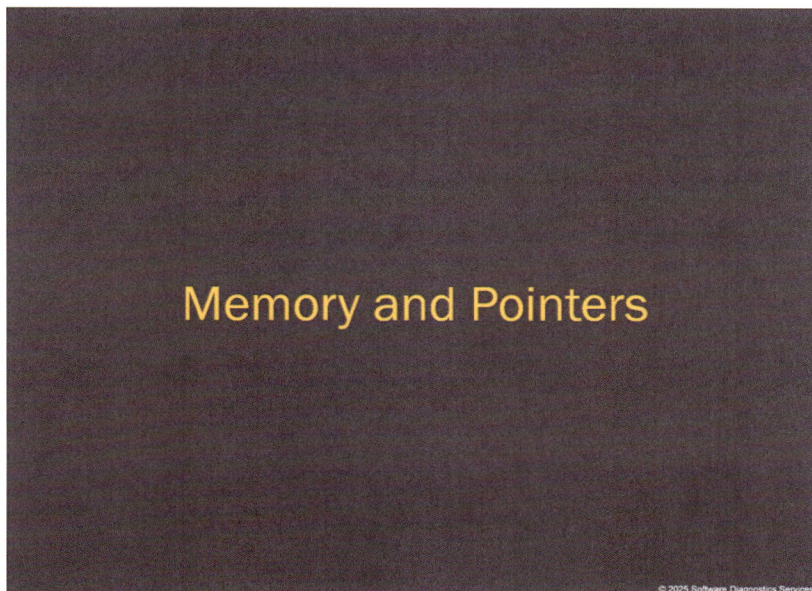

Now, we look at the memory representation of pointers and entities they point to.

The `memory-and-pointers` project can be found in the archive[7]. In the following slide descriptions, we only show relevant code snippets and their output on various platforms.

---

[7] https://www.patterndiagnostics.com/Training/MTRust/MTRust.zip

Mental Exercise

Here, in this picture, entities are the so-called memory cells. Memory cells have addresses that start from 0 and are usually incremented by the so-called pointer size, which is 4 on 32-bit systems and 8 on 64-bit systems. Here, for visual clarity, we use memory cells from a 32-bit system.

Debugger Memory Layout

When we use a debugger, it prints memory cell addresses and their contents in a certain layout shown on this slide. Some debugger commands, such as **x** in GDB, use 2-column and some n-column layouts to print memory.

Memory Dereference Layout

For a 2-column format, some debuggers, such as WinDbg and their commands may interpret the first column as a pointer. In such a case, the second column is a value from a pointer dereference. Also, notice a case when a pointer points to itself. For GDB, it is possible to emulate such behavior using a custom script:

```
define dpp
    set $i = 0
    set $p = $arg0
    while $i < $arg1
        printf "%p: ", $p
        x/gx *(long *)$p
        set $i = $i + 1
        set $p = $p + 8
    end
end
```

Names as Addresses

To repeat, for memory layout, names are interpreted as addresses, and memory cell content (cell value) can also be interpreted as a memory address.

Addresses and Entities

Entities can be either single cells or multicells. Each part of a multicell can be interpreted as having a memory address, if necessary, even if it wasn't meant to have a memory address.

Addresses and Structures

A structure in memory is a sequential collection of memory cells; some may be multicell and themselves substructures. Each part of a structure, its member, or structure field has its own address as well, in addition to the overall address of the structure.

Pointers to Structures

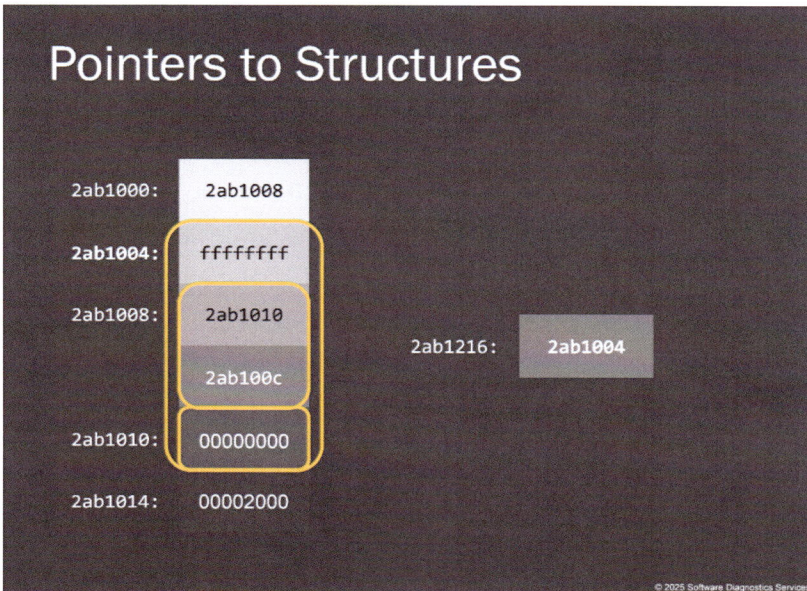

A structure has its address. A pointer to a structure is a memory cell that contains that address. It has its own address.

Arrays

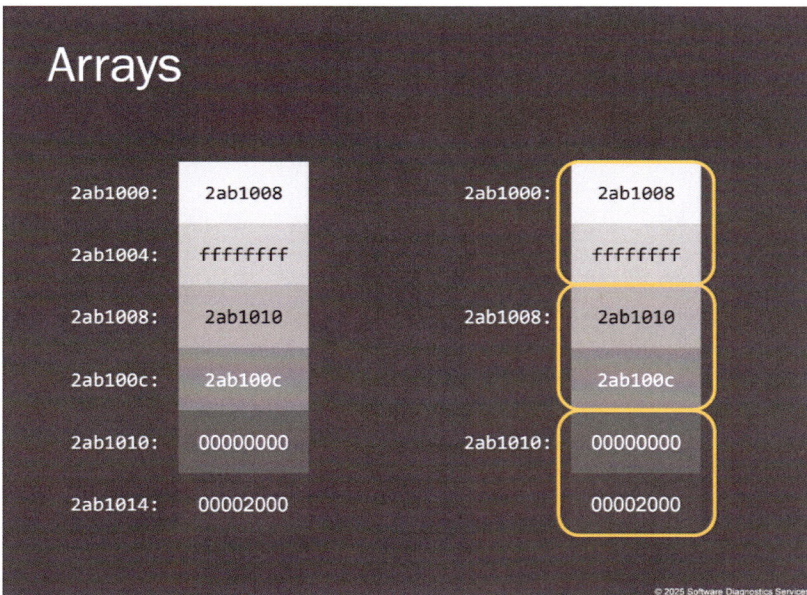

An array is a contiguous sequence of n-cells in memory called array elements. Each array element has its own address. Since the size of each array element is fixed and the same, addressing the random element is fast. Arrays are fixed in size in Rust.

Arrays and Pointers to Arrays

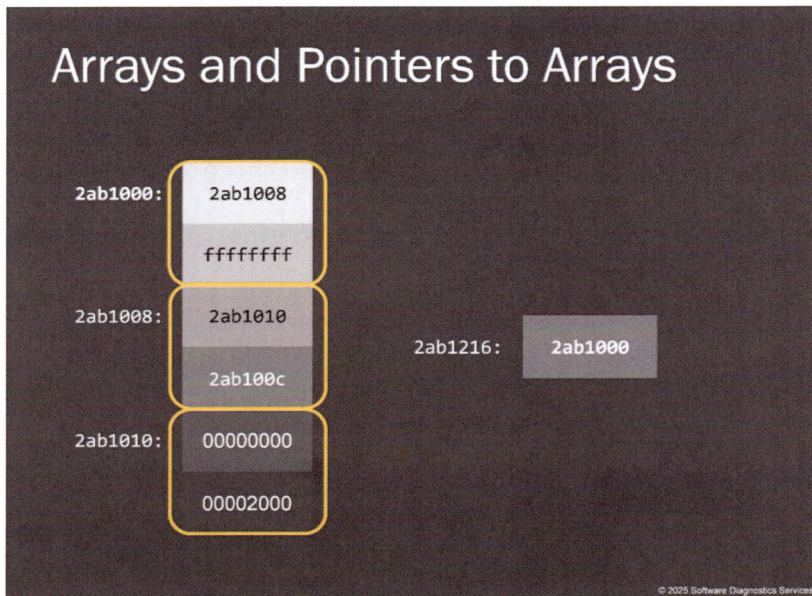

The array address is the address of its first element. But a pointer to an array is a different memory cell that contains the array address. This is similar to structures and pointers to structures. An array can be considered as a structure as well.

Fat Pointers

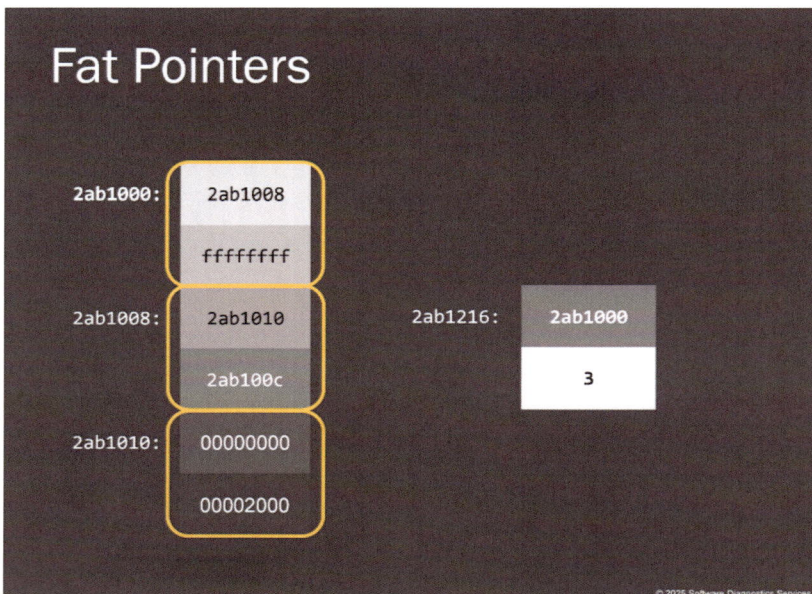

A fat pointer is a pointer that, in addition to a memory address it points to, contains extra information, for example, the size of a memory block in bytes or the count of array elements.

Array Slices

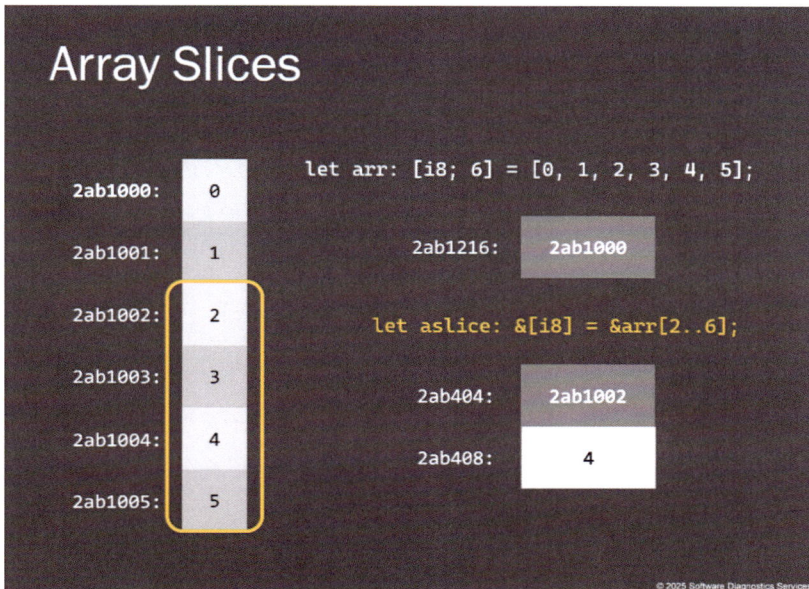

An array slice is a fat pointer to some portion of it.

```rust
println!("--- Arrays and Array Slices ---");
{
    let arr: [i8; 6] = [0, 1, 2, 3, 4, 5];

    println!("address of arr: {:?} address of arr[0]: {:?} address of arr[1]: {:?}
address of arr[2]: {:?}",
        addr_of!(arr), addr_of!(arr[0]),
        addr_of!(arr[1]), addr_of!(arr[2]));

    let mut aslice: &[i8] = &arr[2..6];

    println!("address of aslice: {:?} value of aslice: {aslice:p} address of
aslice[0]: {:?} address of aslice[1]: {:?}",
        addr_of!(aslice), addr_of!(aslice[0]),
        addr_of!(aslice[1]));

    unsafe {
        println!("slice elements: {:?}",
            *(((addr_of!(aslice) as usize) +
            std::mem::size_of::<usize>()) as *const usize));
    }
```

```rust
    aslice = &arr[2..4];

    println!("address of aslice: {:?} value of aslice: {aslice:p} address of
aslice[0]: {:?} address of aslice[1]: {:?}",
        addr_of!(aslice), addr_of!(aslice[0]),
        addr_of!(aslice[1]));

    unsafe {
        println!("slice elements: {:?}",
        *(((addr_of!(aslice) as usize) +
        std::mem::size_of::<usize>()) as *const usize));
    }

    aslice = &arr;

    println!("address of aslice: {:?} value of aslice: {aslice:p} address of
aslice[0]: {:?} address of aslice[1]: {:?}",
        addr_of!(aslice), addr_of!(aslice[0]),
        addr_of!(aslice[1]));

    unsafe {
        println!("slice elements: {:?}",
        *(((addr_of!(aslice) as usize) +
        std::mem::size_of::<usize>()) as *const usize));
    }
}
```

Windows output:

```
--- Arrays and Array Slices ---
address of arr: 0x5d9970e14a address of arr[0]: 0x5d9970e14a address of arr[1]:
0x5d9970e14b address of arr[2]: 0x5d9970e14c
address of aslice: 0x5d9970e1e0 value of aslice: 0x5d9970e14c address of aslice[0]:
0x5d9970e14c address of aslice[1]: 0x5d9970e14d
slice elements: 4
address of aslice: 0x5d9970e1e0 value of aslice: 0x5d9970e14c address of aslice[0]:
0x5d9970e14c address of aslice[1]: 0x5d9970e14d
slice elements: 2
address of aslice: 0x5d9970e1e0 value of aslice: 0x5d9970e14a address of aslice[0]:
0x5d9970e14a address of aslice[1]: 0x5d9970e14b
slice elements: 6
```

x64 Linux output:

```
--- Arrays and Array Slices ---
address of arr: 0x7fffd4c0b0fa address of arr[0]: 0x7fffd4c0b0fa address of arr[1]:
0x7fffd4c0b0fb address of arr[2]: 0x7fffd4c0b0fc
address of aslice: 0x7fffd4c0b190 value of aslice: 0x7fffd4c0b0fc address of
aslice[0]: 0x7fffd4c0b0fc address of aslice[1]: 0x7fffd4c0b0fd
slice elements: 4
address of aslice: 0x7fffd4c0b190 value of aslice: 0x7fffd4c0b0fc address of
aslice[0]: 0x7fffd4c0b0fc address of aslice[1]: 0x7fffd4c0b0fd
slice elements: 2
address of aslice: 0x7fffd4c0b190 value of aslice: 0x7fffd4c0b0fa address of
aslice[0]: 0x7fffd4c0b0fa address of aslice[1]: 0x7fffd4c0b0fb
slice elements: 6
```

A64 Linux output:

```
--- Arrays and Array Slices ---
address of arr: 0xfffff69b1a2a address of arr[0]: 0xfffff69b1a2a address of arr[1]:
0xfffff69b1a2b address of arr[2]: 0xfffff69b1a2c
address of aslice: 0xfffff69b1ac0 value of aslice: 0xfffff69b1a2c address of
aslice[0]: 0xfffff69b1a2c address of aslice[1]: 0xfffff69b1a2d
slice elements: 4
address of aslice: 0xfffff69b1ac0 value of aslice: 0xfffff69b1a2c address of
aslice[0]: 0xfffff69b1a2c address of aslice[1]: 0xfffff69b1a2d
slice elements: 2
address of aslice: 0xfffff69b1ac0 value of aslice: 0xfffff69b1a2a address of
aslice[0]: 0xfffff69b1a2a address of aslice[1]: 0xfffff69b1a2b
slice elements: 6
```

String Literals (UTF-8)

String literals are sequences of UTF-8 encoded characters stored in static memory. The compiler usually avoids duplicating string literals if the same one is referenced in source code in multiple locations. Since a character may occupy several bytes, it is impossible to directly refer to individual characters like in an array, as each indexed array access will require byte sequence parsing from the beginning.

```
println!("--- String Literals ---");
{
    let sl: &str  = "Hello!";

    println!("address of sl: {:?} value of sl: {sl:p}", addr_of!(sl));

    unsafe {
        println!("string literal elements: {:?}",
            *(((addr_of!(sl) as usize) +
            std::mem::size_of::<usize>()) as *const usize));
    }

    let sl: &str  = "Привет!";

    println!("address of sl: {:?} value of sl: {sl:p}",
        addr_of!(sl));

    unsafe {
        println!("string literal elements: {:?}",
            *(((addr_of!(sl) as usize) +
            std::mem::size_of::<usize>()) as *const usize));
    }
```

```
}
```

Windows output:

```
--- String Literals ---
address of sl: 0x5d9970e4f8 value of sl: 0x7ff6939006d0
string literal elements: 6
address of sl: 0x5d9970e5a0 value of sl: 0x7ff693900780
string literal elements: 13
```

x64 Linux output:

```
--- String Literals ---
address of sl: 0x7fffd4c0b4a8 value of sl: 0x55c963380154
string literal elements: 6
address of sl: 0x7fffd4c0b550 value of sl: 0x55c963380190
string literal elements: 13
```

A64 Linux output:

```
--- String Literals ---
address of sl: 0x7fffd4c0b4a8 value of sl: 0x55c963380154
string literal elements: 6
address of sl: 0x7fffd4c0b550 value of sl: 0x55c963380190
string literal elements: 13
```

Byte Strings

If you only work with ASCII characters, you can use byte strings, which are slices of arrays of bytes.

```rust
println!("--- Byte Strings ---");
{
    let bs: &[u8]  = b"Hello!";

    println!("address of bs: {:?} value of bs: {bs:p} address of bs[0]: {:?} address
of bs[1]: {:?}",
        addr_of!(bs), addr_of!(bs[0]),
        addr_of!(bs[1]));

    unsafe {
        println!("byte string elements: {:?}",
            *(((addr_of!(bs) as usize) +
            std::mem::size_of::<usize>()) as *const usize));
    }
}
```

Windows output:

```
--- Byte Strings ---
address of bs: 0x5d9970e678 value of bs: 0x7ff6939006d0 address of bs[0]:
0x7ff6939006d0 address of bs[1]: 0x7ff6939006d1
byte string elements: 6
```

x64 Linux output:

```
--- Byte Strings ---
address of bs: 0x7fffd4c0b628 value of bs: 0x55c963380154 address of bs[0]:
0x55c963380154 address of bs[1]: 0x55c963380155
byte string elements: 6
```

A64 Linux output:

```
--- Byte Strings ---
address of bs: 0xfffff69b1f58 value of bs: 0xaaaab9f01854 address of bs[0]:
0xaaaab9f01854 address of bs[1]: 0xaaaab9f01855
byte string elements: 6
```

Vectors

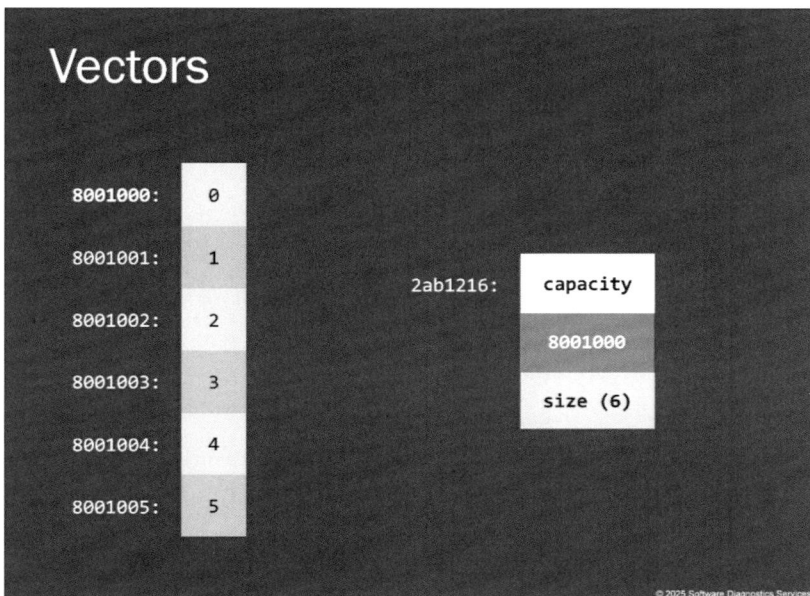

Vectors are a generalization of arrays. They do not have a fixed length. Even if an array is a local stack value, it contains a pointer to heap memory holding vector elements.

Vector Slices

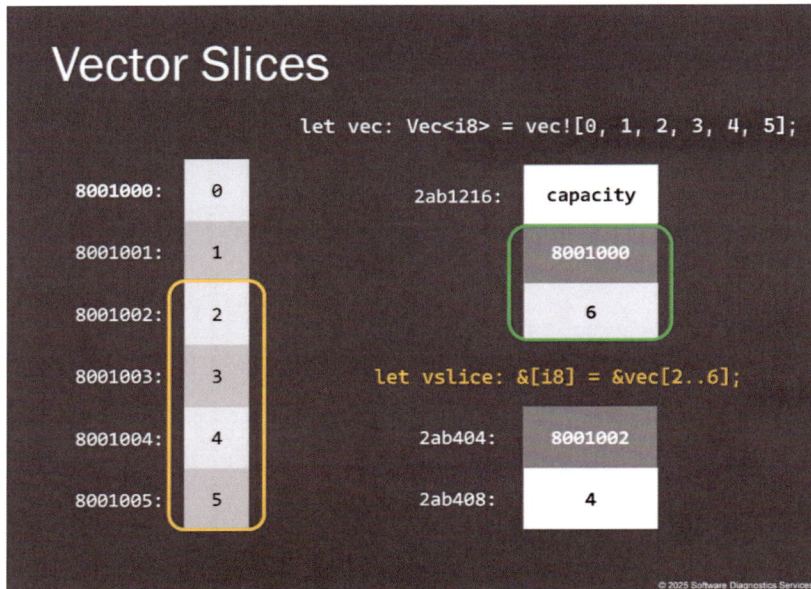

Vector slices are similar to array slices – they are fat pointers.

```rust
println!("--- Vectors and Vector Slices ---");
{
    let mut vec: Vec<i8> = vec![0, 1, 2, 3, 4, 5];

    println!("address of vec: {:?} address of heap allocation: {:?} address of
vec[0]: {:?} address of vec[1]: {:?} address of vec[2]: {:?}",
        addr_of!(vec), vec.as_ptr(), addr_of!(vec[0]), addr_of!(vec[1]),
addr_of!(vec[2]));

    unsafe {
        println!("address of vec: {:?} capacity: {:?} address of heap allocation:
0x{:x} number of elements: {:?}",
            addr_of!(vec), *(((addr_of!(vec) as usize)) as *const usize),
            *(((addr_of!(vec) as usize) + std::mem::size_of::<usize>()) as *const
usize),
            *(((addr_of!(vec) as usize) + 2*std::mem::size_of::<usize>()) as *const
usize)
        );
    }

    vec.push(6);
```

```
    unsafe {
        println!("address of vec: {:?} capacity: {:?} address of heap allocation:
0x{:x} number of elements: {:?}",
            addr_of!(vec), *(((addr_of!(vec) as usize)) as *const usize),
            *(((addr_of!(vec) as usize) + std::mem::size_of::<usize>()) as *const
usize),
            *(((addr_of!(vec) as usize) + 2*std::mem::size_of::<usize>()) as *const
usize)
        );
    }

    let vslice: &[i8] = &vec[2..6];

    println!("address of vslice: {:?} value of vslice: {vslice:p} address of
vslice[0]: {:?} address of vslice[1]: {:?}",
        addr_of!(vslice), addr_of!(vslice[0]), addr_of!(vslice[1]));

    unsafe {
        println!("slice elements: {:?}", *(((addr_of!(vslice) as usize) +
std::mem::size_of::<usize>()) as *const usize));
    }

    let vslice: &[i8] = &vec;

    println!("address of vslice: {:?} value of vslice: {vslice:p} address of
vslice[0]: {:?} address of vslice[1]: {:?}",
        addr_of!(vslice), addr_of!(vslice[0]), addr_of!(vslice[1]));

    unsafe {
        println!("slice elements: {:?}", *(((addr_of!(vslice) as usize) +
std::mem::size_of::<usize>()) as *const usize));
    }
}
```

128

Windows output:

```
--- Vectors and Vector Slices ---
address of vec: 0x3e1419e328 address of heap allocation: 0x1c042d1a730 address of
vec[0]: 0x1c042d1a730 address of vec[1]: 0x1c042d1a731 address of vec[2]:
0x1c042d1a732
address of vec: 0x3e1419e328 capacity: 6 address of heap allocation: 0x1c042d1a730
number of elements: 6
address of vec: 0x3e1419e328 capacity: 12 address of heap allocation: 0x1c042d1a730
number of elements: 7
address of vslice: 0x3e1419e5e0 value of vslice: 0x1c042d1a732 address of vslice[0]:
0x1c042d1a732 address of vslice[1]: 0x1c042d1a733
slice elements: 4
address of vslice: 0x3e1419e730 value of vslice: 0x1c042d1a730 address of vslice[0]:
0x1c042d1a730 address of vslice[1]: 0x1c042d1a731
slice elements: 7
```

x64 Linux output:

```
--- Vectors and Vector Slices ---
address of vec: 0x7fffaeb3aeb8 address of heap allocation: 0x5631f1943a50 address of
vec[0]: 0x5631f1943a50 address of vec[1]: 0x5631f1943a51 address of vec[2]:
0x5631f1943a52
address of vec: 0x7fffaeb3aeb8 capacity: 6 address of heap allocation: 0x5631f1943a50
number of elements: 6
address of vec: 0x7fffaeb3aeb8 capacity: 12 address of heap allocation:
0x5631f1943a50 number of elements: 7
address of vslice: 0x7fffaeb3b150 value of vslice: 0x5631f1943a52 address of
vslice[0]: 0x5631f1943a52 address of vslice[1]: 0x5631f1943a53
slice elements: 4
address of vslice: 0x7fffaeb3b2a0 value of vslice: 0x5631f1943a50 address of
vslice[0]: 0x5631f1943a50 address of vslice[1]: 0x5631f1943a51
slice elements: 7
```

A64 Linux output:

```
--- Vectors and Vector Slices ---
address of vec: 0xffffd49dbb98 address of heap allocation: 0xc38848fd3b10 address of
vec[0]: 0xc38848fd3b10 address of vec[1]: 0xc38848fd3b11 address of vec[2]:
0xc38848fd3b12
address of vec: 0xffffd49dbb98 capacity: 6 address of heap allocation: 0xc38848fd3b10
number of elements: 6
address of vec: 0xffffd49dbb98 capacity: 12 address of heap allocation:
0xc38848fd3b10 number of elements: 7
address of vslice: 0xffffd49dbe50 value of vslice: 0xc38848fd3b12 address of
vslice[0]: 0xc38848fd3b12 address of vslice[1]: 0xc38848fd3b13
slice elements: 4
address of vslice: 0xffffd49dbfa0 value of vslice: 0xc38848fd3b10 address of
vslice[0]: 0xc38848fd3b10 address of vslice[1]: 0xc38848fd3b11
slice elements: 7
```

Strings

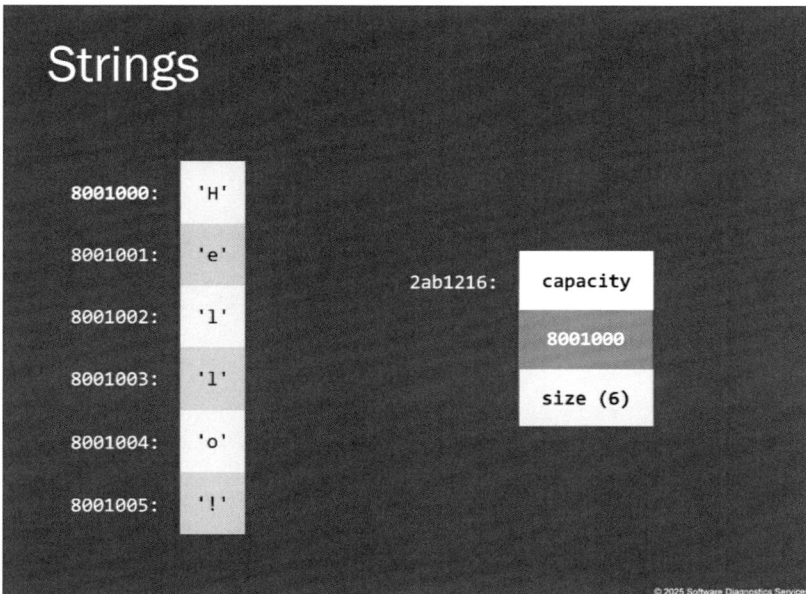

Strings are vectors of UTF-8 characters.

String Slices

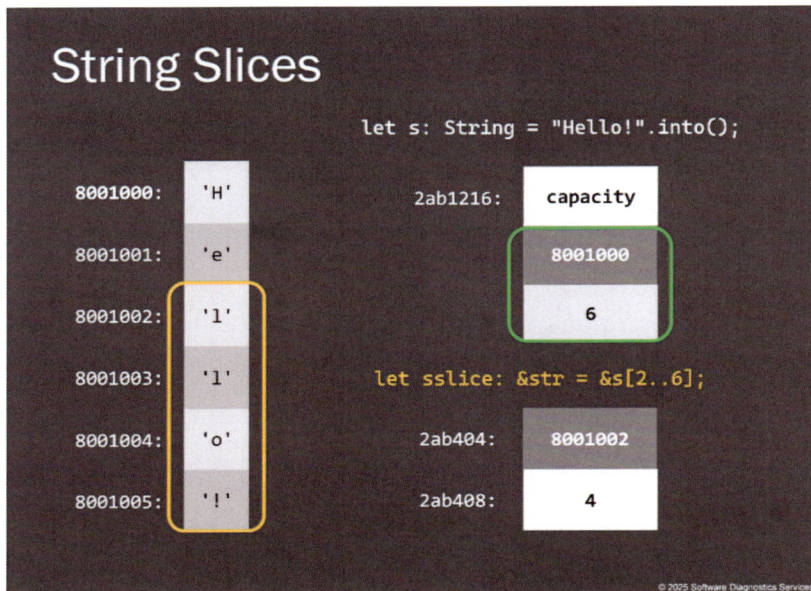

And their slices are like vector slices.

```
println!("--- Strings and String Slices ---");
{
    let s: String = "Hello!".into(); // "Hello!".to_string();

    println!("address of s: {:?} address of heap allocation: {:?}", addr_of!(s),
s.as_ptr());

    unsafe {
        println!("address of s: {:?} capacity: {:?} address of heap allocation:
0x{:x} number of bytes: {:?}",
            addr_of!(s), *(((addr_of!(s) as usize)) as *const usize),
            *(((addr_of!(s) as usize) + std::mem::size_of::<usize>()) as *const
usize),
            *(((addr_of!(s) as usize) + 2*std::mem::size_of::<usize>()) as *const
usize)
        );
    }

    let sslice: &str = &s[2..6];

    println!("address of sslice: {:?} value of sslice: {sslice:p}",
addr_of!(sslice));
```

```rust
    unsafe {
        println!("slice elements: {:?}",
            *(((addr_of!(sslice) as usize) +
            std::mem::size_of::<usize>()) as *const usize));
    }

    let sslice: &str = &s;

    println!("address of sslice: {:?} value of sslice: {sslice:p}",
addr_of!(sslice));

    unsafe {
        println!("slice elements: {:?}",
            *(((addr_of!(sslice) as usize) +
            std::mem::size_of::<usize>()) as *const usize));
    }
}
```

Windows output:

```
--- Strings and String Slices ---
address of s: 0x3e1419e8b8 address of heap allocation: 0x1c042d1a730
address of s: 0x3e1419e8b8 capacity: 6 address of heap allocation: 0x1c042d1a730 num-
ber of bytes: 6
address of sslice: 0x3e1419ea20 value of sslice: 0x1c042d1a732
slice elements: 4
address of sslice: 0x3e1419eb00 value of sslice: 0x1c042d1a730
slice elements: 6
```

x64 Linux output:

```
--- Strings and String Slices ---
address of s: 0x7ffeb9e8f838 address of heap allocation: 0x559c530b3a50
address of s: 0x7ffeb9e8f838 capacity: 6 address of heap allocation: 0x559c530b3a50
number of bytes: 6
address of sslice: 0x7ffeb9e8f990 value of sslice: 0x559c530b3a52
slice elements: 4
address of sslice: 0x7ffeb9e8fa70 value of sslice: 0x559c530b3a50
slice elements: 6
```

A64 Linux output:

```
--- Strings and String Slices ---
address of s: 0xffffda3e6e98 address of heap allocation: 0xaf6a42bdeb10
address of s: 0xffffda3e6e98 capacity: 6 address of heap allocation: 0xaf6a42bdeb10
number of bytes: 6
address of sslice: 0xffffda3e7000 value of sslice: 0xaf6a42bdeb12
slice elements: 4
address of sslice: 0xffffda3e70e0 value of sslice: 0xaf6a42bdeb10
slice elements: 6
```

C-Strings

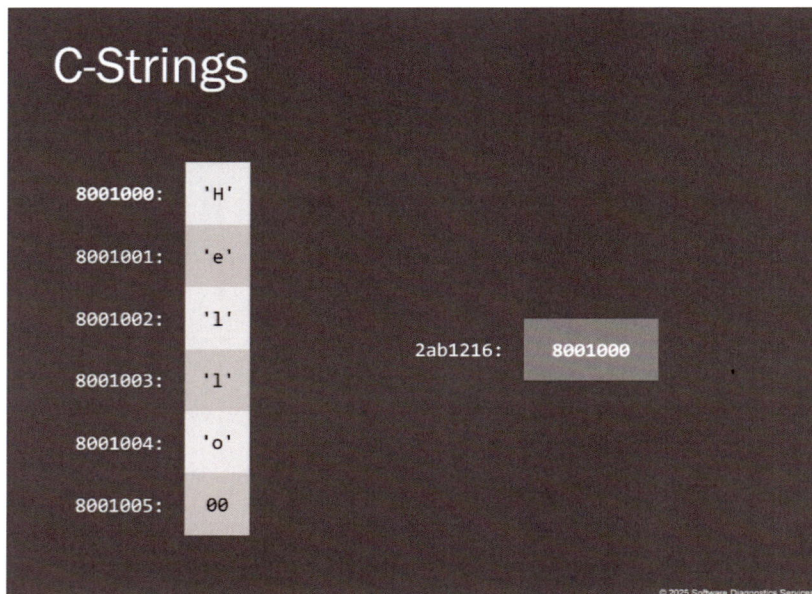

What about zero-terminated strings in C and C++ languages? Such a string is a zero-terminated array of one-byte memory cells. You will need them if you work with OS API or third-party C and C++ libraries.

C-String Slices

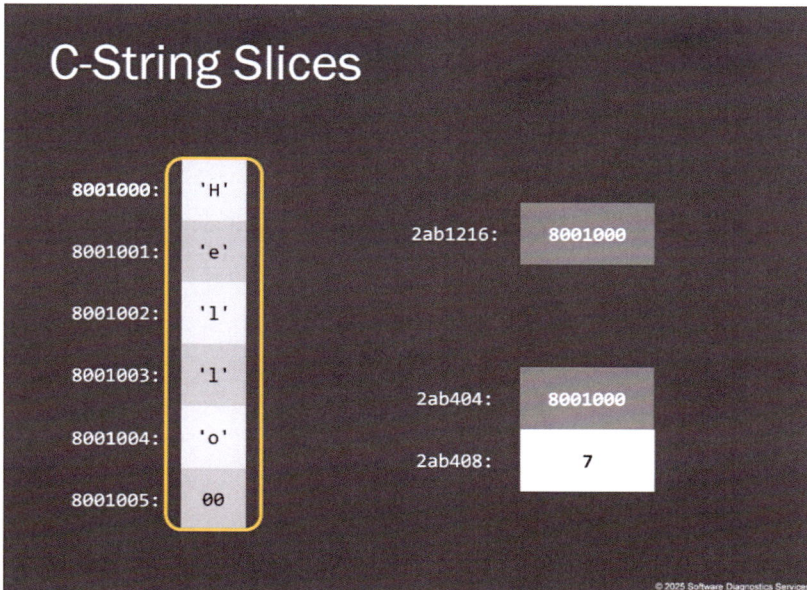

By analogy with String slices, there are slices of C-Strings.

```rust
println!("--- C-Strings and C-String Slices ---");
{
    let sl: &str = "Hello!";

    use std::ffi::CString;
    let cs: CString = CString::new(sl).unwrap();

    println!("address of cs: {:?} address of heap allocation: {:?}", addr_of!(cs),
cs.as_ptr());

    unsafe {
        use std::ffi::CStr;
        let cslice: &CStr = CStr::from_ptr(cs.as_ptr());

        println!("address of cslice: {:?} value of cslice: {cslice:p}",
addr_of!(cslice));

        println!("slice elements: {:?}",
            *(((addr_of!(cslice) as usize) +
            std::mem::size_of::<usize>()) as *const usize));
    }
}
```

Windows output:

```
--- C-Strings and C-String Slices ---
address of cs: 0x5d9970ec98 address of heap allocation: 0x16899e1be00
address of cslice: 0x5d9970ed28 value of cslice: 0x16899e1be00
slice elements: 7
```

x64 Linux output:

```
--- C-Strings and C-String Slices ---
address of cs: 0x7fffd4c0bc48 address of heap allocation: 0x55c964c5cae0
address of cslice: 0x7fffd4c0bcd8 value of cslice: 0x55c964c5cae0
slice elements: 7
```

A64 Linux output:

```
--- C-Strings and C-String Slices ---
address of cs: 0xfffff69b2578 address of heap allocation: 0xaaaaec0e8ad0
address of cslice: 0xfffff69b2608 value of cslice: 0xaaaaec0e8ad0
slice elements: 7
```

Basic Types

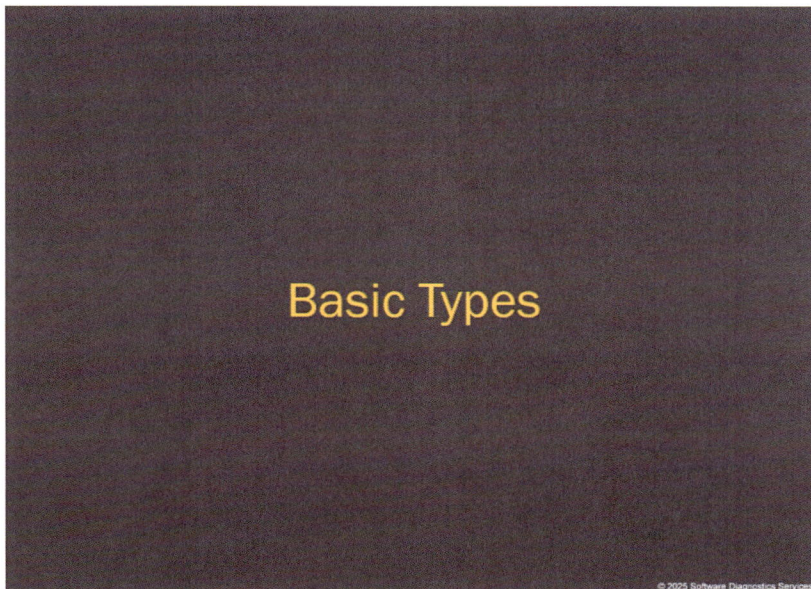

Now, we look at a few fundamental basic types and their relation to memory.

The basic-types project can be found in the archive[8]. In the following slide descriptions, we only show relevant code snippets and their output on various platforms.

---

[8] https://www.patterndiagnostics.com/Training/MTRust/MTRust.zip

Bytes, Pointers, and References

Let's have a byte array and its slice. We can form a pointer to its first element. The pointer arithmetic advance will yield the subsequent bytes.

```rust
println!("--- Bytes, References, and Pointers ---");
{
    let bytes: &[u8] = &[0x12, 0x34, 0x56, 0x78, 0xab, 0xcd];

    println!("address of bytes: {:p} value of bytes: {bytes:p}", &bytes);

    let mut pb: *const u8 = bytes.as_ptr();

    println!("address of pb: {:p} value of pb: {pb:p}",
        &pb);

    let rb: &&[u8] = &bytes;

    println!("address of rb: {:?} value of rb: {rb:p} dereference of rb: {:p}",
addr_of!(rb), *rb);

    unsafe {
        println!("value of pb: {pb:p}, dereference of pb: {:x}", *pb);
    }

    pb = pb.wrapping_add(1);
```

```
    unsafe {
        println!("value of pb: {pb:p}, dereference of pb: {:x}", *pb);
        println!("value of pb: {:?}, dereference of pb: {:x}", pb.wrapping_add(1),
*pb.wrapping_add(1));
    }
}
```

Windows output:

```
--- Bytes, References, and Pointers ---
address of bytes: 0x46a5b6da20 value of bytes: 0x7ff61d21f448
address of pb: 0x46a5b6da88 value of pb: 0x7ff61d21f448
address of rb: 0x46a5b6dae8 value of rb: 0x46a5b6da20 dereference of rb:
0x7ff61d21f448
value of pb: 0x7ff61d21f448, dereference of pb: 12
value of pb: 0x7ff61d21f449, dereference of pb: 34
value of pb: 0x7ff61d21f44a, dereference of pb: 56
```

x64 Linux output:

```
--- Bytes, References, and Pointers ---
address of bytes: 0x7ffc776efcd8 value of bytes: 0x55f4d0e4b0d0
address of pb: 0x7ffc776efd40 value of pb: 0x55f4d0e4b0d0
address of rb: 0x7ffc776efda0 value of rb: 0x7ffc776efcd8 dereference of rb:
0x55f4d0e4b0d0
value of pb: 0x55f4d0e4b0d0, dereference of pb: 12
value of pb: 0x55f4d0e4b0d1, dereference of pb: 34
value of pb: 0x55f4d0e4b0d2, dereference of pb: 56
```

A64 Linux output:

```
--- Bytes, References, and Pointers ---
address of bytes: 0xffffced54f10 value of bytes: 0xaaaacef90f83
address of pb: 0xffffced54f78 value of pb: 0xaaaacef90f83
address of rb: 0xffffced54fd8 value of rb: 0xffffced54f10 dereference of rb:
0xaaaacef90f83
value of pb: 0xaaaacef90f83, dereference of pb: 12
value of pb: 0xaaaacef90f84, dereference of pb: 34
value of pb: 0xaaaacef90f85, dereference of pb: 56
```

u32, Pointers, and References

The second type we look at now is unsigned 32-bit integers. The unsafe technique is the same, but a pointer arithmetic advance takes into consideration the size of u32, which is 4 bytes.

```
println!("--- u32, References, and Pointers ---");
{
    let uints: &[u32] = &[0x2ab1008, 0xffffffff,
        0x2ab1010, 0x2ab100c, 0, 0x2000];

    println!("address of uints: {:p} value of uints: {uints:p}", &uints);

    let mut pu: *const u32 = uints.as_ptr();

    println!("address of pu: {:p} value of pu: {pu:p}",
        &pu);

    let ru: &&[u32] = &uints;

    println!("address of ru: {:?} value of ru: {ru:p} dereference of ru: {:p}",
addr_of!(ru), *ru);

    unsafe {
        println!("value of pu: {pu:p}, dereference of pu: {:x}", *pu);
    }

    pu = pu.wrapping_add(1);
```

```
    unsafe {
        println!("value of pu: {pu:p}, dereference of pu: {:x}", *pu);
        println!("value of pu: {:?}, dereference of pu: {:x}", pu.wrapping_add(1),
*pu.wrapping_add(1));
    }
}
```

Windows output:

```
--- u32, References, and Pointers ---
address of uints: 0x46a5b6dcb8 value of uints: 0x7ff61d21f600
address of pu: 0x46a5b6dd20 value of pu: 0x7ff61d21f600
address of ru: 0x46a5b6dd80 value of ru: 0x46a5b6dcb8 dereference of ru:
0x7ff61d21f600
value of pu: 0x7ff61d21f600, dereference of pu: 2ab1008
value of pu: 0x7ff61d21f604, dereference of pu: ffffffff
value of pu: 0x7ff61d21f608, dereference of pu: 2ab1010
```

x64 Linux output:

```
--- u32, References, and Pointers ---
address of uints: 0x7ffc776eff70 value of uints: 0x55f4d0e4b190
address of pu: 0x7ffc776effd8 value of pu: 0x55f4d0e4b190
address of ru: 0x7ffc776f0038 value of ru: 0x7ffc776eff70 dereference of ru:
0x55f4d0e4b190
value of pu: 0x55f4d0e4b190, dereference of pu: 2ab1008
value of pu: 0x55f4d0e4b194, dereference of pu: ffffffff
value of pu: 0x55f4d0e4b198, dereference of pu: 2ab1010
```

A64 Linux output:

```
--- u32, References, and Pointers ---
address of uints: 0x7ffc776eff70 value of uints: 0x55f4d0e4b190
address of pu: 0x7ffc776effd8 value of pu: 0x55f4d0e4b190
address of ru: 0x7ffc776f0038 value of ru: 0x7ffc776eff70 dereference of ru:
0x55f4d0e4b190
value of pu: 0x55f4d0e4b190, dereference of pu: 2ab1008
value of pu: 0x55f4d0e4b194, dereference of pu: ffffffff
value of pu: 0x55f4d0e4b198, dereference of pu: 2ab1010
```

Little-Endian System

When converting between byte sequences and number values, we need to consider the little-endian system where the least significant digits reside at the lowest memory addresses.

```rust
println!("--- Little-Endian System ---");
{
    let ba: [u8; 4] = [1, 2, 3, 4];
    let u: u32 = u32::from_le_bytes(ba);

    println!("ba: {ba:?} u: {u:x}");

    let pu: *const u32 = ba.as_ptr() as *const u32;

    unsafe {
        println!("address of ba: {:?} value of pu {pu:p} dereference of pu: {:x}",
addr_of!(ba), *pu);
    }
}
```

Windows output:

```
--- Little-Endian System ---
ba: [1, 2, 3, 4] u: 4030201
address of ba: 0x46a5b6df54 value of pu 0x46a5b6df54 dereference of pu: 4030201
```

x64 Linux output:

```
--- Little-Endian System ---
ba: [1, 2, 3, 4] u: 4030201
address of ba: 0x7ffc776f020c value of pu 0x7ffc776f020c dereference of pu: 4030201
```

A64 Linux output:

```
--- Little-Endian System ---
ba: [1, 2, 3, 4] u: 4030201
address of ba: 0xffffced55444 value of pu 0xffffced55444 dereference of pu: 4030201
```

u64 and Pointers

Another example is unsigned 64-bit integers constructed from a slice of a 32-bit integer array, where we also see the little-endian system in action.

```rust
println!("--- u64 and Pointers ---");
{
    let uints: &[u32] = &[0x2ab1008, 0xffffffff,
        0x2ab1010, 0x2ab100c, 0, 0x2000];

    println!("address of uints: {:p} value of uints: {uints:p}", &uints);

    let mut p1: *const u64 = uints.as_ptr() as *const u64;

    unsafe {
        println!("address of p1: {:?} value of p1: {p1:p} dereference of p1: {:x}",
addr_of!(p1), *p1);

        p1 = p1.wrapping_add(1);

        println!("address of p1: {:?} value of p1: {p1:p}, dereference of p1: {:x}",
addr_of!(p1), *p1);
        println!("address of p1: {:?} value of p1: {:?}, dereference of p1: {:x}",
            addr_of!(p1), p1.wrapping_add(1),
            *p1.wrapping_add(1));
    }
}
```

Windows output:

```
--- u64 and Pointers ---
address of uints: 0x46a5b6e068 value of uints: 0x7ff61d21f600
address of p1: 0x46a5b6e0d0 value of p1: 0x7ff61d21f600 dereference of p1:
ffffffff02ab1008
address of p1: 0x46a5b6e0d0 value of p1: 0x7ff61d21f608, dereference of p1:
2ab100c02ab1010
address of p1: 0x46a5b6e0d0 value of p1: 0x7ff61d21f610, dereference of p1:
200000000000
```

x64 Linux output:

```
--- u64 and Pointers ---
address of uints: 0x7ffc776f0320 value of uints: 0x55f4d0e4b190
address of p1: 0x7ffc776f0388 value of p1: 0x55f4d0e4b190 dereference of p1:
ffffffff02ab1008
address of p1: 0x7ffc776f0388 value of p1: 0x55f4d0e4b198, dereference of p1:
2ab100c02ab1010
address of p1: 0x7ffc776f0388 value of p1: 0x55f4d0e4b1a0, dereference of p1:
200000000000
```

A64 Linux output:

```
--- u64 and Pointers ---
address of uints: 0xffffced55558 value of uints: 0xaaaacef91044
address of p1: 0xffffced555c0 value of p1: 0xaaaacef91044 dereference of p1:
ffffffff02ab1008
address of p1: 0xffffced555c0 value of p1: 0xaaaacef9104c, dereference of p1:
2ab100c02ab1010
address of p1: 0xffffced555c0 value of p1: 0xaaaacef91054, dereference of p1:
200000000000
```

Size

Size

◉ std::mem::size_of::<T>()

◉ std::mem::size_of_val(&value)

◉ std::mem::size_of_val(reference)

© 2025 Software Diagnostics Services

There are specific functions to evaluate the size in bytes of types, values (here, we must supply a reference), and values that references refer to.

```rust
println!("--- Size ---");
{
    println!("size of bool: {:?} size of [u32;6]: {:?} size of &[u32]: {:?} size of
Box<[u32;6]>: {:?} size of Box<&[u32]>: {:?}",
        std::mem::size_of::<bool>(),
        std::mem::size_of::<[u32;6]>(),
        std::mem::size_of::<&[u32]>(),
        std::mem::size_of::<Box<[u32;6]>>(),
        std::mem::size_of::<Box<&[u32]>>());

    let uints: [u32; 6] = [0x2ab1008, 0xffffffff,
        0x2ab1010, 0x2ab100c, 0, 0x2000];

    println!("address of uints: {:p} size of uints: {:?} size of reference to uints:
{:?}",
        &uints, std::mem::size_of_val(&uints),
        std::mem::size_of_val(&&uints));

    let ref_uints: &[u32] = &uints;

    println!("address of ref_uints: {:p} size of ref_uints: {:?} size of ref_uints
dereference value: {:?}",
        &ref_uints, std::mem::size_of_val(&ref_uints),
        std::mem::size_of_val(ref_uints));

    let ptr_uints: *const u32 = ref_uints.as_ptr();

    unsafe {
        println!("address of ptr_uints: {:p} size of ptr_uints: {:?} value of
ptr_units: {:x} size of ptr_uints dereference value: {:?}",
            &ptr_uints,
            std::mem::size_of_val(&ptr_uints),
            *ptr_uints,
            std::mem::size_of_val(&*ptr_uints));
    }

    let box_uints: Box<[u32; 6]> = Box::new(uints);

    println!("address of box_uints: {:p} size of box_uints: {:?} value of box_units:
{:p} size of box_uints value: {:?} \
                size of box_uints dereference value: {:?}",
        &box_uints, std::mem::size_of_val(&box_uints),
```

```rust
        box_uints,
        std::mem::size_of_val(&box_uints.as_ptr()),
        std::mem::size_of_val(&*box_uints));

    let box_ref_uints: Box<&[u32; 6]> =
        Box::new(&uints);

    println!("address of box_ref_uints: {:p} size of box_ref_uints: {:?} value of
box_ref_units: {:p} size of box_ref_uints value: {:?} \
        size of box_ref_uints dereference value: {:?}",
        &box_ref_uints,
        std::mem::size_of_val(&box_ref_uints),
        box_ref_uints,
        std::mem::size_of_val(&*box_ref_uints),
        std::mem::size_of_val(&**box_ref_uints));

    let box_slice_uints: Box<[u32]> = Box::new(uints);

    println!("address of box_slice_uints: {:p} size of box_slice_uints: {:?} value of
box_slice_units: {:p} size of box_slice_uints value: {:?}",
        &box_slice_uints,
        std::mem::size_of_val(&box_slice_uints),
        box_slice_uints,
        std::mem::size_of_val(&*box_slice_uints));

    let box_ref_slice_uints: Box<&[u32]> =
        Box::new(&uints[2..5]);

    println!("address of box_ref_slice_uints: {:p} size of box_ref_slice_uints: {:?}
value of box_ref_slice_units: {:p} \
        size of box_ref_slice_uints value: {:?} size of box_ref_slice_uints
dereference value: {:?}",
        &box_ref_slice_uints,
        std::mem::size_of_val(&box_ref_slice_uints),
        box_ref_slice_uints,
        std::mem::size_of_val(&*box_ref_slice_uints),

        std::mem::size_of_val(&**box_ref_slice_uints));
}
```

Windows output:

```
-- Size ---
size of bool: 1 size of [u32;6]: 24 size of &[u32]: 16 size of Box<[u32;6]>: 8 size
of Box<&[u32]>: 8
address of uints: 0x46a5b6e2f8 size of uints: 24 size of reference to uints: 8
address of ref_uints: 0x46a5b6e390 size of ref_uints: 16 size of ref_uints
dereference value: 24
address of ptr_uints: 0x46a5b6e418 size of ptr_uints: 8 value of ptr_units: 2ab1008
size of ptr_uints dereference value: 4
address of box_uints: 0x46a5b6e4a8 size of box_uints: 8 value of box_uints:
0x1f0f6051200 size of box_uints value: 8 size of box_uints dereference value: 24
address of box_ref_uints: 0x46a5b6e578 size of box_ref_uints: 8 value of
box_ref_units: 0x1f0f604bee0 size of box_ref_uints value: 8 size of box_ref_uints
dereference value: 24
address of box_slice_uints: 0x46a5b6e620 size of box_slice_uints: 16 value of
box_slice_units: 0x1f0f6051080 size of box_slice_uints value: 24
address of box_ref_slice_uints: 0x46a5b6e6d8 size of box_ref_slice_uints: 8 value of
box_ref_slice_units: 0x1f0f6050f40 size of box_ref_slice_uints value: 16 size of
box_ref_slice_uints dereference value: 12
```

x64 Linux output:

```
--- Size ---
size of bool: 1 size of [u32;6]: 24 size of &[u32]: 16 size of Box<[u32;6]>: 8 size
of Box<&[u32]>: 8
address of uints: 0x7ffc776f05b0 size of uints: 24 size of reference to uints: 8
address of ref_uints: 0x7ffc776f0648 size of ref_uints: 16 size of ref_uints
dereference value: 24
address of ptr_uints: 0x7ffc776f06d0 size of ptr_uints: 8 value of ptr_units: 2ab1008
size of ptr_uints dereference value: 4
address of box_uints: 0x7ffc776f0760 size of box_uints: 8 value of box_uints:
0x55f4d11b4ae0 size of box_uints value: 8 size of box_uints dereference value: 24
address of box_ref_uints: 0x7ffc776f0810 size of box_ref_uints: 8 value of
box_ref_units: 0x55f4d11b4b00 size of box_ref_uints value: 8 size of box_ref_uints
dereference value: 24
address of box_slice_uints: 0x7ffc776f08b8 size of box_slice_uints: 16 value of
box_slice_units: 0x55f4d11b4b20 size of box_slice_uints value: 24
address of box_ref_slice_uints: 0x7ffc776f0950 size of box_ref_slice_uints: 8 value
of box_ref_slice_units: 0x55f4d11b4b40 size of box_ref_slice_uints value: 16 size of
box_ref_slice_uints dereference value: 12
```

A64 Linux output:

```
--- Size ---
size of bool: 1 size of [u32;6]: 24 size of &[u32]: 16 size of Box<[u32;6]>: 8 size
of Box<&[u32]>: 8
address of uints: 0x7ffc776f05b0 size of uints: 24 size of reference to uints: 8
address of ref_uints: 0x7ffc776f0648 size of ref_uints: 16 size of ref_uints
dereference value: 24
address of ptr_uints: 0x7ffc776f06d0 size of ptr_uints: 8 value of ptr_units: 2ab1008
size of ptr_uints dereference value: 4
address of box_uints: 0x7ffc776f0760 size of box_uints: 8 value of box_uints:
0x55f4d11b4ae0 size of box_uints value: 8 size of box_uints dereference value: 24
address of box_ref_uints: 0x7ffc776f0810 size of box_ref_uints: 8 value of
box_ref_units: 0x55f4d11b4b00 size of box_ref_uints value: 8 size of box_ref_uints
dereference value: 24
address of box_slice_uints: 0x7ffc776f08b8 size of box_slice_uints: 16 value of
box_slice_units: 0x55f4d11b4b20 size of box_slice_uints value: 24
address of box_ref_slice_uints: 0x7ffc776f0950 size of box_ref_slice_uints: 8 value
of box_ref_slice_units: 0x55f4d11b4b40 size of box_ref_slice_uints value: 16 size of
box_ref_slice_uints dereference value: 12
```

Alignment

Values are usually aligned in memory at offsets divisible by their type size in bytes. You can get an alignment of types and values (here, we must supply a reference) using these functions. Again, if you want to get an alignment of a reference value, not an alignment of the value it refers to, then you need to pass a reference to a reference.

```
println!("--- Alignment ---");
{
    let b: bool = true;
    let ul: u64 = 1;
    let rb: &bool = &b;

    println!("alignment of bool type: {:?} alignment of u64 type: {:?}",
        std::mem::align_of::<bool>(),
        std::mem::align_of::<u64>());
    println!("alignment of b: {:?} alignment of ul: {:?} alignment of rb value: {:?}
alignment of rb dereference value: {:?}",
        std::mem::align_of_val(&b),
        std::mem::align_of_val(&ul),
        std::mem::align_of_val(&rb),
        std::mem::align_of_val(rb));
}
```

Output:

```
--- Alignment ---
alignment of bool type: 1 alignment of u64 type: 8
alignment of b: 1 alignment of ul: 8 alignment of rb value: 8 alignment of rb
dereference value: 1
```

Entity Conversion

As you anticipate, the same memory cell addresses and their values are the basis of conversion between different entity types. So, let's look at some examples.

The entity-conversion project can be found in the archive[9]. In the following slide descriptions, we only show relevant code snippets and their output on various platforms.

[9] https://www.patterndiagnostics.com/Training/MTRust/MTRust.zip

Conversion through Pointers

A conversion through pointers is a classic unsafe conversion technique from classic C and C++. Pointers can be converted to each other freely because their value is just a memory address. However, when we dereference them, we get the value based on underlying memory contents, which don't change as illustrated here. Please also note that due to the least significant byte endian convention, the integer value we get differs from the memory layout byte order. You may also get garbage values if the size of the target conversion is larger.

```rust
println!("--- Conversion through Pointers ---");
{
    let _: *const u32 = [0x12_u8, 0x34_u8, 0x56_u8, 0x78_u8].as_ptr() as *const u32;
// for alignment of the next array
    let pu: *const u32 = [0x12_u8, 0x34_u8, 0x56_u8,
        0x78_u8, 0xab_u8, 0xcd_u8].as_ptr() as *const u32;

    let pi: *const i16 = pu as *const i16;

    let pl: *const i64 = pu as *const i64;

    unsafe {
        println!("value of pu: {pu:p} dereference of pu: {:x}", *pu);
        println!("value of pi: {pi:p} dereference of pi: {:x}", *pi);
        println!("value of pl: {pl:p} dereference of pl: {:x}", *pl); // garbage
    }
}
```

Windows output:

```
--- Conversion through Pointers ---
value of pu: 0x7ff60c4ec47c dereference of pu: 78563412
value of pi: 0x7ff60c4ec47c dereference of pi: 3412
value of pl: 0x7ff60c4ec47c dereference of pl: 6176cdab78563412
```

x64 Linux output:

```
--- Conversion through Pointers ---
value of pu: 0x563bccbfd080 dereference of pu: 78563412
value of pi: 0x563bccbfd080 dereference of pi: 3412
value of pl: 0x563bccbfd080 dereference of pl: 6176cdab78563412
```

A64 Linux output:

```
--- Conversion through Pointers ---
value of pu: 0xaaaace1adebf dereference of pu: 78563412
value of pi: 0xaaaace1adebf dereference of pi: 3412
value of pl: 0xaaaace1adebf dereference of pl: 6176cdab78563412
```

Safe Conversion (Explicit Cast)

In Rust, there is also a safe conversion that doesn't involve raw pointers. But this cast must be done explicitly.

```
println!("--- Safe Conversion (Explicit Cast) ---");
{
    let u: u32 = 0x78563412;
    let i: i16 = u as i16;
    let l: i64 = u as i64;

    println!("address of u: {:?} value of u: {u:x}",
        addr_of!(u));
    println!("address of i: {:?} value of i: {i:x}",
        addr_of!(i));
    println!("address of l: {:?} value of l: {l:x}",
        addr_of!(l));

    let ul: u64 = 0xFF;
    let ib: i8 = ul as i8;

    println!("address of ul: {:?} value of ul: {ul:x}",
        addr_of!(ul));
    println!("address of ibL {:?} value of ib: {ib:x} ({ib:?})", addr_of!(ib));
}
```

Windows output:

```
--- Safe Conversion (Explicit Cast) ---
address of u: 0xbc120ff1e8 value of u: 78563412
address of i: 0xbc120ff1ee value of i: 3412
address of l: 0xbc120ff1f0 value of l: 78563412
address of ul: 0xbc120ff300 value of ul: ff
address of ibL 0xbc120ff30f value of ib: ff (-1)
```

x64 Linux output:

```
--- Safe Conversion (Explicit Cast) ---
address of u: 0x7ffcd63954a8 value of u: 78563412
address of i: 0x7ffcd63954ae value of i: 3412
address of l: 0x7ffcd63954b0 value of l: 78563412
address of ul: 0x7ffcd63955c0 value of ul: ff
address of ibL 0x7ffcd63955cf value of ib: ff (-1)
```

A64 Linux output:

```
--- Safe Conversion (Explicit Cast) ---
address of u: 0xffffea967600 value of u: 78563412
address of i: 0xffffea967606 value of i: 3412
address of l: 0xffffea967608 value of l: 78563412
address of ul: 0xffffea967718 value of ul: ff
address of ibL 0xffffea967727 value of ib: ff (-1)
```

Safe Conversion (Coercion)

In Rust, there is also safe implicit coercion between some related types.

```rust
println!("--- Safe Conversion (Coercion) ---");
{
    let mut mi: i32 = 0;
    let pmi: *mut i32 = &mut mi; // addr_of_mut!(mi);

    let mri: &mut i32 = &mut mi;
    let ri: &i32 = mri;

    println!("address of mi: {:?}", pmi);

    println!("address of mri: {:?} value of mri: {mri:p}", addr_of!(mri));
    println!("address of ri: {:?} value of ri: {ri:p}", addr_of!(ri));

    let pi: *const i32 = ri;

    println!("address of pi: {:?} value of pi: {pi:p}", addr_of!(pi));

    let aslice: &[i32] = &[0, 1, 2, 3, 4, 5];

    println!("address of aslice: {:?} value of aslice: {aslice:p} address of
aslice[0]: {:?} address of aslice[1]: {:?}",
        addr_of!(aslice), addr_of!(aslice[0]), addr_of!(aslice[1]));

    unsafe {
        println!("slice elements: {:?}", *(((addr_of!(aslice) as usize) +
std::mem::size_of::<usize>()) as *const usize));
    }
}
```

Windows output:

```
--- Safe Conversion (Coercion) ---
address of mi: 0xe2b5afeedc
address of mri: 0xe2b5afeee8 value of mri: 0xe2b5afeedc
address of ri: 0xe2b5afeef0 value of ri: 0xe2b5afeedc
address of pi: 0xe2b5afead0 value of pi: 0xe2b5afeedc
address of aslice: 0xe2b5aff038 value of aslice: 0x7ff696c3b7b0 address of aslice[0]:
0x7ff696c3b7b0 address of aslice[1]: 0x7ff696c3b7b4
slice elements: 6
```

x64 Linux output:

```
--- Safe Conversion (Coercion) ---
address of mi: 0x7ffdedca812c
address of mri: 0x7ffdedca8138 value of mri: 0x7ffdedca812c
address of ri: 0x7ffdedca8140 value of ri: 0x7ffdedca812c
address of pi: 0x7ffdedca8080 value of pi: 0x7ffdedca812c
address of aslice: 0x7ffdedca8288 value of aslice: 0x556ecd550270 address of
aslice[0]: 0x556ecd550270 address of aslice[1]: 0x556ecd550274
slice elements: 6
```

A64 Linux output:

```
--- Safe Conversion (Coercion) ---
address of mi: 0xffffc22a5474
address of mri: 0xffffc22a5480 value of mri: 0xffffc22a5474
address of ri: 0xffffc22a5488 value of ri: 0xffffc22a5474
address of pi: 0xffffc22a5440 value of pi: 0xffffc22a5474
address of aslice: 0xffffc22a55e0 value of aslice: 0xc4d77f9c06d0 address of
aslice[0]: 0xc4d77f9c06d0 address of aslice[1]: 0xc4d77f9c06d4
slice elements: 6
```

Forcing

There are several unsafe techniques to force conversion between incompatible types, such as integers and references. Unions can be used to interpret raw memory contents.

```
println!("--- Forcing ---");
{
    // let ri: &i32 = 1 as &i32;

    unsafe {
        let pi: *const i32 = 4 as *const i32;
        let ri: &i32 = &*pi; // no crash because we don't do real dereference

        println!("value of ri: {ri:p}");
        // let i: i32 = *ri; // crash
    }

    union InvalidReference<'a> {
        i: i32,
        ri: &'a i32
    }

    let ir: InvalidReference = InvalidReference { i: 1 };

    unsafe {
        println!("value of ir.i: {:?} value of ir.ri: {:p}", ir.i, ir.ri);
        // let i: i32 = *ir.ri; // crash
    }
}
```

Windows output:

```
--- Forcing ---
value of ri: 0x4
value of ir.i: 1 value of ir.ri: 0x1
```

x64 Linux output:

```
--- Forcing ---
value of ri: 0x4
value of ir.i: 1 value of ir.ri: 0x7f5a00000001
```

A64 Linux output:

```
--- Forcing ---
value of ri: 0x1
value of ir.i: 1 value of ir.ri: 0xaaaa00000001
```

Tuples

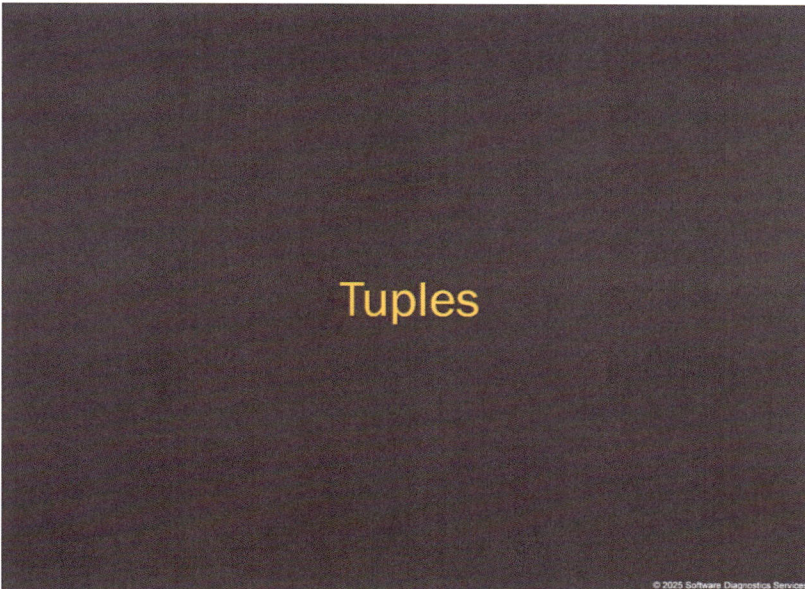

various platforms.

Tuples are sequences of values of different types. Tuples have the alignment of the greatest element alignment and size divisible by that alignment. Although tuple elements are accessible in the order they are declared in the tuple list, their memory addresses may be different. This curious observation was the base for the declarative memory concept we coined while working on this section[10].

The `tuples` project can be found in the archive[11]. In the following slide descriptions, we only show relevant code snippets and their output on

---

[10] https://dumpanalysis.org/declarative-memory

[11] https://www.patterndiagnostics.com/Training/MTRust/MTRust.zip

```
println!("--- Tuples ---");
{
    let i: i32 = 1;

    // #[repr(C)]
    let tuple: (bool, bool, i32, &i32) = (false, true,
        0x12345678, &i);

    println!("size of tuple: {:?} alignment of tuple: {:?}",
std::mem::size_of_val(&tuple),
        std::mem::align_of_val(&tuple));


    println!("address of tuple: {:?} addresses of fields: {:?}, {:?}, {:?}, {:?}",
        addr_of!(tuple), addr_of!(tuple.0),
        addr_of!(tuple.1), addr_of!(tuple.2),
        addr_of!(tuple.3));
}
```

Windows output:

```
--- Tuples ---
size of tuple: 16 alignment of tuple: 8
address of tuple: 0x298459f2b8 addresses of fields: 0x298459f2bc, 0x298459f2bd,
0x298459f2b8, 0x298459f2c0
```

x64 Linux output:

```
--- Tuples ---
size of tuple: 16 alignment of tuple: 8
address of tuple: 0x7ffebde01418 addresses of fields: 0x7ffebde0141c, 0x7ffebde0141d,
0x7ffebde01418, 0x7ffebde01420
```

A64 Linux output:

```
--- Tuples ---
size of tuple: 16 alignment of tuple: 8
address of tuple: 0xffffd0020908 addresses of fields: 0xffffd002090c, 0xffffd002090d,
0xffffd0020908, 0xffffd0020910
```

Structs

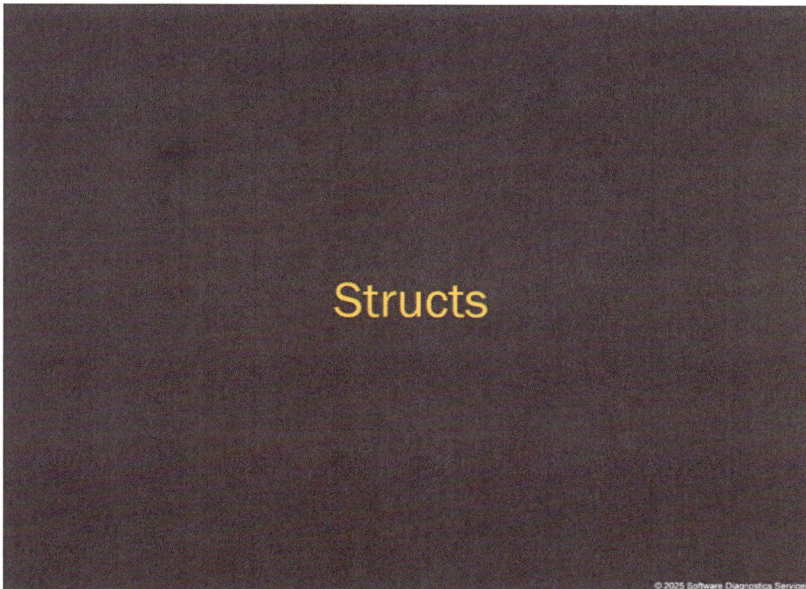

Now, we cover structs and their instances.

The `structs` project can be found in the archive[12]. In the following slide descriptions, we only show relevant code snippets and their output on various platforms.

160

Tuple-like Structs

We can view structs as collections of fields laid out in memory. Such fields may be anonymous, as in the case of tuple-like structs. Like tuples, fields of such structs can be reordered by a compiler.

```rust
println!("--- Tuple-like Structs ---");
{
    struct Tuple (bool, bool, i32, );

    let tuple: Tuple = Tuple(false, true, 0x12345678, );

    println!("size of tuple: {:?} alignment of tuple: {:?}",
std::mem::size_of_val(&tuple), std::mem::align_of_val(&tuple));

    println!("address of tuple: {:?} addresses of fields: {:?}, {:?}, {:?}",
        addr_of!(tuple), addr_of!(tuple.0), addr_of!(tuple.1),
addr_of!(tuple.2));

    #[repr(C)]
    struct TupleC (bool, bool, i32, );

    let tuple: TupleC = TupleC(false, true, 0x12345678, );

    println!("size of tuple: {:?} alignment of tuple: {:?}",
std::mem::size_of_val(&tuple), std::mem::align_of_val(&tuple));

    println!("address of tuple: {:?} addresses of fields: {:?}, {:?}, {:?}",
```

```rust
        addr_of!(tuple), addr_of!(tuple.0), addr_of!(tuple.1),
addr_of!(tuple.2));

    struct TupleWithRef<'a> (bool, bool, i32, &'a i32);

    let i: i32 = 1;

    let tuple: TupleWithRef<'_> = TupleWithRef(false, true, 0x12345678, &i);

    println!("size of tuple: {:?} alignment of tuple: {:?}",
std::mem::size_of_val(&tuple), std::mem::align_of_val(&tuple));

    println!("address of tuple: {:?} addresses of fields: {:?}, {:?}, {:?}, {:?}",
        addr_of!(tuple), addr_of!(tuple.0), addr_of!(tuple.1), addr_of!(tuple.2),
addr_of!(tuple.3));

    let tuple_ref: &TupleWithRef = &tuple;

    println!("address of tuple_ref: {:?} value of tuple_ref: {tuple_ref:p}",
addr_of!(tuple_ref));

    let tuple_ptr: *const TupleWithRef = addr_of!(tuple);

    println!("address of tuple_ptr: {:?} value of tuple_ptr: {tuple_ptr:p}",
addr_of!(tuple_ptr));
}
```

Windows output:

```
--- Tuple-like Structs ---
size of tuple: 8 alignment of tuple: 4
address of tuple: 0x979c2fd668 addresses of fields: 0x979c2fd66c, 0x979c2fd66d,
0x979c2fd668
size of tuple: 8 alignment of tuple: 4
address of tuple: 0x979c2fd7e8 addresses of fields: 0x979c2fd7e8, 0x979c2fd7e9,
0x979c2fd7ec
size of tuple: 16 alignment of tuple: 8
address of tuple: 0x979c2fd970 addresses of fields: 0x979c2fd97c, 0x979c2fd97d,
0x979c2fd978, 0x979c2fd970
address of tuple_ref: 0x979c2fdb28 value of tuple_ref: 0x979c2fd970
address of tuple_ptr: 0x979c2fdbb8 value of tuple_ptr: 0x979c2fd970
```

x64 Linux output:

```
--- Tuple-like Structs ---
size of tuple: 8 alignment of tuple: 4
address of tuple: 0x7ffe6eaca0f8 addresses of fields: 0x7ffe6eaca0fc, 0x7ffe6eaca0fd,
0x7ffe6eaca0f8
size of tuple: 8 alignment of tuple: 4
address of tuple: 0x7ffe6eaca278 addresses of fields: 0x7ffe6eaca278, 0x7ffe6eaca279,
0x7ffe6eaca27c
size of tuple: 16 alignment of tuple: 8
address of tuple: 0x7ffe6eaca400 addresses of fields: 0x7ffe6eaca40c, 0x7ffe6eaca40d,
0x7ffe6eaca408, 0x7ffe6eaca400
address of tuple_ref: 0x7ffe6eaca5b8 value of tuple_ref: 0x7ffe6eaca400
address of tuple_ptr: 0x7ffe6eaca648 value of tuple_ptr: 0x7ffe6eaca400
```

A64 Linux output:

```
--- Tuple-like Structs ---
size of tuple: 8 alignment of tuple: 4
address of tuple: 0xffffe5730a78 addresses of fields: 0xffffe5730a7c, 0xffffe5730a7d,
0xffffe5730a78
size of tuple: 8 alignment of tuple: 4
address of tuple: 0xffffe5730bf8 addresses of fields: 0xffffe5730bf8, 0xffffe5730bf9,
0xffffe5730bfc
size of tuple: 16 alignment of tuple: 8
address of tuple: 0xffffe5730d80 addresses of fields: 0xffffe5730d8c, 0xffffe5730d8d,
0xffffe5730d88, 0xffffe5730d80
address of tuple_ref: 0xffffe5730f38 value of tuple_ref: 0xffffe5730d80
address of tuple_ptr: 0xffffe5730fc8 value of tuple_ptr: 0xffffe5730d80
```

Newtypes

Tuple-like structs with one anonymous field are useful for the so-called *newtypes* that encapsulate existing types. The benefit of *newtypes* is that they allow strict type checking, which is not possible if their underlying existing types are used.

```rust
println!("--- Newtypes ---");
{
    struct MyVector (Vec<i32>);

    let mut my_vector: MyVector = MyVector(Vec::new());
    my_vector.0.push(0);

    println!("address of my_vector: {:?} value of my_vector: {:?}",
addr_of!(my_vector), my_vector.0.as_ptr());

    let my_vector_ref: &MyVector = &my_vector;

    println!("address of my_vector_ref: {:?} value of my_vector_ref:
{my_vector_ref:p} dereference of my_vector_ref: {:?}",
        addr_of!(my_vector_ref),
        my_vector_ref.0.as_ptr()
        /* (*my_vector_ref).0.as_ptr() */);

    let my_vector_ptr: *const MyVector =
        addr_of!(my_vector);

    unsafe {
```

```
        println!("address of my_vector_ptr: {:?} value of my_vector_ptr:
{my_vector_ptr:p} dereference of my_vector_ptr: {:?}",
            addr_of!(my_vector_ptr),
            (*my_vector_ptr).0.as_ptr());
    }
}
```

Windows output:

```
--- Newtypes ---
address of my_vector: 0x7a711be300 value of my_vector: 0x2618aaf4bf0
address of my_vector_ref: 0x7a711be390 value of my_vector_ref: 0x7a711be300
dereference of my_vector_ref: 0x2618aaf4bf0
address of my_vector_ptr: 0x7a711be420 value of my_vector_ptr: 0x7a711be300
dereference of my_vector_ptr: 0x2618aaf4bf0
```

x64 Linux output:

```
--- Newtypes ---
address of my_vector: 0x7ffcba50d050 value of my_vector: 0x5639686cd9e0
address of my_vector_ref: 0x7ffcba50d0e0 value of my_vector_ref: 0x7ffcba50d050
dereference of my_vector_ref: 0x5639686cd9e0
address of my_vector_ptr: 0x7ffcba50d170 value of my_vector_ptr: 0x7ffcba50d050
dereference of my_vector_ptr: 0x5639686cd9e0
```

A64 Linux output:

```
--- Newtypes ---
address of my_vector: 0x7ffcba50d050 value of my_vector: 0x5639686cd9e0
address of my_vector_ref: 0x7ffcba50d0e0 value of my_vector_ref: 0x7ffcba50d050
dereference of my_vector_ref: 0x5639686cd9e0
address of my_vector_ptr: 0x7ffcba50d170 value of my_vector_ptr: 0x7ffcba50d050
dereference of my_vector_ptr: 0x5639686cd9e0
```

Newtypes (Binary Compatible)

We can also ask for a guarantee that the overall size is the same as the underlying basic type.

```
println!("--- Newtypes (Binary Compatible) ---");
{
    #[repr(transparent)]
    struct MyBool
    (
        bool
    );

    let my_bool: MyBool = MyBool(true);

    println!("size of bool: {:?} size of MyBool: {:?} size of my_bool: {:?}",
        std::mem::size_of::<bool>(), std::mem::size_of::<MyBool>(),
std::mem::size_of_val(&my_bool));
}
```

Output:

```
--- Newtypes (Binary Compatible) ---
size of bool: 1 size of MyBool: 1 size of my_bool: 1
```

Named-field Structs

Named-field structs are similar to those in other system programming languages, such as C and C++. The difference is that you need to specify field names when creating struct instances.

```rust
println!("--- Named-field Structs ---");
{
    #[derive(Debug)]
    struct MyStruct {
        field1: bool,
        field2: bool,
        field3: i32,
        field4: u64,
    }

    let my_struct: MyStruct = MyStruct { field1: false,
        field2: true, field3: 0x12345678,
        field4: 0x123456789abcdef, };

    println!("address of my_struct: {:?} address of field1, field2, field3, field4:
{:?}, {:?}, {:?}, {:?}",
        addr_of!(my_struct),
        addr_of!(my_struct.field1),
        addr_of!(my_struct.field2),
        addr_of!(my_struct.field3),
        addr_of!(my_struct.field4));
```

```rust
    let my_struct_ref: &MyStruct = &my_struct;

    println!("address of my_struct_ref: {:?} value of my_struct_ref:
{my_struct_ref:p} dereference of my_struct_ref: {:?}",
        addr_of!(my_struct_ref), my_struct_ref
        /* *my_struct_ref */);

    let my_struct_ptr: *const MyStruct =
        addr_of!(my_struct);

    unsafe {
        println!("address of my_struct_ptr: {:?} value of my_struct_ptr:
{my_struct_ptr:p} dereference of my_struct_ptr: {:?}",
            addr_of!(my_struct_ptr), *my_struct_ptr);
    }

    let my_struct: Box<MyStruct> = Box::new(MyStruct {
        field1: false, field2: true,
        field3: 0x12345678,
        field4: 0x123456789abcdef, });

    println!("address of my_struct: {:?} value of my_struct as pointer: {my_struct:p}
value of my_struct: {:?} \
    address of field1, field2, field3, field4: {:?}, {:?}, {:?}, {:?}",
        addr_of!(my_struct), my_struct
        /* *my_struct */,
        addr_of!(my_struct.field1),
        addr_of!(my_struct.field2),
        addr_of!(my_struct.field3),
        addr_of!(my_struct.field4)
        /* addr_of!((*my_struct).field1),
            addr_of!((*my_struct).field2),
            addr_of!((*my_struct).field3),
            addr_of!((*my_struct).field4) */);
}
```

Windows output:

```
--- Named-field Structs ---
address of my_struct: 0x7a711be4e0 address of field1, field2, field3, field4:
0x7a711be4ec, 0x7a711be4ed, 0x7a711be4e8, 0x7a711be4e0
address of my_struct_ref: 0x7a711be598 value of my_struct_ref: 0x7a711be4e0
dereference of my_struct_ref: MyStruct { field1: false, field2: true, field3:
305419896, field4: 81985529216486895 }
address of my_struct_ptr: 0x7a711be620 value of my_struct_ptr: 0x7a711be4e0
dereference of my_struct_ptr: MyStruct { field1: false, field2: true, field3:
305419896, field4: 81985529216486895 }
address of my_struct: 0x7a711be6a8 value of my_struct as pointer: 0x2618aaf4c90 value
of my_struct: MyStruct { field1: false, field2: true, field3: 305419896, field4:
81985529216486895 } address of field1, field2, field3, field4: 0x2618aaf4c9c,
0x2618aaf4c9d, 0x2618aaf4c98, 0x2618aaf4c90
```

x64 Linux output:

```
--- Named-field Structs ---
address of my_struct: 0x7ffcba50d230 address of field1, field2, field3, field4:
0x7ffcba50d23c, 0x7ffcba50d23d, 0x7ffcba50d238, 0x7ffcba50d230
address of my_struct_ref: 0x7ffcba50d2e8 value of my_struct_ref: 0x7ffcba50d230
dereference of my_struct_ref: MyStruct { field1: false, field2: true, field3:
305419896, field4: 81985529216486895 }
address of my_struct_ptr: 0x7ffcba50d370 value of my_struct_ptr: 0x7ffcba50d230
dereference of my_struct_ptr: MyStruct { field1: false, field2: true, field3:
305419896, field4: 81985529216486895 }
address of my_struct: 0x7ffcba50d3f8 value of my_struct as pointer: 0x5639686cd9e0
value of my_struct: MyStruct { field1: false, field2: true, field3: 305419896,
field4: 81985529216486895 } address of field1, field2, field3, field4:
0x5639686cd9ec, 0x5639686cd9ed, 0x5639686cd9e8, 0x5639686cd9e0
```

A64 Linux output:

```
--- Named-field Structs ---
address of my_struct: 0xffffdff868b0 address of field1, field2, field3, field4:
0xffffdff868bc, 0xffffdff868bd, 0xffffdff868b8, 0xffffdff868b0
address of my_struct_ref: 0xffffdff86968 value of my_struct_ref: 0xffffdff868b0
dereference of my_struct_ref: MyStruct { field1: false, field2: true, field3:
305419896, field4: 81985529216486895 }
address of my_struct_ptr: 0xffffdff869f0 value of my_struct_ptr: 0xffffdff868b0
dereference of my_struct_ptr: MyStruct { field1: false, field2: true, field3:
305419896, field4: 81985529216486895 }
address of my_struct: 0xffffdff86a78 value of my_struct as pointer: 0xaaaaf330ead0
value of my_struct: MyStruct { field1: false, field2: true, field3: 305419896,
field4: 81985529216486895 } address of field1, field2, field3, field4:
0xaaaaf330eadc, 0xaaaaf330eadd, 0xaaaaf330ead8, 0xaaaaf330ead0
```

Reference/Pointer to Struct

Here, we revisit our conceptual philosophy of pointer pictures and annotate them with Rust code. I provide examples of both references and raw pointers.

Ref/Ptr to Struct Dereference

Here, we dereference a reference and a pointer to a struct. We get the new struct value if Clone and Copy traits are defined. It is not possible to move the value since the old reference to it still exists at the time of the move, and this will violate lifetime rules.

Dereference with Replacement

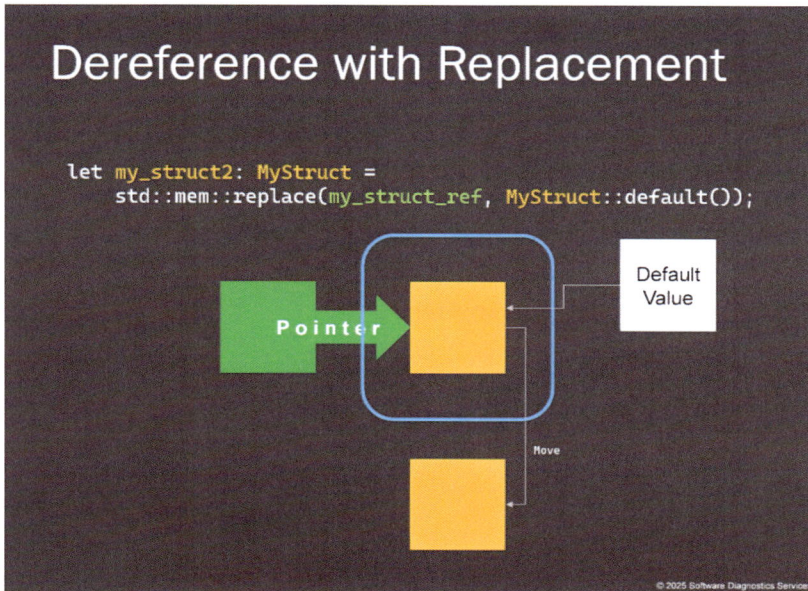

However, if you have a reference to a mutable struct, it is possible to replace its value with a default value while moving the original value out.

```rust
println!("--- Dereference with Replacement---");
{
    #[derive(Debug, Default)]
    struct MyStruct {
        field1: bool,
        field2: bool,
        field3: i32,
        field4: u64,
    }

    let mut my_struct: MyStruct = MyStruct {
        field1: false, field2: true,
        field3: 0x12345678, field4: 0x123456789abcdef,
    };

    let my_struct_ref: &mut MyStruct = &mut my_struct;
    let my_struct2: MyStruct =
        std::mem::replace(my_struct_ref,
        MyStruct::default());
    println!("address of my_struct: {:?} value of my_struct: {my_struct:?} address of
my_struct2: {:?} \
        value of my_struct2: {my_struct2:?}",
```

```
        addr_of!(my_struct), addr_of!(my_struct2));
}
```

Windows output:

```
--- Dereference with Replacement---
address of my_struct: 0x7a711bebf8 value of my_struct: MyStruct { field1: false,
field2: false, field3: 0, field4: 0 } address of my_struct2: 0x7a711bec08 value of
my_struct2: MyStruct { field1: false, field2: true, field3: 305419896, field4:
81985529216486895 }
```

x64 Linux output:

```
--- Dereference with Replacement---
address of my_struct: 0x7ffcba50d948 value of my_struct: MyStruct { field1: false,
field2: false, field3: 0, field4: 0 } address of my_struct2: 0x7ffcba50d958 value of
my_struct2: MyStruct { field1: false, field2: true, field3: 305419896, field4:
81985529216486895 }
```

A64 Linux output:

```
--- Dereference with Replacement---
address of my_struct: 0x7ffcba50d948 value of my_struct: MyStruct { field1: false,
field2: false, field3: 0, field4: 0 } address of my_struct2: 0x7ffcba50d958 value of
my_struct2: MyStruct { field1: false, field2: true, field3: 305419896, field4:
81985529216486895 }
```

One Ref/Ptr to Many Structs

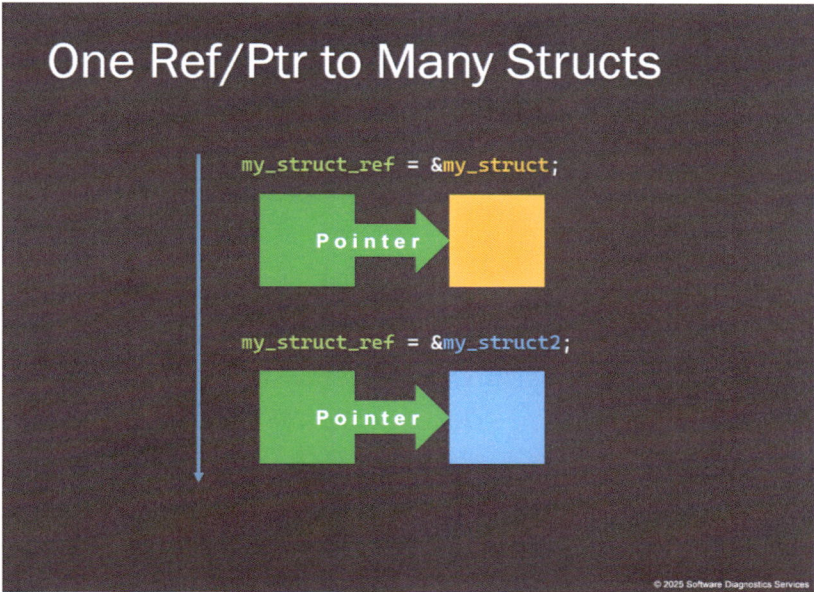

Memory Leak

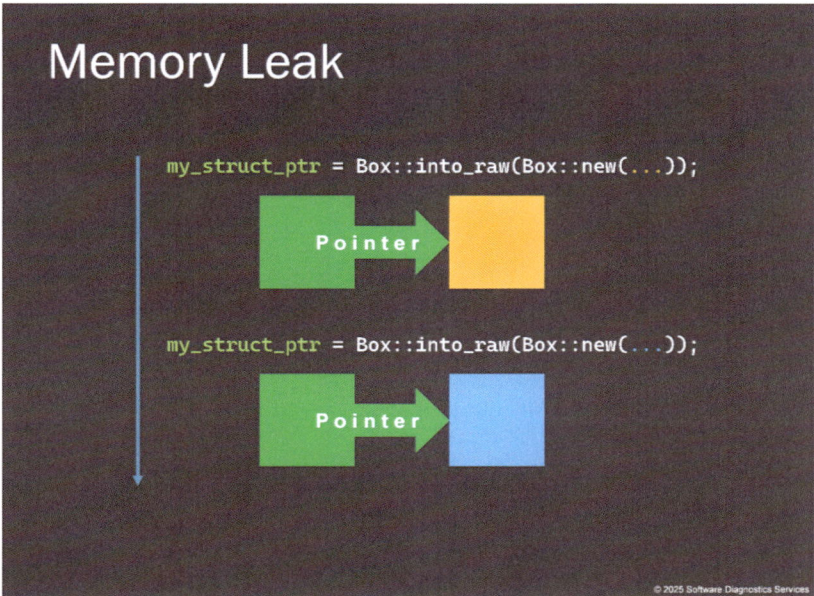

Many Ref/Ptr to One Struct

Here, we assign the value of one pointer or reference to another pointer and reference, and both now point to the same struct.

Many to One Dereference

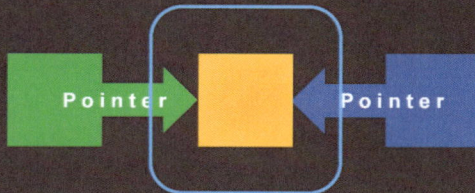

If we dereference both references or pointers, we get the same value with the same address.

Ref/Ptr to Ref/Ptr to Struct

We can also have references to references and pointers to pointers to structs, and so on, with double and more dereferences needed to get the value. We'll see why we need double-pointers or double-references later when we talk about passing parameters to functions.

Ref/Ptr to Ref/Ptr Dereference

Here, we have double dereference illustrated.

176

```rust
    println!("--- One Ref/Ptr to Many Structs ---");
    println!("--- Many Ref/Ptr to One Struct ---");
    println!("--- Many to One Dereference ---");
    println!("--- Ref/Ptr to Ref/Ptr to Struct ---");
    println!("--- Ref/Ptr to Ref/Ptr Dereference ---");
    {
        #[derive(PartialEq, Debug, Clone, Copy)]
        struct MyStruct {
            field1: bool,
            field2: bool,
            field3: i32,
            field4: u64,
        }

        let my_struct: MyStruct = MyStruct { field1: false, field2: true, field3:
    0x12345678, field4: 0x123456789abcdef, };

        let my_struct_ref: &MyStruct = &my_struct;
        let my_struct_ptr: *const MyStruct = addr_of!(my_struct);

        let my_struct_ref2: &MyStruct = my_struct_ref;
        let my_struct_ptr2: *const MyStruct = my_struct_ptr;

        println!("address of my_struct_ref: {:?} value of my_struct_ref:
    {my_struct_ref:p} address of my_struct_ref dereference: {:p}",
            addr_of!(my_struct_ref), &*my_struct_ref);
        println!("address of my_struct_ref2: {:?} value of my_struct_ref2:
    {my_struct_ref2:p} address of my_struct_ref2 dereference: {:p}",
            addr_of!(my_struct_ref2), &*my_struct_ref2);
        println!("address of my_struct_ptr: {:?} value of my_struct_ptr:
    {my_struct_ptr:p} address of my_struct_ptr dereference: {:?}",
            addr_of!(my_struct_ptr), addr_of!(*my_struct_ptr));
        println!("address of my_struct_ptr2: {:?} value of my_struct_ptr2:
    {my_struct_ptr2:p} address of my_struct_ptr2 dereference: {:?}",
            addr_of!(my_struct_ptr2), addr_of!(*my_struct_ptr2));

        assert_eq!(&*my_struct_ref, &*my_struct_ref2);
        assert_eq!(addr_of!(*my_struct_ptr), addr_of!(*my_struct_ptr2));

        let my_struct_ref_ref: &&MyStruct = &my_struct_ref;
        let my_struct_ptr_ptr: *const *const MyStruct = addr_of!(my_struct_ptr);
```

```
    let my_struct_ref: &MyStruct = *my_struct_ref_ref;
    unsafe {
        let my_struct_ptr: *const MyStruct = *my_struct_ptr_ptr;
    }


    let my_struct_ref2: &MyStruct = *my_struct_ref_ref;
    let my_struct2: MyStruct = *my_struct_ref2;
    let my_struct2: MyStruct = **my_struct_ref_ref;
    unsafe {
        let my_struct_ptr2: *const MyStruct = *my_struct_ptr_ptr;
        let my_struct3: MyStruct = *my_struct_ptr2;
        let my_struct3: MyStruct = **my_struct_ptr_ptr;
    }
}
```

Windows output:

```
--- One Ref/Ptr to Many Structs ---
--- Many Ref/Ptr to One Struct ---
--- Many to One Dereference ---
--- Ref/Ptr to Ref/Ptr to Struct ---
--- Ref/Ptr to Ref/Ptr Dereference ---
address of my_struct_ref: 0x979c2fe690 value of my_struct_ref: 0x979c2fe680 address
of my_struct_ref dereference: 0x979c2fe680
address of my_struct_ref2: 0x979c2fe6a0 value of my_struct_ref2: 0x979c2fe680 address
of my_struct_ref2 dereference: 0x979c2fe680
address of my_struct_ptr: 0x979c2fe698 value of my_struct_ptr: 0x979c2fe680 address
of my_struct_ptr dereference: 0x979c2fe680
address of my_struct_ptr2: 0x979c2fe6a8 value of my_struct_ptr2: 0x979c2fe680 address
of my_struct_ptr2 dereference: 0x979c2fe680
```

x64 Linux output:

```
--- One Ref/Ptr to Many Structs ---
--- Many Ref/Ptr to One Struct ---
--- Many to One Dereference ---
--- Ref/Ptr to Ref/Ptr to Struct ---
--- Ref/Ptr to Ref/Ptr Dereference ---
address of my_struct_ref: 0x7ffe6eacb0f8 value of my_struct_ref: 0x7ffe6eacb0e8 ad-
dress of my_struct_ref dereference: 0x7ffe6eacb0e8
address of my_struct_ref2: 0x7ffe6eacb108 value of my_struct_ref2: 0x7ffe6eacb0e8 ad-
dress of my_struct_ref2 dereference: 0x7ffe6eacb0e8
address of my_struct_ptr: 0x7ffe6eacb100 value of my_struct_ptr: 0x7ffe6eacb0e8 ad-
dress of my_struct_ptr dereference: 0x7ffe6eacb0e8
address of my_struct_ptr2: 0x7ffe6eacb110 value of my_struct_ptr2: 0x7ffe6eacb0e8 ad-
dress of my_struct_ptr2 dereference: 0x7ffe6eacb0e8
```

A64 Linux output:

```
--- One Ref/Ptr to Many Structs ---
--- Many Ref/Ptr to One Struct ---
--- Many to One Dereference ---
--- Ref/Ptr to Ref/Ptr to Struct ---
--- Ref/Ptr to Ref/Ptr Dereference ---
address of my_struct_ref: 0xffffe5731ab0 value of my_struct_ref: 0xffffe5731aa0 ad-
dress of my_struct_ref dereference: 0xffffe5731aa0
address of my_struct_ref2: 0xffffe5731ac0 value of my_struct_ref2: 0xffffe5731aa0 ad-
dress of my_struct_ref2 dereference: 0xffffe5731aa0
address of my_struct_ptr: 0xffffe5731ab8 value of my_struct_ptr: 0xffffe5731aa0 ad-
dress of my_struct_ptr dereference: 0xffffe5731aa0
address of my_struct_ptr2: 0xffffe5731ac8 value of my_struct_ptr2: 0xffffe5731aa0 ad-
dress of my_struct_ptr2 dereference: 0xffffe5731aa0
```

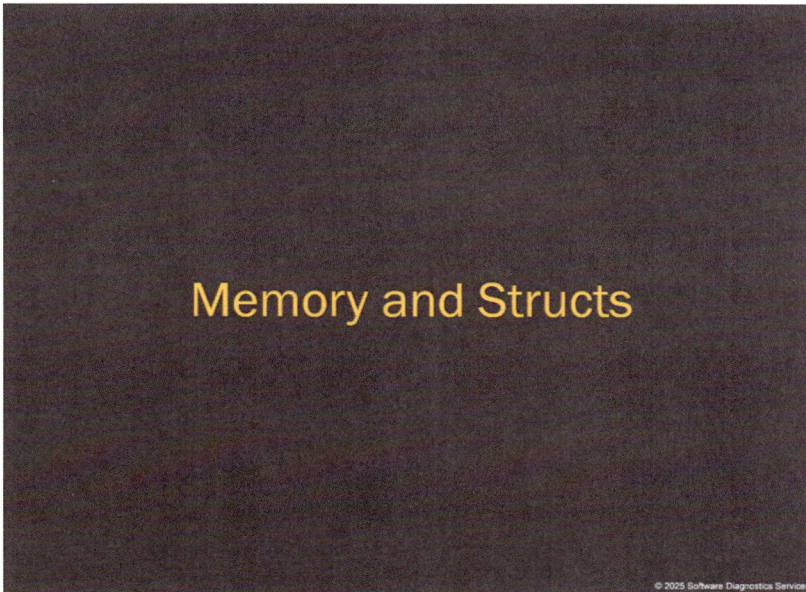

Memory and Structs

© 2025 Software Diagnostics Services

Now, we look at the memory representation of structs.

The `memory-and-structs` project can be found in the archive[13]. In the following slide descriptions, we only show relevant code snippets and their output on various platforms.

[13] https://www.patterndiagnostics.com/Training/MTRust/MTRust.zip

Addresses and Structs

A struct in memory is a sequential collection of memory cells; some may be multicell and themselves substructs. Each part of a struct, its member, or struct field, has its own address as well in addition to the overall address of the struct. However, please bear in mind that a compiler may rearrange fields to make a more compact struct. If you want full compatibility with legacy code written in C and C++, you can specify an attribute to control it.

Struct Field Addresses

This example shows field addresses when we have a struct value.

```
println!("--- Addresses and Structs ---");
println!("--- Struct Field Addresses ---");
{
    #[repr(C)]
    struct InnerStruct1 {
        field1: i32,
        field2: i32,
    }

    struct InnerStruct2 {
        field: i32,
    }

    #[repr(C)]
    struct OuterStruct {
        field1: i32,
        field2: InnerStruct1,
        field3: InnerStruct2,
    }

    let my_struct: OuterStruct = OuterStruct {field1: 0,
        field2: InnerStruct1{field1: 1, field2: 2},
        field3: InnerStruct2{field: 3}, };

    println!("address of my_struct: {:p}", &my_struct);
    println!("address of my_struct.field1: {:p}",
        &my_struct.field1);
    println!("value of my_struct.field1: {:?}",
        my_struct.field1);
    println!("address of my_struct.field2: {:p}",
        &my_struct.field2);
    println!("address of my_struct.field2.field1: {:p}", &my_struct.field2.field1);
    println!("value of my_struct.field2.field1: {:?}",
        my_struct.field2.field1);
    println!("address of my_struct.field2.field2: {:p}", &my_struct.field2.field2);
    println!("value of my_struct.field2.field2: {:?}",
        my_struct.field2.field2);
    println!("address of my_struct.field3: {:p}",
        &my_struct.field3);
    println!("address of my_struct.field3.field: {:p}",
        &my_struct.field3.field);
```

```
    println!("value of my_struct.field3.field: {:?}",
        my_struct.field3.field);
}
```

Windows output:

```
--- Addresses and Structs ---
--- Struct Field Addresses ---
address of my_struct: 0x9101bcca1c
address of my_struct.field1: 0x9101bcca1c
value of my_struct.field1: 0
address of my_struct.field2: 0x9101bcca20
address of my_struct.field2.field1: 0x9101bcca20
value of my_struct.field2.field1: 1
address of my_struct.field2.field2: 0x9101bcca24
value of my_struct.field2.field2: 2
address of my_struct.field3: 0x9101bcca28
address of my_struct.field3.field: 0x9101bcca28
value of my_struct.field3.field: 3
```

x64 Linux output:

```
--- Addresses and Structs ---
--- Struct Field Addresses ---
address of my_struct: 0x7ffccd7b2a18
address of my_struct.field1: 0x7ffccd7b2a18
value of my_struct.field1: 0
address of my_struct.field2: 0x7ffccd7b2a1c
address of my_struct.field2.field1: 0x7ffccd7b2a1c
value of my_struct.field2.field1: 1
address of my_struct.field2.field2: 0x7ffccd7b2a20
value of my_struct.field2.field2: 2
address of my_struct.field3: 0x7ffccd7b2a24
address of my_struct.field3.field: 0x7ffccd7b2a24
value of my_struct.field3.field: 3
```

A64 Linux output:

```
--- Addresses and Structs ---
--- Struct Field Addresses ---
address of my_struct: 0x7ffccd7b2a18
address of my_struct.field1: 0x7ffccd7b2a18
value of my_struct.field1: 0
address of my_struct.field2: 0x7ffccd7b2a1c
address of my_struct.field2.field1: 0x7ffccd7b2a1c
value of my_struct.field2.field1: 1
address of my_struct.field2.field2: 0x7ffccd7b2a20
value of my_struct.field2.field2: 2
address of my_struct.field3: 0x7ffccd7b2a24
address of my_struct.field3.field: 0x7ffccd7b2a24
value of my_struct.field3.field: 3
```

Ref/Ptr to Structs

A struct has its address. A pointer or a reference to a struct is a memory cell that contains that address. It has its own address.

Ref/Ptr to Struct and Fields

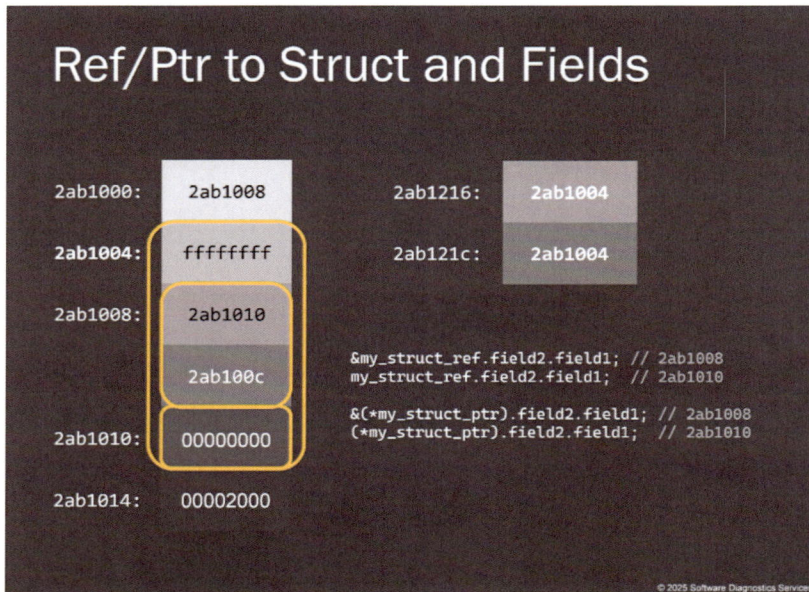

This example shows field addresses when we have a pointer to a struct value.

```rust
println!("--- Ref/Ptr to Structs ---");
println!("--- Ref/Ptr to Struct and Fields ---");
{
    #[repr(C)]
    struct InnerStruct1 {
        field1: i32,
        field2: i32,
    }

    struct InnerStruct2 {
        field: i32,
    }

    #[repr(C)]
    struct OuterStruct {
        field1: i32,
        field2: InnerStruct1,
        field3: InnerStruct2,
    }

    let my_struct: OuterStruct = OuterStruct {field1: 0,
        field2: InnerStruct1{field1: 1, field2: 2},
```

```
        field3: InnerStruct2{field: 3}, };

    let my_struct_ref: &OuterStruct = &my_struct;
    let my_struct_ptr: *const OuterStruct =
        addr_of!(my_struct);

    println!("address of my_struct: {:?} address of my_struct_ref: {:?} value of
my_struct_ref: {my_struct_ref:p} \
address of my_struct_ptr: {:?} value of my_struct_ptr: {my_struct_ptr:p}",
        addr_of!(my_struct), addr_of!(my_struct_ref),
        addr_of!(my_struct_ptr));

    println!("address of my_struct_ref.field2.field1: {:p}",
&my_struct_ref.field2.field1);
    println!("value of my_struct_ref.field2.field1: {:?}",
my_struct_ref.field2.field1);
    unsafe {
        println!("address of my_struct_ptr.field2.field1: {:p}",
            &(*my_struct_ptr).field2.field1);
        println!("value of my_struct_ptr.field2.field1: {:?}",
(*my_struct_ptr).field2.field1);
    }
}
```

Windows output:

```
--- Ref/Ptr to Structs ---
--- Ref/Ptr to Struct and Fields ---
address of my_struct: 0x9101bccd94 address of my_struct_ref: 0x9101bccdb0 value of
my_struct_ref: 0x9101bccd94 address of my_struct_ptr: 0x9101bccdb8 value of
my_struct_ptr: 0x9101bccd94
address of my_struct_ref.field2.field1: 0x9101bccd98
value of my_struct_ref.field2.field1: 1
address of my_struct_ptr.field2.field1: 0x9101bccd98
value of my_struct_ptr.field2.field1: 1
```

x64 Linux output:

```
--- Ref/Ptr to Structs ---
--- Ref/Ptr to Struct and Fields ---
address of my_struct: 0x7ffccd7b2d90 address of my_struct_ref: 0x7ffccd7b2db0 value
of my_struct_ref: 0x7ffccd7b2d90 address of my_struct_ptr: 0x7ffccd7b2db8 value of
my_struct_ptr: 0x7ffccd7b2d90
address of my_struct_ref.field2.field1: 0x7ffccd7b2d94
value of my_struct_ref.field2.field1: 1
address of my_struct_ptr.field2.field1: 0x7ffccd7b2d94
value of my_struct_ptr.field2.field1: 1
```

A64 Linux output:

```
--- Ref/Ptr to Structs ---
--- Ref/Ptr to Struct and Fields ---
address of my_struct: 0xffffdefdbd94 address of my_struct_ref: 0xffffdefdbdb0 value
of my_struct_ref: 0xffffdefdbd94 address of my_struct_ptr: 0xffffdefdbdb8 value of
my_struct_ptr: 0xffffdefdbd94
address of my_struct_ref.field2.field1: 0xffffdefdbd98
value of my_struct_ref.field2.field1: 1
address of my_struct_ptr.field2.field1: 0xffffdefdbd98
value of my_struct_ptr.field2.field1: 1
```

External Struct Alignment

It is possible to align struct values on specific address boundaries, for example, the second struct is aligned on a page boundary.

Internal Struct Alignment (WinDbg)

It is also possible to change a struct internal alignment through packing while preserving its C-type layout. This slide and the next slide provide examples using WinDbg and GDB debuggers.

Internal Struct Alignment (GDB)

```rust
println!("--- External Struct Alignment ---");
println!("--- Internal Struct Alignment ---");
{
    #[repr(C)]
    struct Struct {
        field1: bool,
        field2: i16,
        field8: i64,
    }

    #[repr(C, align(4096))]
    struct StructAligned {
        field1: bool,
        field2: i16,
        field8: i64,
    }

    let my_struct: Struct = Struct { field1: false,
        field2: 1, field8: 2,  };
    let my_struct_aligned: StructAligned =
        StructAligned { field1: false, field2: 1,
            field8: 2,  };
```

```rust
    println!("alignment of Struct: {:?} alignment of StructAligned: {:?}",
        std::mem::align_of::<Struct>(),
        std::mem::align_of::<StructAligned>());
    println!("address of my_struct: {:?} address of my_struct_aligned: {:?}",
addr_of!(my_struct),
        addr_of!(my_struct_aligned));

    #[repr(C, packed)]
    struct StructPacked {
        field1: bool,
        field2: i16,
        field8: i64,
    }

    let my_struct_packed: StructPacked = StructPacked {
        field1: false, field2: 1, field8: 2,  };

    println!("size of Struct: {:?} size of StructPacked: {:?} size of StructAligned:
{:?}",
        std::mem::size_of::<Struct>(), std::mem::size_of::<StructPacked>(),
        std::mem::size_of::<StructAligned>());

    println!("size of my_struct: {:?} size of my_struct_packed: {:?} size of
my_struct_aligned: {:?}",
        std::mem::size_of_val(&my_struct), std::mem::size_of_val(&my_struct_packed),
        std::mem::size_of_val(&my_struct_aligned));
}
```

Windows output:

```
--- External Struct Alignment ---
--- Internal Struct Alignment ---
alignment of Struct: 8 alignment of StructAligned: 4096
address of my_struct: 0x9101bccff0 address of my_struct_aligned: 0x9101bcd000
size of Struct: 16 size of StructPacked: 11 size of StructAligned: 4096
size of my_struct: 16 size of my_struct_packed: 11  size of my_struct_aligned: 4096
```

x64 Linux output:

```
--- External Struct Alignment ---
--- Internal Struct Alignment ---
alignment of Struct: 8 alignment of StructAligned: 4096
address of my_struct: 0x7ffccd7b2ff0 address of my_struct_aligned: 0x7ffccd7b3000
size of Struct: 16 size of StructPacked: 11 size of StructAligned: 4096
size of my_struct: 16 size of my_struct_packed: 11  size of my_struct_aligned: 4096
```

A64 Linux output:

```
--- External Struct Alignment ---
--- Internal Struct Alignment ---
alignment of Struct: 8 alignment of StructAligned: 4096
address of my_struct: 0xffffdefdbff0 address of my_struct_aligned: 0xffffdefdc000
size of Struct: 16 size of StructPacked: 11 size of StructAligned: 4096
size of my_struct: 16 size of my_struct_packed: 11  size of my_struct_aligned: 4096
```

Enums

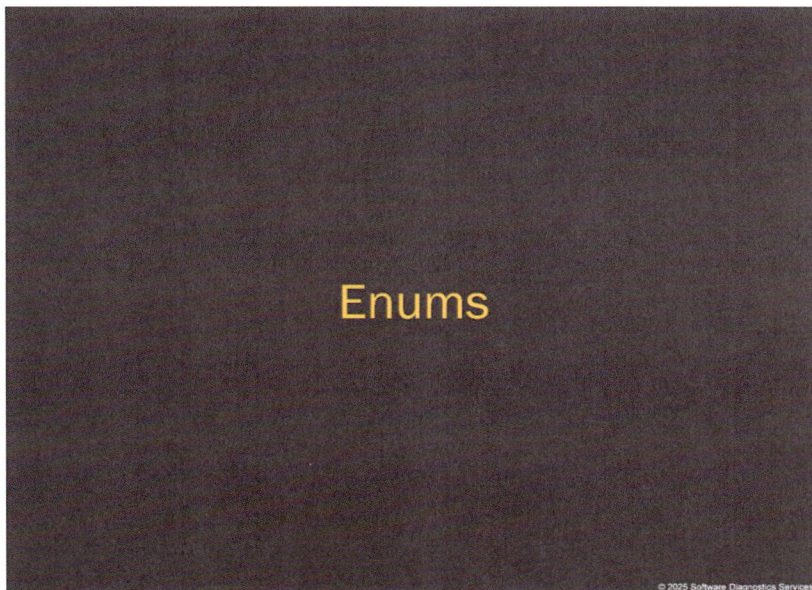

At a memory level, a Rust enum is a collection of memory cells to accommodate the largest value with an optional additional memory cell discriminating between different interpretations of these memory cells.

The enums project can be found in the archive[14]. In the following slide descriptions, we only show relevant code snippets and their output on various platforms.

---

[14] https://www.patterndiagnostics.com/Training/MTRust/MTRust.zip

Simple Enums

The size of simple enums values in bytes accommodates the largest variant value. Such enums may be unaligned. If explicitly aligned, their size is at least the size of the alignment.

```rust
println!("--- Simple Enums ---");
{
    #[derive(Debug)]
    enum MySimpleEnum {
        Variant1,
        Variant2,
        Variant3,
    }

    let my_simple_enum: MySimpleEnum = MySimpleEnum::Variant3;
    let my_simple_enum_ptr: *const MySimpleEnum = addr_of!(my_simple_enum);

    unsafe {
        let raw_value: usize = read_unaligned(my_simple_enum_ptr as *const usize);

        println!("address of my_simple_enum: {:?} size: {} value: {:?} raw memory
value: 0x{:x}",
            my_simple_enum_ptr, std::mem::size_of_val(&my_simple_enum),
&my_simple_enum, raw_value);
    }
```

```rust
#[derive(Debug)]
enum MySimpleEnum2 {
    Variant1 = 1,
    Variant2 = 2,
    Variant3 = 35636,
}


let my_simple_enum2: MySimpleEnum2 = MySimpleEnum2::Variant2;
let my_simple_enum2_ptr: *const MySimpleEnum2 = addr_of!(my_simple_enum2);


unsafe {
    let raw_value: usize = read_unaligned(my_simple_enum2_ptr as *const usize);

    println!("address of my_simple_enum2: {:?} size: {} value: {:?} raw memory
value: 0x{:x}",
            my_simple_enum2_ptr, std::mem::size_of_val(&my_simple_enum2),
&my_simple_enum2, raw_value);
}


#[derive(Debug)]
#[repr(align(8))]
enum MySimpleEnumAligned {
    Variant1,
    Variant2,
    Variant3,
}


let my_simple_enum_aligned: MySimpleEnumAligned = MySimpleEnumAligned::Variant2;
let my_simple_enum_aligned_ptr: *const MySimpleEnumAligned =
addr_of!(my_simple_enum_aligned);


unsafe {
    let raw_value: usize = *(my_simple_enum_aligned_ptr as *const usize);

    println!("address of my_simple_enum_aligned: {:?} size: {} value: {:?} raw
memory value: 0x{:x}",
            my_simple_enum_aligned_ptr,
std::mem::size_of_val(&my_simple_enum_aligned), &my_simple_enum_aligned,
            raw_value);
}
}
```

Windows output:

```
--- Simple Enums ---
address of my_simple_enum: 0xf50d5be89f size: 1 value: Variant3 raw memory value:
0xf50d5be89f02
address of my_simple_enum2: 0xf50d5be976 size: 2 value: Variant2 raw memory value:
0xf50d5be9760002
address of my_simple_enum_aligned: 0xf50d5bea48 size: 8 value: Variant2 raw memory
value: 0x1
```

x64 Linux output:

```
--- Simple Enums ---
address of my_simple_enum: 0x7ffe0a87584f size: 1 value: Variant3 raw memory value:
0x7ffe0a87584f02
address of my_simple_enum2: 0x7ffe0a875926 size: 2 value: Variant2 raw memory value:
0x7ffe0a8759260002
address of my_simple_enum_aligned: 0x7ffe0a8759f8 size: 8 value: Variant2 raw memory
value: 0x1
```

A64 Linux output:

```
--- Simple Enums ---
address of my_simple_enum: 0xffffc4e2078f size: 1 value: Variant3 raw memory value:
0xffffc4e2078f02
address of my_simple_enum2: 0xffffc4e2087e size: 2 value: Variant2 raw memory value:
0xffffc4e2087e0002
address of my_simple_enum_aligned: 0xffffc4e20968 size: 8 value: Variant2 raw memory
value: 0x1
```

Enums with Structs

The size of enums in bytes that have variants with fields accommodates the largest variant value plus a byte that records the variant index. If a variant value occupies less memory space than the largest variant value, the rest of the memory space is undefined: it may contain garbage bytes.

```
println!("--- Enums with Structs ---");
{
    #[derive(Debug)]
    enum MyDataEnum {
        Variant0,
        Variant1(bool),
        Variant2 {
            field1: bool,
            field2: u32,
        },
        Variant3 {
            field1: bool,
            field2: u32,
            field3: u64,
        },
    }

    let mut my_data_enum: MyDataEnum = MyDataEnum::Variant0;
    let my_data_enum_ptr: *const MyDataEnum = addr_of_mut!(my_data_enum);

    unsafe {
```

```rust
        let raw_value: usize = *(my_data_enum_ptr as *const usize);
        let raw_value2: usize =
*((my_data_enum_ptr as *const usize).wrapping_add(1));

        println!("address of my_data_enum: {:?} size: {} value: {:?} raw memory
values: 0x{:x} 0x{:x}",
            my_data_enum_ptr, std::mem::size_of_val(&my_data_enum), &my_data_enum,
            raw_value2, raw_value);
    }


    my_data_enum = MyDataEnum::Variant1(true);

    unsafe {
        let raw_value: usize = *(my_data_enum_ptr as *const usize);
        let raw_value2: usize =
*((my_data_enum_ptr as *const usize).wrapping_add(1));

        println!("address of my_data_enum: {:?} size: {} value: {:?} raw memory
values: 0x{:x} 0x{:x}",
            my_data_enum_ptr, std::mem::size_of_val(&my_data_enum), &my_data_enum,
            raw_value2, raw_value);
    }


    my_data_enum = MyDataEnum::Variant2 {field1: true, field2: 2};

    unsafe {
        let raw_value: usize = *(my_data_enum_ptr as *const usize);
        let raw_value2: usize =
*((my_data_enum_ptr as *const usize).wrapping_add(1));

        println!("address of my_data_enum: {:?} size: {} value: {:?} raw memory
values: 0x{:x} 0x{:x}",
            my_data_enum_ptr, std::mem::size_of_val(&my_data_enum), &my_data_enum,
            raw_value2, raw_value);
    }

    my_data_enum = MyDataEnum::Variant3 {field1: true, field2: 2, field3: 3};

    unsafe {
        let raw_value: usize = *(my_data_enum_ptr as *const usize);
        let raw_value2: usize =
*((my_data_enum_ptr as *const usize).wrapping_add(1));
```

```
        println!("address of my_data_enum: {:?} size: {} value: {:?} raw memory
values: 0x{:x} 0x{:x}",
            my_data_enum_ptr, std::mem::size_of_val(&my_data_enum), &my_data_enum,
            raw_value2, raw_value);
    }

    my_data_enum = MyDataEnum::Variant1(true);

    unsafe {
        let raw_value: usize = *(my_data_enum_ptr as *const usize);
        let raw_value2: usize =
*((my_data_enum_ptr as *const usize).wrapping_add(1));

        println!("address of my_data_enum: {:?} size: {} value: {:?} raw memory
values: 0x{:x} 0x{:x}",
            my_data_enum_ptr, std::mem::size_of_val(&my_data_enum), &my_data_enum,
            raw_value2, raw_value);
    }
}
```

Windows output:

```
--- Enums with Structs ---
address of my_data_enum: 0xf50d5beb50 size: 16 value: Variant0 raw memory values: 0x0
0x0
address of my_data_enum: 0xf50d5beb50 size: 16 value: Variant1(true) raw memory
values: 0x0 0x101
address of my_data_enum: 0xf50d5beb50 size: 16 value: Variant2 { field1: true,
field2: 2 } raw memory values: 0xf50d5bee90 0x200000102
address of my_data_enum: 0xf50d5beb50 size: 16 value: Variant3 { field1: true,
field2: 2, field3: 3 } raw memory values: 0x3 0x20d5b0103
address of my_data_enum: 0xf50d5beb50 size: 16 value: Variant1(true) raw memory
values: 0x0 0x101
```

x64 Linux output:

```
--- Enums with Structs ---
address of my_data_enum: 0x7ffe0a875b00 size: 16 value: Variant0 raw memory values:
0x22000 0x0
address of my_data_enum: 0x7ffe0a875b00 size: 16 value: Variant1(true) raw memory
values: 0x2000 0x101
address of my_data_enum: 0x7ffe0a875b00 size: 16 value: Variant2 { field1: true,
field2: 2 } raw memory values: 0x7ffe0a875e80 0x200000102
address of my_data_enum: 0x7ffe0a875b00 size: 16 value: Variant3 { field1: true,
field2: 2, field3: 3 } raw memory values: 0x3 0x267e90103
address of my_data_enum: 0x7ffe0a875b00 size: 16 value: Variant1(true) raw memory
values: 0x7f1a15e275e0 0x7ffe0a870101
```

A64 Linux output:

```
--- Enums with Structs ---
address of my_data_enum: 0xffffc4e20a80 size: 16 value: Variant0 raw memory values:
0x19c6e0 0x19d000
address of my_data_enum: 0xffffc4e20a80 size: 16 value: Variant1(true) raw memory
values: 0xe8f974c33c6c 0xffffc4e20101
address of my_data_enum: 0xffffc4e20a80 size: 16 value: Variant2 { field1: true,
field2: 2 } raw memory values: 0xe8f974c63000 0x274c60102
address of my_data_enum: 0xffffc4e20a80 size: 16 value: Variant3 { field1: true,
field2: 2, field3: 3 } raw memory values: 0x3 0x200000103
address of my_data_enum: 0xffffc4e20a80 size: 16 value: Variant1(true) raw memory
values: 0x0 0x3010102464c0101
```

Enum Null Pointer Optimization

If we have two variants and one is a pointer, then the other variant value can be a NULL pointer value. In this way we can remove an additional variant discriminator byte.

```rust
println!("--- Enum Null Pointer Optimization ---");
{
    #[derive(Debug)]
    enum MyEnum {
        Nothing,
        Something(Box<u64>),
    }

    let mut my_enum: MyEnum = MyEnum::Nothing;
    let my_enum_ptr: *const MyEnum = addr_of_mut!(my_enum);

    unsafe {
        let raw_value: usize = *(my_enum_ptr as *const usize);

        println!("address of my_enum: {:?} size: {} value: {:?} raw memory value:
0x{:x}",
            my_enum_ptr, std::mem::size_of_val(&my_enum), &my_enum, raw_value);
    }

    my_enum = MyEnum::Something(Box::new(1));
```

```rust
    unsafe {
        let raw_value: usize = *(my_enum_ptr as *const usize);

        println!("address of my_enum: {:?} size: {} value: {:?} raw memory value:
0x{:x}",
            my_enum_ptr, std::mem::size_of_val(&my_enum), &my_enum, raw_value);
    }
}
```

Windows output:

```
--- Enum Null Pointer Optimization ---
address of my_enum: 0xf50d5bf088 size: 8 value: Nothing raw memory value: 0x0
address of my_enum: 0xf50d5bf088 size: 8 value: Something(1) raw memory value:
0x2bd67cba6c0
```

x64 Linux output:

```
--- Enum Null Pointer Optimization ---
address of my_enum: 0x7ffe0a876038 size: 8 value: Nothing raw memory value: 0x0
address of my_enum: 0x7ffe0a876038 size: 8 value: Something(1) raw memory value:
0x5587c939e950
```

A64 Linux output:

```
--- Enum Null Pointer Optimization ---
address of my_enum: 0xffffc4e21018 size: 8 value: Nothing raw memory value: 0x0
address of my_enum: 0xffffc4e21018 size: 8 value: Something(1) raw memory value:
0xb35294433b10
```

Now, we briefly discuss Rust source code organization and its relation to debugging symbolic information. We divide the solution workspace design into 3 levels.

The `source-code-and-symbols` project can be found in the archive[15]. In the following slide descriptions, we only show relevant code snippets and their output on various platforms.

---

[15] https://www.patterndiagnostics.com/Training/MTRust/MTRust.zip

Conceptual Layer (Modules)

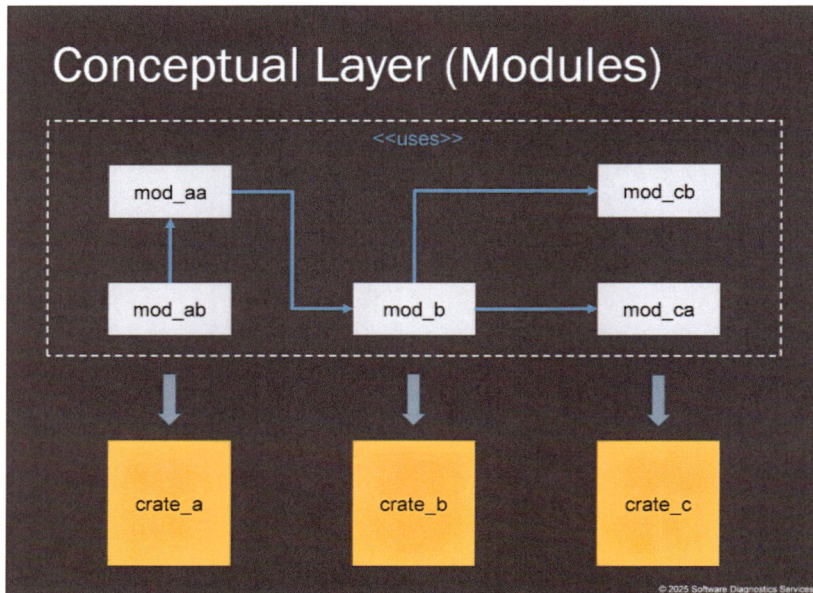

The first level is conceptual, where we have a "uses" relationship between workspace modules.

Logical Layer (Crates)

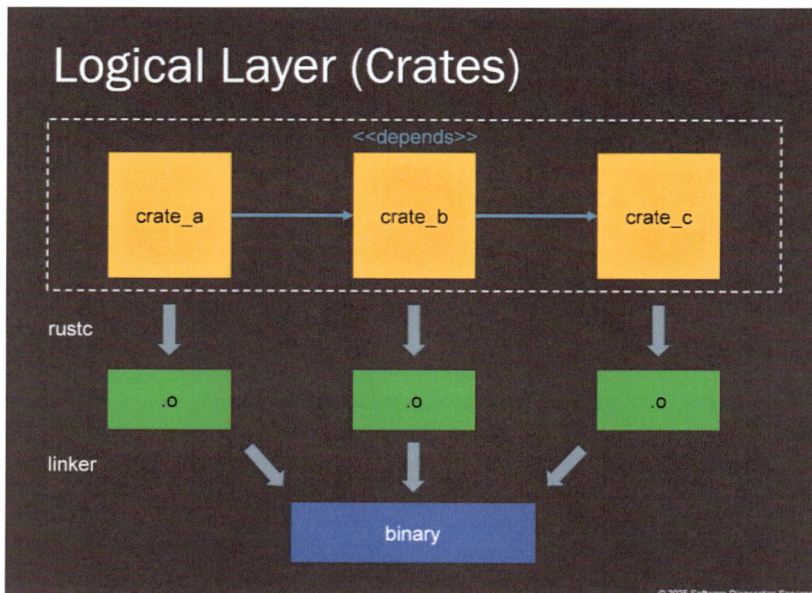

From a compiler perspective, it works with a crate unit as a whole and converts source code to an object file. Several object files are combined by a linker into an executable file. We have a "depends" relationship between crates.

Physical Layer (Source Files)

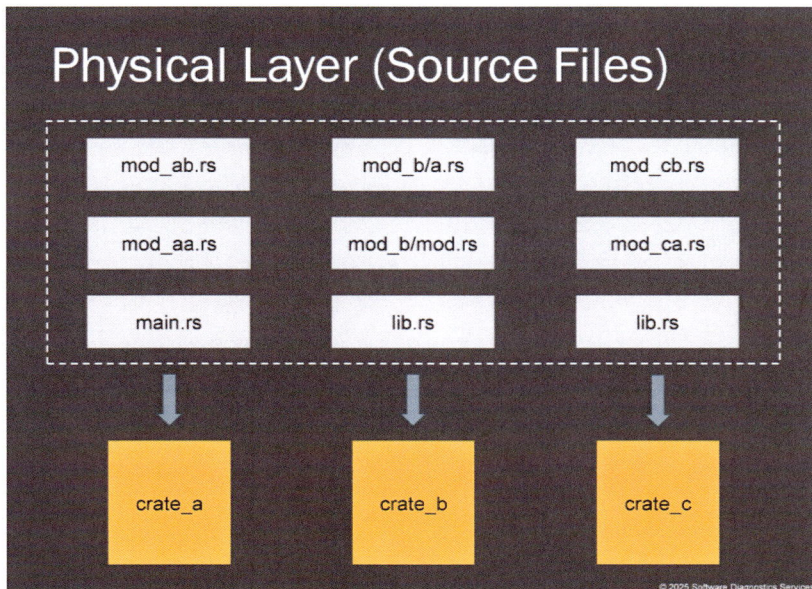

The last layer is a physical layer of source code files where modules can be split across several files.

Name Isolation

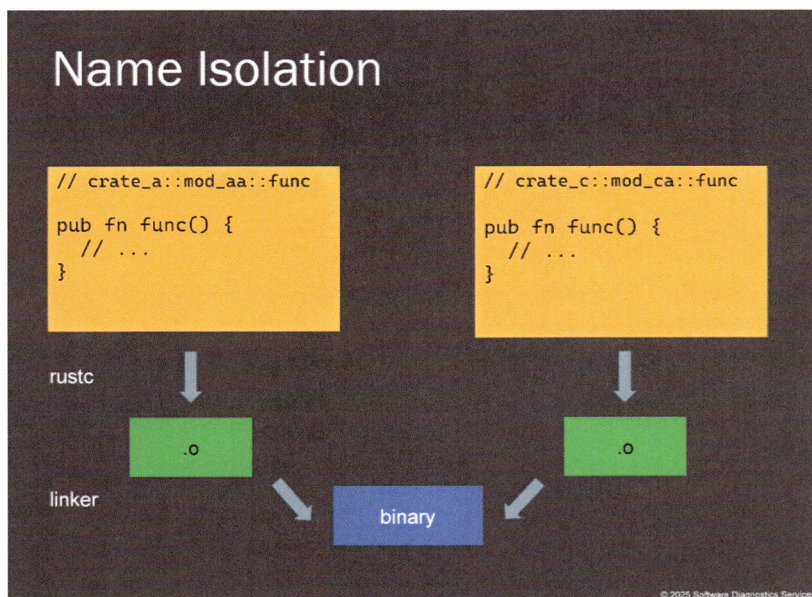

To isolate similar names, the compiler uses namespaces starting from the crate name and continuing with module names. We can see that in WinDbg and GDB debuggers.

```rust
// crate_a/main.rs
mod mod_ab;
mod mod_aa;

fn main() {
    mod_ab::func();
}

// crate_a/mod_aa.rs
use crate_b::mod_b;

pub fn func() {
    println!("mod_aa: func");
    mod_b::func();
}

// crate_a/mod_ab.rs
use crate::mod_aa;

pub fn func() {
    println!("mod_ab: func");
    mod_aa::func();
}

// crate_b/lib.rs
pub mod mod_b;

// crate_b/mod_b/mod.rs
use crate_c::mod_ca;
use crate_c::mod_cb;

mod a;

pub fn func() {
    println!("mod_b: func");
    a::func();
    mod_ca::func();
    mod_cb::func();
}
```

```rust
// crate_b/mod_b/a.rs
pub fn func() {
    println!("a: func");
    b::func();
}

mod b {
    pub fn func() {
        println!("b: func");
    }
}

// crate_c/lib.rs
pub mod mod_ca;
pub mod mod_cb;

// crate_c/mod_ca.rs
pub fn func() {
    println!("mod_ca: func");
}

// crate_c/mod_cb.rs
pub fn func() {
    println!("mod_cb: func");
}
```

Output:

```
mod_ab: func
mod_aa: func
mod_b: func
a: func
b: func
mod_ca: func
mod_cb: func
```

Functions

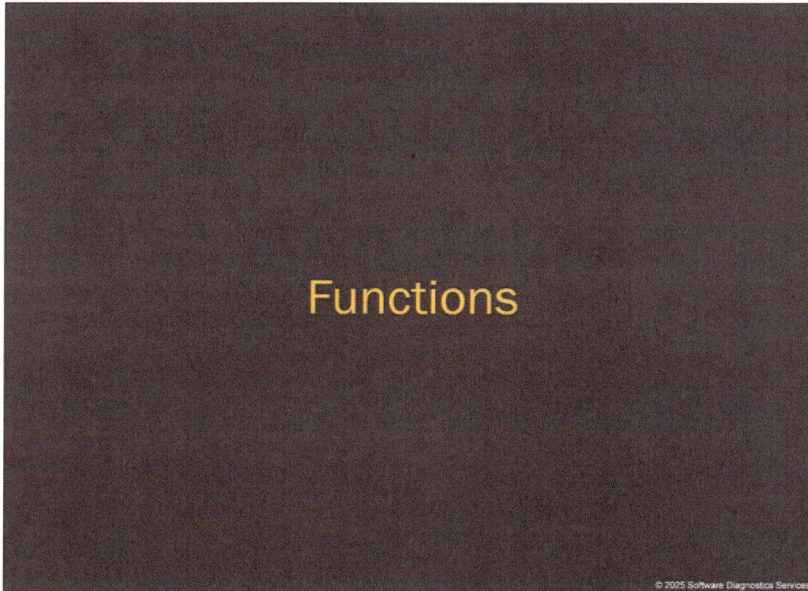

The next two parts of this training are about functions.

The `functions` project can be found in the archive[16]. In the following slide descriptions, we only show relevant code snippets and their output on various platforms.

Pointers to Functions

Functions are code bytes and, therefore, occupy some memory locations with their start addresses. Therefore, pointers to functions contain the start addresses of the functions.

```rust
fn func (i: i32) -> i32 {
    i
}

println!("--- Pointers to Functions ---");
{
    let func_ptr: fn(i32) -> i32 = func;
    let func_ptr_const: *const fn(i32) -> i32 =
        func as *const fn(i32) -> i32;
    let func_ptr_mut: *mut fn(i32) -> i32 =
        func as *mut fn(i32) -> i32;

    println!("address of func_ptr: {:?} value of func_ptr: {func_ptr:p}",
addr_of!(func_ptr));
    println!("address of func_ptr_const: {:?} value of func_ptr_const:
{func_ptr_const:p}",
        addr_of!(func_ptr_const));
    println!("address of func_ptr_mut: {:?} value of func_ptr_mut: {func_ptr_mut:p}",
        addr_of!(func_ptr_mut));
```

```
    func_ptr(0);
    // unsafe {
    //     (*func_ptr_const)(0); // crash
    //     (*func_ptr_mut)(0);   // crash
    // }
}
```

Windows output:

```
--- Pointers to Functions ---
address of func_ptr: 0x562f2fdb68 value of func_ptr: 0x7ff69cad5550
address of func_ptr_const: 0x562f2fdb70 value of func_ptr_const: 0x7ff69cad5550
address of func_ptr_mut: 0x562f2fdb78 value of func_ptr_mut: 0x7ff69cad5550
```

x64 Linux output:

```
--- Pointers to Functions ---
address of func_ptr: 0x7ffd86cdc0e8 value of func_ptr: 0x556a1f5b6150
address of func_ptr_const: 0x7ffd86cdc0f0 value of func_ptr_const: 0x556a1f5b6150
address of func_ptr_mut: 0x7ffd86cdc0f8 value of func_ptr_mut: 0x556a1f5b6150
```

A64 Linux output:

```
--- Pointers to Functions ---
address of func_ptr: 0xffffdec03348 value of func_ptr: 0xaaaaaf61bbf4
address of func_ptr_const: 0xffffdec03350 value of func_ptr_const: 0xaaaaaf61bbf4
address of func_ptr_mut: 0xffffdec03358 value of func_ptr_mut: 0xaaaaaf61bbf4
```

References to Functions

References to functions are actually references to pointers to functions. When we dereference them, we get pointers to functions.

```
println!("--- References to Functions ---");
{
    let func_ref: &fn(i32) -> i32 =
        &(func as fn(i32) -> i32);
    let func_ref_mut: &mut fn(i32) -> i32 =
        &mut (func as fn(i32) -> i32);

    println!("address of func_ref: {:?} value of func_ref: {func_ref:p} dereference
of func_ref {:p}",
        addr_of!(func_ref), *func_ref);
    println!("address of func_ref_mut: {:?} value of func_ref_mut: {func_ref_mut:p}
dereference of func_ref_mut {:p}",
        addr_of!(func_ref_mut), *func_ref_mut);

    func_ref(0);
    (*func_ref)(0);
    func_ref_mut(0);
    (*func_ref_mut)(0);
}
```

Windows output:

```
--- References to Functions ---
address of func_ref: 0x562f2fdcb8 value of func_ref: 0x7ff69caf15f0 dereference of
func_ref 0x7ff69cad5550
address of func_ref_mut: 0x562f2fdcc0 value of func_ref_mut: 0x562f2fdcc8 dereference
of func_ref_mut 0x7ff69cad5550
```

x64 Linux output:

```
--- References to Functions ---
address of func_ref: 0x7ffd86cdc238 value of func_ref: 0x556a1f5fd638 dereference of
func_ref 0x556a1f5b6150
address of func_ref_mut: 0x7ffd86cdc240 value of func_ref_mut: 0x7ffd86cdc248
dereference of func_ref_mut 0x556a1f5b6150
```

A64 Linux output:

```
--- References to Functions ---
address of func_ref: 0xffffdec03498 value of func_ref: 0xaaaaaf672b08 dereference of
func_ref 0xaaaaaf61bbf4
address of func_ref_mut: 0xffffdec034a0 value of func_ref_mut: 0xffffdec034a8
dereference of func_ref_mut 0xaaaaaf61bbf4
```

Function Pointer Types

To simplify signatures, we can name function pointer types.

```
println!("--- Function Pointer Types ---");
{
    type MyFuncPtr = fn(i32) -> i32;

    let func_ptr: MyFuncPtr = func;

    func_ptr(0);
}
```

Struct Function Fields

Structs may contain fields that are pointers to functions: this mimics OOP implementation in C.

```rust
println!("--- Stuct Function Fields ---");
{
    type PF = fn(i32) -> i32;

    struct MyStruct {
        field: i32,
        func_ptr: PF,
    }

    let my_struct: MyStruct = MyStruct { field: 0,
        func_ptr: func, };

    (my_struct.func_ptr)(0);

    println!("value of my_struct.func_ptr: {:p}",
        my_struct.func_ptr);
}
```

Windows output:

```
--- Stuct Function Fields ---
value of my_struct.func_ptr: 0x7ff69cad5550
```

x64 Linux output:

```
--- Stuct Function Fields ---
value of my_struct.func_ptr: 0x556a1f5b6150
```

A64 Linux output:

```
--- Stuct Function Fields ---
value of my_struct.func_ptr: 0x556a1f5b6150
```

Associated Functions

```
Associated Functions

struct MyStruct {
    field: i32,
    func_ptr: PF,
}

impl MyStruct {
    fn method (&self, i: i32) -> i32 { i }
}

my_struct.method(0);
```

© 2025 Software Diagnostics Services

We can associate functions we structs similar to class methods in OOP. But we have to provide a reference to self to differentiate between struct instances when we call such functions. In contrast to C++, we need to specify self explicitly when we define associated functions. We will also talk about self when we cover function parameters.

```
println!("--- Associated Functions ---");
{
    type PF = fn(i32) -> i32;

    struct MyStruct {
        field: i32,
        func_ptr: PF,
    }

    impl MyStruct {
        fn method (&self, i: i32) -> i32 { i }
    }

    let my_struct: MyStruct = MyStruct { field: 0,
        func_ptr: func, };

    my_struct.method(0);

    println!("address of method: {:p}",
        MyStruct::method as fn(&MyStruct, i32) -> i32);
}
```

Windows output:

```
--- Associated Functions ---
address of method: 0x7ff69cad5560
```

x64 Linux output:

```
--- Associated Functions ---
address of method: 0x556a1f5b6160
```

A64 Linux output:

```
--- Associated Functions ---
address of method: 0x556a1f5b6160
```

Pointers to Associated Functions

Similar to free functions, it is also possible to have pointers to associated functions, but we need to explicitly specify concrete instances of self as a parameter.

```rust
println!("--- Pointers to Associated Functions ---");
{
    type PF = fn(i32) -> i32;

    struct MyStruct {
        field: i32,
        func_ptr: PF,
    }

    impl MyStruct {
        fn method (&self, i: i32) -> i32 { i }
    }

    let my_struct: MyStruct = MyStruct { field: 0,
        func_ptr: func, };

    let method_ptr: fn(&MyStruct, i32) -> i32 =
        MyStruct::method;

    method_ptr(&my_struct, 0);
```

```rust
    println!("address of method: {:p}",
        MyStruct::method as fn(&MyStruct, i32) -> i32);
    println!("address of method_ptr: {:?} value of method_ptr {method_ptr:p}",
addr_of!(method_ptr));
}
```

Windows output:

```
--- Pointers to Associated Functions ---
address of method: 0x7ff69cad5580
address of method_ptr: 0x562f2fdf40 value of method_ptr 0x7ff69cad5580
```

x64 Linux output:

```
--- Pointers to Associated Functions ---
address of method: 0x556a1f5b6170
address of method_ptr: 0x7ffd86cdc4c0 value of method_ptr 0x556a1f5b6170
```

A64 Linux output:

```
--- Pointers to Associated Functions ---
address of method: 0xaaaaaf61bc20
address of method_ptr: 0xffffdec03720 value of method_ptr 0xaaaaaf61bc20
```

Type-associated Functions

Like static class methods in OOP languages, it is possible to associate functions with a struct type. Such type-associated functions don't have self parameters. It is also possible to have pointers to them.

```rust
println!("--- Type-associated Functions ---");
{
    type PF = fn(i32) -> i32;

    struct MyStruct {
        field: i32,
        func_ptr: PF,
    }

    impl MyStruct {
        fn method_type (i: i32) -> i32 { i }
    }

    MyStruct::method_type(0);

    let method_type_ptr: fn(i32) -> i32 =
        MyStruct::method_type;

    method_type_ptr(0);

    println!("address of method_type: {:p}",
        MyStruct::method_type as fn(i32) -> i32);
```

```
    println!("address of method_type_ptr: {:?} value of method_type_ptr
{method_type_ptr:p}",
        addr_of!(method_type_ptr));
}
```

Windows output:

```
--- Type-associated Functions ---
address of method_type: 0x7ff69cad55a0
address of method_type_ptr: 0x562f2fe010 value of method_type_ptr 0x7ff69cad55a0
```

x64 Linux output:

```
--- Type-associated Functions ---
address of method_type: 0x556a1f5b6180
address of method_type_ptr: 0x7ffd86cdc590 value of method_type_ptr 0x556a1f5b6180
```

A64 Linux output:

```
--- Type-associated Functions ---
address of method_type: 0xaaaaaf61bc3c
address of method_type_ptr: 0xffffdec037f0 value of method_type_ptr 0xaaaaaf61bc3c
```

Trait Functions

```
Trait Functions

trait Base {
    fn method (i: i32) -> i32;
}

struct Derived {}

impl Base for Derived {
    fn method (i: i32) -> i32 { i }
}

my_derived.method(0);
```

© 2025 Software Diagnostics Services

Instead of class hierarchy in traditional OOP languages, Rust uses an interface-type approach via the so-called traits. In structs, we implement associated or type-associated methods declared in traits. On this slide, we model a base-derived hierarchy using a trait and a struct. It is also possible to inherit one trait from another.

Trait Objects

```
Trait Objects

trait Base {
    fn method (i: i32) -> i32;
}

impl Base for Derived {
    fn method (i: i32) -> i32 { i }
}

let my_base: &dyn Base = &my_derived;

my_base.method(0); // (*my_base).method(0);
```

© 2025 Software Diagnostics Services

We can also define the so-called trait objects, which represent trait implementations. Since different structs may implement the same trait functions differently, trait objects must differentiate between them, and dynamically dispatch to the appropriate function and supply the correct reference to self.

```rust
println!("--- Trait Functions and Objects ---");
{
    trait Base {
        fn method (&self, i: i32) -> i32;
    }

    struct Derived {}

    impl Base for Derived {
        fn method (&self, i: i32) -> i32 { i }
    }

    let my_derived: Derived = Derived {};

    my_derived.method(0);

    let my_base: &dyn Base = &my_derived;

    my_base.method(0);
      (*my_base).method(0);

    println!("address of method: {:p}",
        Derived::method as fn(&Derived, i32) -> i32);
}
```

Windows output:

```
--- Trait Functions and Objects ---
address of method: 0x7ff69cad55b0
```

x64 Linux output:

```
--- Trait Functions and Objects ---
address of method: 0x556a1f5b6190
```

A64 Linux output:

```
--- Trait Functions and Objects ---
address of method: 0xaaaaaf61bc4c
```

vtable Memory Layout

These dynamic dispatch function calls are implemented uniformly by having a specific (vtable) virtual function table for each trait object where the addresses of the trait methods are replaced with those of the implementation struct methods. This is similar to virtual function tables (VTBL) in languages such as C++.

Trait Object Memory Layout

Every trait object has an address of implementation struct and a virtual function table pointer (vtable). Therefore, each trait function call from a trait object is a type-independent call where the target function address is easily calculated based on the address of the virtual function table and virtual function offset.

```rust
println!("--- vtable and Trait Object Memory Layout ---");
{
    trait Base {
        fn method1 (&self);
        fn method2 (&self);
    }

    struct Derived {
        data: u32,
    }

    struct Derived2 {
        data: u64,
    }

    impl Base for Derived {
        fn method1 (&self) {}
        fn method2 (&self) {}
    }

    impl Base for Derived2 {
        fn method1 (&self) {}
        fn method2 (&self) {}
    }

    let my_derived: Derived = Derived { data: 1, };
    let my_derived2: Derived2 = Derived2 { data: 2, };

    println!("address of my_derived: {:?} address of method1: {:p} address of
method2: {:p}",
        addr_of!(my_derived),
        Derived::method1 as fn(&Derived),
        Derived::method2 as fn(&Derived));
    println!("address of my_derived2: {:?} address of method: {:p} address of
method2: {:p}",
        addr_of!(my_derived2),
        Derived2::method1 as fn(&Derived2),
        Derived2::method2 as fn(&Derived2));

    let mut my_base: &dyn Base = &my_derived;

    unsafe {
```

```
        let vtable_addr: *const usize =
        *(((addr_of!(my_base) as usize) +
        std::mem::size_of::<usize>()) as *const usize) as *const usize;
        println!("address of my_base: {:?} value of my_base (data): {my_base:p} value
of my_base+usize (address of vtable): {:p}",
        addr_of!(my_base), vtable_addr);
        println!("address of destructor: {:p} size: {:?} alignment: {:?} address of
method1: {:p} address of method2: {:p}",
            *vtable_addr as *const usize,
            *(((vtable_addr as usize) +
                std::mem::size_of::<usize>()) as *const usize),
            *(((vtable_addr as usize) +
                2*std::mem::size_of::<usize>()) as *const usize),
            *(((vtable_addr as usize) +
                3*std::mem::size_of::<usize>()) as *const usize) as *const usize,
            *(((vtable_addr as usize) +
                4*std::mem::size_of::<usize>()) as *const usize) as *const
usize);
    }

    my_base = &my_derived2;

    unsafe {
        let vtable_addr: *const usize =
            *(((addr_of!(my_base) as usize) +
                std::mem::size_of::<usize>()) as *const usize) as *const usize;
        println!("address of my_base: {:?} value of my_base (data): {my_base:p} value
of my_base+usize (address of vtable): {:p}",
            addr_of!(my_base), vtable_addr);
        println!("address of destructor: {:p} size: {:?} alignment: {:?} address of
method1: {:p} address of method2: {:p}",
            *vtable_addr as *const usize,
            *(((vtable_addr as usize) +
                std::mem::size_of::<usize>()) as *const usize),
            *(((vtable_addr as usize) +
                2*std::mem::size_of::<usize>()) as *const usize),
            *(((vtable_addr as usize) +
                3*std::mem::size_of::<usize>()) as *const usize) as *const usize,
            *(((vtable_addr as usize) +
                4*std::mem::size_of::<usize>()) as *const usize) as *const
usize);
    }
```

```
}
```

Windows output:

```
--- vtable and Trait Object Memory Layout ---
address of my_derived: 0x562f2fe15c address of method1: 0x7ff69cad55d0 address of
method2: 0x7ff69cad55e0
address of my_derived2: 0x562f2fe160 address of method: 0x7ff69cad55f0 address of
method2: 0x7ff69cad5600
address of my_base: 0x562f2fe238 value of my_base (data): 0x562f2fe15c value of
my_base+usize (address of vtable): 0x7ff69caf1b60
address of destructor: 0x7ff69cad6ad0 size: 4 alignment: 4 address of method1:
0x7ff69cad55d0 address of method2: 0x7ff69cad55e0
address of my_base: 0x562f2fe238 value of my_base (data): 0x562f2fe160 value of
my_base+usize (address of vtable): 0x7ff69caf1e30
address of destructor: 0x7ff69cad6b50 size: 8 alignment: 8 address of method1:
0x7ff69cad55f0 address of method2: 0x7ff69cad5600
```

x64 Linux output:

```
--- vtable and Trait Object Memory Layout ---
address of my_derived: 0x7ffd86cdc6dc address of method1: 0x556a1f5b61a0 address of
method2: 0x556a1f5b61b0
address of my_derived2: 0x7ffd86cdc6e0 address of method: 0x556a1f5b61c0 address of
method2: 0x556a1f5b61d0
address of my_base: 0x7ffd86cdc7b8 value of my_base (data): 0x7ffd86cdc6dc value of
my_base+usize (address of vtable): 0x556a1f5fd8d0
address of destructor: 0x556a1f5b70d0 size: 4 alignment: 4 address of method1:
0x556a1f5b61a0 address of method2: 0x556a1f5b61b0
address of my_base: 0x7ffd86cdc7b8 value of my_base (data): 0x7ffd86cdc6e0 value of
my_base+usize (address of vtable): 0x556a1f5fdad0
address of destructor: 0x556a1f5b7160 size: 8 alignment: 8 address of method1:
0x556a1f5b61c0 address of method2: 0x556a1f5b61d0
```

A64 Linux output:

```
--- vtable and Trait Object Memory Layout ---
address of my_derived: 0xffffdec0393c address of method1: 0xaaaaaf61bc68 address of
method2: 0xaaaaaf61bc78
address of my_derived2: 0xffffdec03940 address of method: 0xaaaaaf61bc88 address of
method2: 0xaaaaaf61bc98
address of my_base: 0xffffdec03a18 value of my_base (data): 0xffffdec0393c value of
my_base+usize (address of vtable): 0xaaaaaf672da0
address of destructor: 0xaaaaaf61d14c size: 4 alignment: 4 address of method1:
0xaaaaaf61bc68 address of method2: 0xaaaaaf61bc78
address of my_base: 0xffffdec03a18 value of my_base (data): 0xffffdec03940 value of
my_base+usize (address of vtable): 0xaaaaaf672f88
address of destructor: 0xaaaaaf61d1b4 size: 8 alignment: 8 address of method1:
0xaaaaaf61bc88 address of method2: 0xaaaaaf61bc98
```

Boxed Trait Object Layout

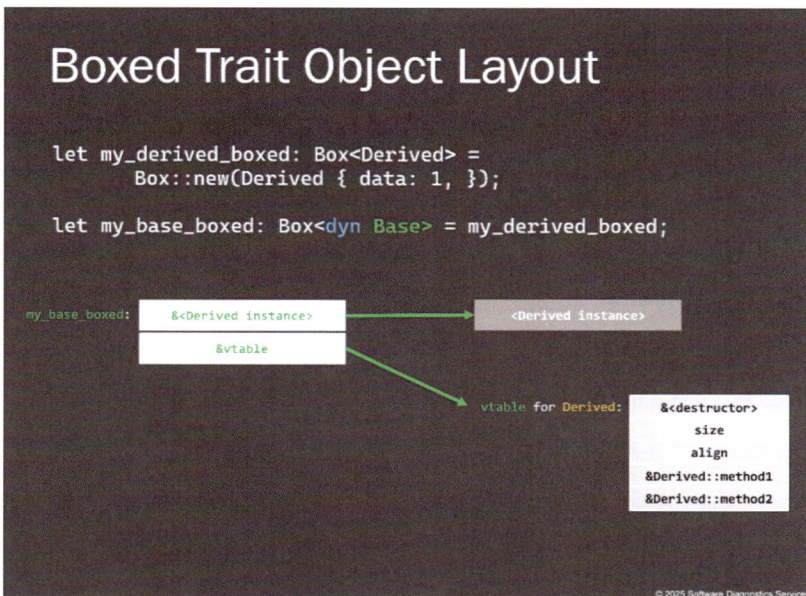

If an implementation struct was created dynamically and placed in the heap region, its trait object layout is similar.

```rust
println!("--- Boxed Trait Object Layout ---");
{
    trait Base {
        fn method1 (&self);
        fn method2 (&self);
    }

    struct Derived {
        data: u32,
    }

    impl Base for Derived {
        fn method1 (&self) {}
        fn method2 (&self) {}
    }

    let my_derived_boxed: Box<Derived> =
        Box::new(Derived { data: 1, });

    println!("address of my_derived_boxed: {:?} address of method1: {:p} address of
method2: {:p}",
        addr_of!(my_derived_boxed),
        Derived::method1 as fn(&Derived),
        Derived::method2 as fn(&Derived));

    let my_base_boxed: Box<dyn Base> =
        my_derived_boxed;

    unsafe {
        let vtable_addr: *const usize =
            *(((addr_of!(my_base_boxed) as usize) +
                std::mem::size_of::<usize>()) as *const usize) as *const usize;
        println!("address of my_base_boxed: {:?} value of my_base_boxed (data):
{my_base_boxed:p} value of my_base_boxed+usize (address of vtable): {:p}",
            addr_of!(my_base_boxed), vtable_addr);
        println!("address of destructor: {:p} size: {:?} alignment: {:?} address of
method1: {:p} address of method2: {:p}",
            *vtable_addr as *const usize,
            *(((vtable_addr as usize) +
                std::mem::size_of::<usize>()) as *const usize),
            *(((vtable_addr as usize) +
                2*std::mem::size_of::<usize>()) as *const usize),
```

```
        *(((vtable_addr as usize) +
            3*std::mem::size_of::<usize>()) as *const usize) as *const usize,
        *(((vtable_addr as usize) +
            4*std::mem::size_of::<usize>()) as *const usize) as *const
usize);
    }
}
```

Windows output:

```
--- Boxed Trait Object Layout ---
address of my_derived_boxed: 0x562f2fe4b8 address of method1: 0x7ff69cad5610 address
of method2: 0x7ff69cad5620
address of my_base_boxed: 0x562f2fe530 value of my_base_boxed (data): 0x18eaaf7beb0
value of my_base_boxed+usize (address of vtable): 0x7ff69caf2020
address of destructor: 0x7ff69cad6ae0 size: 4 alignment: 4 address of method1:
0x7ff69cad5610 address of method2: 0x7ff69cad5620
```

x64 Linux output:

```
--- Boxed Trait Object Layout ---
address of my_derived_boxed: 0x7ffd86cdca38 address of method1: 0x556a1f5b61e0
address of method2: 0x556a1f5b61f0
address of my_base_boxed: 0x7ffd86cdcab0 value of my_base_boxed (data):
0x556a1ff4dae0 value of my_base_boxed+usize (address of vtable): 0x556a1f5fdc90
address of destructor: 0x556a1f5b70e0 size: 4 alignment: 4 address of method1:
0x556a1f5b61e0 address of method2: 0x556a1f5b61f0
```

A64 Linux output:

```
--- Boxed Trait Object Layout ---
address of my_derived_boxed: 0xffffdec03c98 address of method1: 0xaaaaaf61bca8
address of method2: 0xaaaaaf61bcb8
address of my_base_boxed: 0xffffdec03d10 value of my_base_boxed (data):
0xaaaac031bad0 value of my_base_boxed+usize (address of vtable): 0xaaaaaf673130
address of destructor: 0xaaaaaf61d13c size: 4 alignment: 4 address of method1:
0xaaaaaf61bca8 address of method2: 0xaaaaaf61bcb8
```

Struct Constructors

```
Struct Constructors

struct MyStruct {
    field: i32,
}

impl MyStruct {
    fn new (i: i32) -> Self {
        MyStruct { field: i+10 }
    }
}

let my_struct: MyStruct = MyStruct::new(0);
```
© 2025 Software Diagnostics Services

Now we come to constructors. These are just type-associated functions that return Self. Their names can be anything, new is just a convention.

```rust
println!("--- Struct Constructors ---");
{
    struct MyStruct {
        field: i32,
    }

    impl MyStruct {
        fn new (i: i32) -> Self {
            MyStruct { field: i+10 }
        }

        fn new_debug (i: i32) -> Self {
            let new_val: MyStruct = MyStruct { field: i+10 };
            println!("address of new_val: {:?}", addr_of!(new_val));
            new_val
        }
    }

    let my_struct: MyStruct = MyStruct::new(0);

    println!("address of my_struct: {:?}",
        addr_of!(my_struct));
```

```
    let my_struct: MyStruct = MyStruct::new_debug(0);

    println!("address of my_struct: {:?}",
        addr_of!(my_struct));

    let my_struct_ref: &MyStruct =
        &MyStruct::new_debug(0);

    println!("address of my_struct_ref: {:?} value of my_struct_ref:
{my_struct_ref:p} dereference of my_struct_ref: {:?}",
        addr_of!(my_struct_ref), (*my_struct_ref).field);
}
```

Windows output:

```
--- Struct Constructors ---
address of my_struct: 0x562f2fe694
address of new_val: 0x562f2fd7f4
address of my_struct: 0x562f2fe6e4
address of new_val: 0x562f2fd7f4
address of my_struct_ref: 0x562f2fe750 value of my_struct_ref: 0x562f2fe73c
dereference of my_struct_ref: 10
```

x64 Linux output:

```
--- Struct Constructors ---
address of my_struct: 0x7ffd86cdcc14
address of new_val: 0x7ffd86cdbaa4
address of my_struct: 0x7ffd86cdcc64
address of new_val: 0x7ffd86cdbaa4
address of my_struct_ref: 0x7ffd86cdccd0 value of my_struct_ref: 0x7ffd86cdccbc
dereference of my_struct_ref: 10
```

A64 Linux output:

```
--- Struct Constructors ---
address of my_struct: 0xffffdec03e74
address of new_val: 0xffffdec02b1c
address of my_struct: 0xffffdec03ec4
address of new_val: 0xffffdec02b1c
address of my_struct_ref: 0xffffdec03e30 value of my_struct_ref: 0xffffdec03f1c
dereference of my_struct_ref: 10
```

Struct Destructor

If we need specialized destructors with custom logic, we can implement the Drop trait for our structs. The default destructor will call destructors for each struct field.

```
println!("--- Struct Destructors ---");
{
    trait Base {}

    struct MyStruct {
        field: i32,
    }

    impl Base for MyStruct {}

    let my_struct: MyStruct = MyStruct { field: 0 };

    let mut my_base: &dyn Base = &my_struct;

    unsafe {
        let vtable_addr: *const usize =
            *(((addr_of!(my_base) as usize) +
            std::mem::size_of::<usize>()) as *const usize) as *const usize;
        println!("address of MyStruct destructor: {:p}", *vtable_addr as *const
usize);
    }

    struct MyStruct2 {
        field: i32,
    }

    impl Base for MyStruct2 {}

    impl Drop for MyStruct2 {
        fn drop (&mut self) {
            println!("drop for MyStruct2 instance address: {self:p}");
        }
    }

    let my_struct2: MyStruct2 = MyStruct2 { field: 0 };
    println!("address of my_struct2: {:?}",
        addr_of!(my_struct2));

    my_base = &my_struct2;

    unsafe {
        let vtable_addr: *const usize =
```

```
                *(((addr_of!(my_base) as usize) +
                std::mem::size_of::<usize>()) as *const usize) as *const usize;
            println!("address of MyStruct2 destructor: {:p}", *vtable_addr as *const
    usize);
        }

        let my_struct2_boxed: Box<MyStruct2> =
            Box::new(MyStruct2 { field: 0 });
        println!("value of my_struct2_boxed: {:p}", my_struct2_boxed);

        let my_base_boxed: Box<dyn Base> =
            my_struct2_boxed;

        unsafe {
            let vtable_addr: *const usize =
                *(((addr_of!(my_base) as usize) +
                std::mem::size_of::<usize>()) as *const usize) as *const usize;
            println!("address of MyStruct2 destructor: {:p}", *vtable_addr as *const
    usize);
        }

#[repr(C)]
    struct MyStruct3 {
        field1: i32,
        field2: String,
    }

    impl Base for MyStruct3 {}

    let my_struct3: MyStruct3 = MyStruct3 { field1: 0,
        field2: "MyStruct3 instance".into() };
    println!("address of my_struct3: {:?}",
        addr_of!(my_struct3));

    my_base = &my_struct3;

    unsafe {
        let vtable_addr: *const usize =
            *(((addr_of!(my_base) as usize) +
            std::mem::size_of::<usize>()) as *const usize) as *const usize;
        println!("address of MyStruct3 destructor: {:p}", *vtable_addr as *const
    usize);
```

```
        }
}
```

Windows output:

```
--- Struct Destructors ---
address of MyStruct destructor: 0x7ff69cad6b60
address of my_struct2: 0x562f2fe854
address of MyStruct2 destructor: 0x7ff69cad6b90
value of my_struct2_boxed: 0x18eaaf7beb0
address of MyStruct2 destructor: 0x7ff69cad6b90
address of my_struct3: 0x562f2fe948
address of MyStruct3 destructor: 0x7ff69cad6bb0
drop for MyStruct2 instance address: 0x18eaaf7beb0
drop for MyStruct2 instance address: 0x562f2fe854
```

x64 Linux output:

```
--- Struct Destructors ---
address of MyStruct destructor: 0x556a1f5b7170
address of my_struct2: 0x7ffd86cdcdd4
address of MyStruct2 destructor: 0x556a1f5b7190
value of my_struct2_boxed: 0x556a1ff4dae0
address of MyStruct2 destructor: 0x556a1f5b7190
address of my_struct3: 0x7ffd86cdcec8
address of MyStruct3 destructor: 0x556a1f5b71a0
drop for MyStruct2 instance address: 0x556a1ff4dae0
drop for MyStruct2 instance address: 0x7ffd86cdcdd4
```

A64 Linux output:

```
--- Struct Destructors ---
address of MyStruct destructor: 0xaaaaaf61d1e4
address of my_struct2: 0xffffdec04034
address of MyStruct2 destructor: 0xaaaaaf61d1f4
value of my_struct2_boxed: 0xaaaac031bad0
address of MyStruct2 destructor: 0xaaaaaf61d1f4
address of my_struct3: 0xffffdec04128
address of MyStruct3 destructor: 0xaaaaaf61d214
drop for MyStruct2 instance address: 0xaaaac031bad0
drop for MyStruct2 instance address: 0xffffdec04034
```

Struct Clone

If we don't want to move values when we assign them to new variables, we can either derive the default implementation of the Clone trait or write our own. Clone does a deep copy; for example, a String buffer is duplicated.

```rust
println!("--- Struct Clone ---");
{
    #[derive(Clone)]
    struct MyStruct {
        field: String,
    }

    let my_struct: MyStruct = MyStruct { field: "MyStruct instance".into() };
    let my_struct2: MyStruct = my_struct.clone();

    assert_ne!(my_struct.field.as_ptr(),
        my_struct2.field.as_ptr());

    println!("address of my_struct: {:?} String contents address: {:p}",
addr_of!(my_struct),
        my_struct.field.as_ptr());
    println!("address of my_struct2: {:?} String contents address: {:p}",
addr_of!(my_struct2),
        my_struct2.field.as_ptr());
}
```

Windows output:

```
--- Struct Clone ---
address of my_struct: 0x562f2fea40 String contents address: 0x18eaaf80fa0
address of my_struct2: 0x562f2fea70 String contents address: 0x18eaaf810e0
```

x64 Linux output:

```
--- Struct Clone ---
address of my_struct: 0x7ffd86cdcfc0 String contents address: 0x556a1ff4dae0
address of my_struct2: 0x7ffd86cdcff8 String contents address: 0x556a1ff4db00
```

A64 Linux output:

```
--- Struct Clone ---
address of my_struct: 0xffffdec04220 String contents address: 0xaaaac031bad0
address of my_struct2: 0xffffdec04258 String contents address: 0xaaaac031baf0
```

Struct Copy

```
Struct Copy

let i: i32 = 0;

#[derive(Clone, Copy)]
struct MyStruct<'a> {
    field: &'a i32,
}

let my_struct: MyStruct = MyStruct { field: &i };

let my_struct2: MyStruct = my_struct;

assert_eq!(my_struct.field, my_struct2.field);
```

When we only need a bitwise shallow copy, we can derive the Copy trait for our structs. If fields contain addresses, they will be identical.

```
println!("--- Struct Copy ---");
{
    let i: i32 = 0;

    #[derive(Clone, Copy)]
    struct MyStruct<'a> {
        field: &'a i32,
    }

    let my_struct: MyStruct = MyStruct { field: &i };
    let my_struct2: MyStruct = my_struct;

    assert_eq!(my_struct.field, my_struct2.field);
    assert_eq!(my_struct.field as *const i32, my_struct2.field as *const i32);

    println!("address of my_struct: {:?} String contents address: {:p}",
addr_of!(my_struct),
        my_struct.field);
    println!("address of my_struct2: {:?} String contents address: {:p}",
addr_of!(my_struct2),
        my_struct2.field);
}
```

Windows output:

```
--- Struct Copy ---
address of my_struct: 0x562f2febd8 String contents address: 0x562f2febd4
address of my_struct2: 0x562f2febe0 String contents address: 0x562f2febd4
```

x64 Linux output:

```
--- Struct Copy ---
address of my_struct: 0x7ffd86cdd160 String contents address: 0x7ffd86cdd15c
address of my_struct2: 0x7ffd86cdd168 String contents address: 0x7ffd86cdd15c
```

A64 Linux output:

```
--- Struct Copy ---
address of my_struct: 0xffffdec043c0 String contents address: 0xffffdec043bc
address of my_struct2: 0xffffdec043c8 String contents address: 0xffffdec043bc
```

Parameters by Value

A few words about passing parameters. If we pass a value to a function parameter, the latter will take ownership if the Copy trait is not derived. Passing numeric values is efficient since they implement the Copy trait by default. However, passing instances of structs by value is not efficient since the copy is required.

```rust
println!("--- Parameters by Value ---");
{
    struct MyStruct {
        field: i32,
    }

    let my_struct: MyStruct = MyStruct { field: 0 };

    println!("address of my_struct: {:?}",
        addr_of!(my_struct));

    fn func (val: MyStruct) {
        println!("address of val: {:?}",
            addr_of!(val));
    }

    func(my_struct);
    // func(my_struct);

    #[derive(Clone, Copy)]
    struct MyStruct2 {
        field: i32,
```

```rust
    }

    let my_struct2: MyStruct2 = MyStruct2 { field: 0 };

    println!("address of my_struct2: {:?}",
        addr_of!(my_struct2));

    fn func2 (val: MyStruct2) {
        println!("address of val: {:?}",
            addr_of!(val));
    }

    func2(my_struct2);
    func2(my_struct2);

    #[derive(Clone)]
    struct MyStruct3 {
        field: i32,
    }

    let my_struct3: MyStruct3 = MyStruct3 { field: 0 };

    println!("address of my_struct3: {:?}",
        addr_of!(my_struct3));

    fn func3 (val: MyStruct3) {
        println!("address of val: {:?}",
            addr_of!(val));
    }

    func3(my_struct3.clone());
    func3(my_struct3.clone());
}
```

Windows output:

```
--- Parameters by Value ---
address of my_struct: 0x562f2fed14
address of val: 0x562f2fd7fc
address of my_struct2: 0x562f2fed64
address of val: 0x562f2fd7fc
address of val: 0x562f2fd7fc
address of my_struct3: 0x562f2fedb4
address of val: 0x562f2fd7fc
address of val: 0x562f2fd7fc
```

x64 Linux output:

```
--- Parameters by Value ---
address of my_struct: 0x7ffd86cdd29c
address of val: 0x7ffd86cdbaac
address of my_struct2: 0x7ffd86cdd2ec
address of val: 0x7ffd86cdbaac
address of val: 0x7ffd86cdbaac
address of my_struct3: 0x7ffd86cdd33c
address of val: 0x7ffd86cdbaac
address of val: 0x7ffd86cdbaac
```

A64 Linux output:

```
--- Parameters by Value ---
address of my_struct: 0xffffdec044fc
address of val: 0xffffdec02b24
address of my_struct2: 0xffffdec0454c
address of val: 0xffffdec02b24
address of val: 0xffffdec02b24
address of my_struct3: 0xffffdec0459c
address of val: 0xffffdec02b24
address of val: 0xffffdec02b24
```

Parameters by Ref/Ptr

If we need to modify the original mut value, we can pass it by mut reference. But this is not a good practice. Structs are more efficient to pass by reference or pointer since only their addresses need to be copied. Passing numeric values by reference may not be efficient since it involves taking their addresses and then dereferencing them inside functions.

```rust
println!("--- Parameters by Ref/Ptr ---");
{
    struct MyStruct {
        field: i32,
    }

    let my_struct: MyStruct = MyStruct { field: 0 };

    println!("address of my_struct: {:?}",
        addr_of!(my_struct));

    fn func (val_ref: &MyStruct) {
        println!("address of val_ref: {:?} value of val_ref {val_ref:p}",
addr_of!(val_ref));
    }

    func(&my_struct);
    func(&my_struct);

    fn func2 (val_ptr: *const MyStruct) {
        println!("address of val_ptr: {:?} value of val_ptr {val_ptr:p}",
addr_of!(val_ptr));
```

```
    }

    func2(&my_struct);
    func2(addr_of!(my_struct));
}
```

Windows output:

```
--- Parameters by Ref/Ptr ---
address of my_struct: 0x562f2fee34
address of val_ref: 0x562f2fd7c8 value of val_ref 0x562f2fee34
address of val_ref: 0x562f2fd7c8 value of val_ref 0x562f2fee34
address of val_ptr: 0x562f2fd7c8 value of val_ptr 0x562f2fee34
address of val_ptr: 0x562f2fd7c8 value of val_ptr 0x562f2fee34
```

x64 Linux output:

```
--- Parameters by Ref/Ptr ---
address of my_struct: 0x7ffd86cdd3bc
address of val_ref: 0x7ffd86cdba98 value of val_ref 0x7ffd86cdd3bc
address of val_ref: 0x7ffd86cdba98 value of val_ref 0x7ffd86cdd3bc
address of val_ptr: 0x7ffd86cdba98 value of val_ptr 0x7ffd86cdd3bc
address of val_ptr: 0x7ffd86cdba98 value of val_ptr 0x7ffd86cdd3bc
```

A64 Linux output:

```
--- Parameters by Ref/Ptr ---
address of my_struct: 0xffffdec0461c
address of val_ref: 0xffffdec02af0 value of val_ref 0xffffdec0461c
address of val_ref: 0xffffdec02af0 value of val_ref 0xffffdec0461c
address of val_ptr: 0xffffdec02af0 value of val_ptr 0xffffdec0461c
address of val_ptr: 0xffffdec02af0 value of val_ptr 0xffffdec0461c
```

self

```
self

struct MyStruct {
    field: i32,
}

impl MyStruct {
    fn func (&self, i: i32) {
    }
}

let my_struct: MyStruct = MyStruct { field: 0 };

my_struct.func(0);
MyStruct::func(&my_struct, 0);
```

A few words about self. It is implicitly passed if we use a struct instance for an associated function call. But we can also use an explicit type-associated call and specify a reference to self explicitly.

```
println!("--- self ---");
{
    struct MyStruct {
        field: i32,
    }

    impl MyStruct {
        fn func (&self, i: i32) {
            println!("address of self: {:?} value of self {self:p}",
addr_of!(self));
        }
    }

    let my_struct: MyStruct = MyStruct { field: 0 };

    println!("address of my_struct: {:?}",
        addr_of!(my_struct));

    my_struct.func(0);
    MyStruct::func(&my_struct, 0);
}
```

Windows output:

```
--- self ---
address of my_struct: 0x562f2feeb4
address of self: 0x562f2fd7c0 value of self 0x562f2feeb4
address of self: 0x562f2fd7c0 value of self 0x562f2feeb4
```

x64 Linux output:

```
--- self ---
address of my_struct: 0x7ffd86cdd43c
address of self: 0x7ffd86cdba90 value of self 0x7ffd86cdd43c
address of self: 0x7ffd86cdba90 value of self 0x7ffd86cdd43c
```

A64 Linux output:

```
--- self ---
address of my_struct: 0xffffdec0469c
address of self: 0xffffdec02ae8 value of self 0xffffdec0469c
address of self: 0xffffdec02ae8 value of self 0xffffdec0469c
```

Trait Objects as Parameters

When a trait object is passed as a parameter, the address of its implementation vtable is passed as a separate implicit parameter.

```rust
trait Base {
    fn method (i: i32) -> i32;
}

impl Base for Derived {
    fn method (i: i32) -> i32 { i }
}

let my_derived: Derived = Derived {};

fn foo(func: &dyn Base, i: i32) -> i32 {
    func.method(i)
}

foo(&my_derived, /* address of vtable, */ 1);
```

© 2025 Software Diagnostics Services

```rust
println!("--- Trait Objects as Parameters ---");
{
    trait Base {
        fn method (&self, i: i32) -> i32;
    }

    struct Derived {}

    impl Base for Derived {
        fn method (&self, i: i32) -> i32 { i }
    }

    let my_derived: Derived = Derived {};

    fn foo(func: &dyn Base, i: i32) -> i32 {
        func.method(i)
    }

    foo(&my_derived, 1);
}
```

Struct as Return Value

```rust
Struct as Return Value

struct MyStruct {
    field1: u64,
    field2: u64,
    field3: u64,
}

fn foo(param: u64) -> MyStruct {
    MyStruct { ... }
}

let my_struct: MyStruct =
    foo(/* address to copy the returned struct,*/ 5);
```

© 2025 Software Diagnostics Services

Finally, a few words about structs as return values. If a struct is allocated on the stack inside a function, we cannot return its address in RAX or X0 since it is a local value that is invalid outside the function scope. Instead, we need to assign its field values to some external memory in the outer scope. Such a memory address is implicitly passed as the first function parameter and, also returned in RAX or X0.

```
println!("--- Struct as Return Value ---");
{
    struct MyStruct {
        field1: u64,
        field2: u64,
        field3: u64,
        field4: u64,
    }

    fn foo(param: u64) -> MyStruct {
        MyStruct { field1: 1, field2: 2, field3: 3, field4: 4 }
    }

    let my_struct: MyStruct = foo(5);
}
```

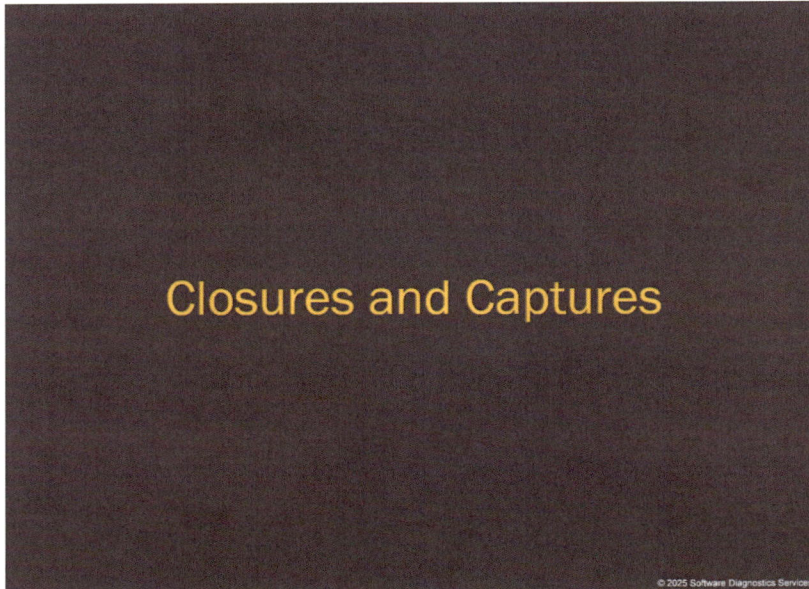

Closures and Captures

© 2025 Software Diagnostics Services

Closures are intersections between functions and structs, as we will see in the following slides.

The `closures` project can be found in the archive[17]. In the following slide descriptions, we only show relevant code snippets and their output on various platforms.

---

[17] https://www.patterndiagnostics.com/Training/MTRust/MTRust.zip

Closure Struct

```
struct closures::main::closure$0 // closures::main::{{closure}}
{
}

let negate = |x: i32| -x;
negate(10);

// Windows
mov      dword ptr [rsp+64h],0Ah
mov      edx,dword ptr [rsp+64h]
lea      rcx,[rsp+63h]
call     closures::main::closure$0

// Linux (x64)
movl     $0xa,0x3c(%rsp)
mov      0x3c(%rsp),%esi
lea      0x38(%rsp),%rdi
callq    <closures::main::{{closure}}>
```

© 2025 Software Diagnostics Services

While outside, a closure appears just as a function; it is implemented internally as a struct with an associated function. In disassembly, we can see that an address of the struct is passed as a first &self parameter.

```
println!("--- Closure Struct ---");
{
    let negate = |x: i32| -x;
    negate(10);

    println!("address of negate closure struct: {:?}", addr_of!(negate));
}
```

Windows output:

```
--- Closure Struct ---
address of negate closure struct: 0x120e8ff7c3
```

x64 Linux output:

```
--- Closure Struct ---
address of negate closure struct: 0x7fff55076de0
```

A64 Linux output:

```
--- Closure Struct ---
address of negate closure struct: 0xffffeafd490b
```

A64 Closure Struct Example

```
A64 Closure Struct Example

struct closures::main::{{closure}}
{
}

let negate = |x: i32| -x;
negate(10);

// Linux (arm64)
mov     w8, #0xa
str     w8, [sp, #100]
ldr     w1, [sp, #100]
add     x0, sp, #0x63
bl      <closures::main::{{closure}}>
```

This is another disassembly example but from arm64 Linux.

Captures (Borrowing)

```
Captures (Borrowing)

struct closures::main::closure$1
{
        ref_b: &i32,
}

let b: i32 = 0;
let negate = |x: i32| b-x;
negate(10);

// x64 Windows
mov     dword ptr [rsp+144h],0
lea     rax,[rsp+144h]
mov     qword ptr [rsp+148h],rax
mov     dword ptr [rsp+154h],0Ah
mov     edx,dword ptr [rsp+154h]
lea     rcx,[rsp+148h]
call    closures!closures::main::closure$1
```

Since a closure is implemented as a struct with an associated function, references to captured values are simply struct fields. That an address of the value is stored inside a struct can be seen in this x64 Windows disassembly.

Captures (Borrowing) x64 Linux

Here is the same code, but the disassembly is from x64 Linux.

```rust
println!("--- Captures (Borrowing) ---");
{
    let b: i32 = 0;

    let negate = |x: i32| b-x;
    negate(10);

    unsafe {
        println!("address of b: {:?} address of negate closure struct: {:?}, struct
value: {:?}",
            addr_of!(b), addr_of!(negate),
            *(addr_of!(negate) as *const *const i32));
    }
}
```

Windows output:

```
--- Captures (Borrowing) ---
address of b: 0x120e8ff844 address of negate closure struct: 0x120e8ff848, struct
value: 0x120e8ff844
```

x64 Linux output:

```
--- Captures (Borrowing) ---
address of b: 0x7fff55076e64 address of negate closure struct: 0x7fff55076e68, struct
value: 0x7fff55076e64
```

A64 Linux output:

```
--- Captures (Borrowing) ---
address of b: 0xffffeafd498c address of negate closure struct: 0xffffeafd4990, struct
value: 0xffffeafd498c
```

Captures (Move)

When we have move capture, the values are moved to closure struct, as can be seen in this x64 Windows disassembly.

Captures (Move) x64 Linux

Here is the same disassembly example but from x64 Linux.

```rust
println!("--- Captures (Move) ---");
{
    let b: i32 = 0;

    let negate = move |x: i32| b-x;
    negate(10);

     unsafe {
         println!("address of b: {:?} address of negate closure struct: {:?}, struct value: {:?}",
             addr_of!(b), addr_of!(negate),
             *(addr_of!(negate) as *const i32));
     }
}
```

Windows output:

```
--- Captures (Move) ---
address of b: 0x120e8ff8fc address of negate closure struct: 0x120e8ff900, struct
value: 0
```

x64 Linux output:

```
--- Captures (Move) ---
address of b: 0x7fff55076f1c address of negate closure struct: 0x7fff55076f20, struct
value: 0
```

A64 Linux output:

```
--- Captures (Move) ---
address of b: 0xffffeafd4a44 address of negate closure struct: 0xffffeafd4a48, struct
value: 7
```

Smart Pointers

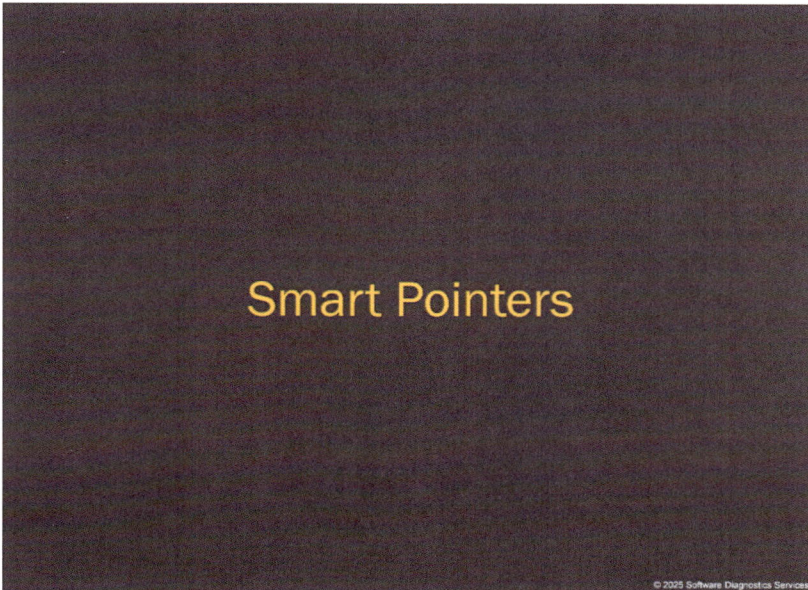

Smart pointers are needed to overcome strict ownership and borrowing rules of ordinary pointers and references.

The smart-pointers project can be found in the archive[18]. In the following slide descriptions, we only show relevant code snippets and their output on various platforms.

---

[18] https://www.patterndiagnostics.com/Training/MTRust/MTRust.zip

Why Smart Pointers?

The purpose of smart pointers is to automate memory management, for example, to release memory when a pointer goes out-of-scope. Ordinary (non-smart) pointers and references contain the address of a value without owning it, thus having separate lifetimes. A value can be owned by only one smart pointer, the so-called single ownership, or it can be owned by several smart pointers, the so-called shared ownership. When such smart pointers go out of scope one by one, a non-zero reference count keeps the value alive. Smart pointers with interior mutability allow a mutable shared state between different threads or when we occasionally need to mutate some substructure while having references to generally immutable values.

Types of Smart Pointers

A value can only be owned by a single Box<T> or RefCell<T>. The latter smart pointer type allows interior mutation on demand. If we want a value to be owned by several smart pointers while having a reference count, we should use Rc<T> (for single-threaded code) and Arc<T> (for multi-threaded code). In the latter case, a reference count is protected for simultaneous thread access.

Interior Immutable Single Owner

With Box<T>, we can only mutate a value when it is explicitly declared mutable.

```
println!("--- Interior Immutable Single Owner ---");
{
    let so: Box<i32> = Box::new(0);

    println!("address of so: {:?} address of heap allocation: {so:p} value of heap
allocation {}", addr_of!(so), so);

    let mut mso: Box<i32> = Box::new(0);

    println!("address of mso: {:?} address of heap allocation: {mso:p} value of heap
allocation {}", addr_of!(mso), mso);

    *mso += 1;

    println!("address of mso: {:?} address of heap allocation: {mso:p} value of heap
allocation {}", addr_of!(mso), mso);
}
```

Windows output:

```
--- Interior Immutable Single Owner ---
address of so: 0x529e8fd888 address of heap allocation: 0x1b97621a6d0 value of heap
allocation 0
address of mso: 0x529e8fd948 address of heap allocation: 0x1b976226c20 value of heap
allocation 0
address of mso: 0x529e8fd948 address of heap allocation: 0x1b976226c20 value of heap
allocation 1
```

x64 Linux output:

```
--- Interior Immutable Single Owner ---
address of so: 0x7ffe89f04998 address of heap allocation: 0x55f59d230a50 value of
heap allocation 0
address of mso: 0x7ffe89f04a58 address of heap allocation: 0x55f59d230a70 value of
heap allocation 0
address of mso: 0x7ffe89f04a58 address of heap allocation: 0x55f59d230a70 value of
heap allocation 1
```

A64 Linux output:

```
--- Interior Immutable Single Owner ---
address of so: 0xffffdd8c46f8 address of heap allocation: 0xaf99fef8cb10 value of
heap allocation 0
address of mso: 0xffffdd8c47b8 address of heap allocation: 0xaf99fef8cb30 value of
heap allocation 0
address of mso: 0xffffdd8c47b8 address of heap allocation: 0xaf99fef8cb30 value of
heap allocation 1
```

Interior Mutable Single Ownership

With RefCell<T>, we can borrow mutable references at runtime. Compared to Box<T>, if used alone, it stores the value on a stack.

```
println!("--- Interior Mutable Single Ownership ---");
{
    let imso: RefCell<i32> = RefCell::new(0);

    unsafe {
        println!("address of imso: {:?} address of value: {:p} value {} value from
pointer {}",
            addr_of!(imso), imso.as_ptr(), *imso.borrow(), *imso.as_ptr());
    }

    *imso.borrow_mut() += 1;

    unsafe {
        println!("address of imso: {:?} address of value: {:p} value {} value from
pointer {}",
            addr_of!(imso), imso.as_ptr(), *imso.borrow(), *imso.as_ptr());
    }

    let imso: Box<RefCell<i32>> = Box::new(RefCell::new(0));

    unsafe {
```

```rust
        println!("address of imso: {:?} address of heap allocation {:p} address of
value: {:p} value {} value from pointer {}",
            addr_of!(imso), *addr_of!(imso), imso.as_ptr(), *imso.borrow(),
*imso.as_ptr());
    }

    *imso.borrow_mut() += 1;

    unsafe {
        println!("address of imso: {:?} address of heap allocation {:p} address of
value: {:p} value {} value from pointer {}",
            addr_of!(imso), *addr_of!(imso), imso.as_ptr(), *imso.borrow(),
*imso.as_ptr());
    }

    let imso: RefCell<Box<i32>> = RefCell::new(Box::new(0));

    unsafe {
        println!("address of imso: {:?} address of RefCell value: {:p} Box address
{:p} Box value {} value {}",
            addr_of!(imso), imso.as_ptr(), *(imso.as_ptr() as *const Box<i32>),
            **(imso.as_ptr() as *const Box<i32>), *imso.borrow());
    }

    *imso.borrow_mut() = Box::new(1);

    unsafe {
        println!("address of imso: {:?} address of RefCell value: {:p} Box address
{:p} Box value {} value {}",
            addr_of!(imso), imso.as_ptr(), *(imso.as_ptr() as *const Box<i32>),
            **(imso.as_ptr() as *const Box<i32>), *imso.borrow());
    }

    let imso: RefCell<Box<RefCell<i32>>> = RefCell::new(Box::new(RefCell::new(0)));

    unsafe {
        println!("address of imso: {:?} address of RefCell value: {:p} Box address
{:p} Box value {:?} value {}",
            addr_of!(imso), imso.as_ptr(), *(imso.as_ptr() as *const Box<Ref-
Cell<i32>>),
            **(imso.as_ptr() as *const Box<RefCell<i32>>), *imso.borrow().borrow());
    }
```

```
    *imso.borrow().borrow_mut() += 1;

    unsafe {
        println!("address of imso: {:?} address of RefCell value: {:p} Box address
{:p} Box value {:?} value {}",
            addr_of!(imso), imso.as_ptr(), *(imso.as_ptr() as *const Box<Ref-
Cell<i32>>),
            **(imso.as_ptr() as *const Box<RefCell<i32>>), *imso.borrow().borrow());
    }
}
```

Windows output:

```
--- Interior Mutable Single Ownership ---
address of imso: 0x529e8fdae0 address of value: 0x529e8fdae8 value 0 value from
pointer 0
address of imso: 0x529e8fdae0 address of value: 0x529e8fdae8 value 1 value from
pointer 1
address of imso: 0x529e8fdcc8 address of heap allocation 0x1b976222ff0 address of
value: 0x1b976222ff8 value 0 value from pointer 0
address of imso: 0x529e8fdcc8 address of heap allocation 0x1b976222ff0 address of
value: 0x1b976222ff8 value 1 value from pointer 1
address of imso: 0x529e8fdee0 address of RefCell value: 0x529e8fdee8 Box address
0x1b97621a6d0 Box value 0 value 0
address of imso: 0x529e8fdee0 address of RefCell value: 0x529e8fdee8 Box address
0x1b976226c20 Box value 1 value 1
address of imso: 0x529e8fe110 address of RefCell value: 0x529e8fe118 Box address
0x1b976222f90 Box value RefCell { value: 0 } value 0
address of imso: 0x529e8fe110 address of RefCell value: 0x529e8fe118 Box address
0x1b976222f90 Box value RefCell { value: 1 } value 1
```

x64 Linux output:

```
--- Interior Mutable Single Ownership ---
address of imso: 0x7ffe89f04bf0 address of value: 0x7ffe89f04bf8 value 0 value from
pointer 0
address of imso: 0x7ffe89f04bf0 address of value: 0x7ffe89f04bf8 value 1 value from
pointer 1
address of imso: 0x7ffe89f04dc8 address of heap allocation 0x55f59d230a50 address of
value: 0x55f59d230a58 value 0 value from pointer 0
address of imso: 0x7ffe89f04dc8 address of heap allocation 0x55f59d230a50 address of
value: 0x55f59d230a58 value 1 value from pointer 1
address of imso: 0x7ffe89f04fc0 address of RefCell value: 0x7ffe89f04fc8 Box address
0x55f59d230a70 Box value 0 value 0
address of imso: 0x7ffe89f04fc0 address of RefCell value: 0x7ffe89f04fc8 Box address
0x55f59d230a90 Box value 1 value 1
address of imso: 0x7ffe89f051d0 address of RefCell value: 0x7ffe89f051d8 Box address
0x55f59d230a70 Box value RefCell { value: 0 } value 0
address of imso: 0x7ffe89f051d0 address of RefCell value: 0x7ffe89f051d8 Box address
0x55f59d230a70 Box value RefCell { value: 1 } value 1
```

A64 Linux output:

```
--- Interior Mutable Single Ownership ---
address of imso: 0xffffdd8c4950 address of value: 0xffffdd8c4958 value 0 value from
pointer 0
address of imso: 0xffffdd8c4950 address of value: 0xffffdd8c4958 value 1 value from
pointer 1
address of imso: 0xffffdd8c4b38 address of heap allocation 0xaf99fef8cb10 address of
value: 0xaf99fef8cb18 value 0 value from pointer 0
address of imso: 0xffffdd8c4b38 address of heap allocation 0xaf99fef8cb10 address of
value: 0xaf99fef8cb18 value 1 value from pointer 1
address of imso: 0xffffdd8c4d50 address of RefCell value: 0xffffdd8c4d58 Box address
0xaf99fef8cb30 Box value 0 value 0
address of imso: 0xffffdd8c4d50 address of RefCell value: 0xffffdd8c4d58 Box address
0xaf99fef8cb50 Box value 1 value 1
address of imso: 0xffffdd8c4f80 address of RefCell value: 0xffffdd8c4f88 Box address
0xaf99fef8cb30 Box value RefCell { value: 0 } value 0
address of imso: 0xffffdd8c4f80 address of RefCell value: 0xffffdd8c4f88 Box address
0xaf99fef8cb30 Box value RefCell { value: 1 } value 1
```

Shared Ownership

Rc<T> (and Arc<T>) is similar to Box<T> but with a reference count. It is also possible to have interior mutability when combined with RefCell.

```
println!("--- Shared Ownership ---");
{
    let rc: Rc<i32> = Rc::new(0);

    println!("address of rc: {:?} address of value: {rc:p} value {}", addr_of!(rc),
rc);

    unsafe {
        println!("address of reference count {:p} value of reference count {} from
pointer {}",
            *(addr_of!(rc) as *const *const usize), Rc::strong_count(&rc),
            **(addr_of!(rc) as *const *const usize));
    }

    let rc2: Rc<i32> = Rc::clone(&rc);

    println!("address of rc2: {:?} address of value: {rc2:p} value {}",
addr_of!(rc2), rc2);

    unsafe {
```

```
            println!("value of reference count {} from pointer {}",
Rc::strong_count(&rc2),
                **(addr_of!(rc2) as *const *const usize));
    }


    fn foo(param: Rc<i32>) {
        println!("foo: address of param: {:?} address of value: {param:p} value  {}",
addr_of!(param), param);

        unsafe {
            println!("foo: value of reference count {} from pointer {}",
Rc::strong_count(&param),
                **(addr_of!(param) as *const *const usize));
        }
    }

    foo(Rc::clone(&rc2));

    unsafe {
        println!("value of reference count {} from pointer {}",
Rc::strong_count(&rc),
            **(addr_of!(rc) as *const *const usize));
    }

    foo(rc2);

    unsafe {
        println!("value of reference count {} from pointer {}",
Rc::strong_count(&rc),
            **(addr_of!(rc) as *const *const usize));
    }

    // foo(rc2);
    foo(rc);
    // foo(rc);

    let imrc: Rc<RefCell<i32>> = Rc::new(RefCell::new(0));

    println!("address of imrc: {:?} address of value: {imrc:p} value {:?}",
addr_of!(imrc), imrc);

    unsafe {
```

```
        println!("address of reference count {:p} value of reference count {} from
pointer {}",
            *(addr_of!(imrc) as *const *const usize), Rc::strong_count(&imrc),
            **(addr_of!(imrc) as *const *const usize));
    }

    let imrc2: Rc<RefCell<i32>> = Rc::clone(&imrc);

    *imrc2.borrow_mut() += 1;

    println!("address of imrc: {:?} address of value: {imrc:p} value {:?}",
addr_of!(imrc), imrc);

    unsafe {
        println!("address of reference count {:p} value of reference count {} from
pointer {}",
            *(addr_of!(imrc) as *const *const usize), Rc::strong_count(&imrc),
            **(addr_of!(imrc) as *const *const usize));
    }
}
```

Windows output:

```
--- Shared Ownership ---
address of rc: 0x529e8fe398 address of value: 0x1b976222e80 value 0
address of reference count 0x1b976222e70 value of reference count 1 from pointer 1
address of rc2: 0x529e8fe4f8 address of value: 0x1b976222e80 value 0
value of reference count 2 from pointer 2
foo: address of param: 0x529e8fd2f8 address of value: 0x1b976222e80 value  0
foo: value of reference count 3 from pointer 3
value of reference count 2 from pointer 2
foo: address of param: 0x529e8fd2f8 address of value: 0x1b976222e80 value  0
foo: value of reference count 2 from pointer 2
value of reference count 1 from pointer 1
foo: address of param: 0x529e8fd2f8 address of value: 0x1b976222e80 value  0
foo: value of reference count 1 from pointer 1
address of imrc: 0x529e8fe738 address of value: 0x1b976223be0 value RefCell { value:
0 }
address of reference count 0x1b976223bd0 value of reference count 1 from pointer 1
address of imrc: 0x529e8fe738 address of value: 0x1b976223be0 value RefCell { value:
1 }
address of reference count 0x1b976223bd0 value of reference count 2 from pointer 2
```

x64 Linux output:

```
--- Shared Ownership ---
address of rc: 0x7ffe89f05438 address of value: 0x55f59d230a60 value 0
address of reference count 0x55f59d230a50 value of reference count 1 from pointer 1
address of rc2: 0x7ffe89f05588 address of value: 0x55f59d230a60 value 0
value of reference count 2 from pointer 2
foo: address of param: 0x7ffe89f043e8 address of value: 0x55f59d230a60 value  0
foo: value of reference count 3 from pointer 3
value of reference count 2 from pointer 2
foo: address of param: 0x7ffe89f043e8 address of value: 0x55f59d230a60 value  0
foo: value of reference count 2 from pointer 2
value of reference count 1 from pointer 1
foo: address of param: 0x7ffe89f043e8 address of value: 0x55f59d230a60 value  0
foo: value of reference count 1 from pointer 1
address of imrc: 0x7ffe89f057b8 address of value: 0x55f59d230a30 value RefCell {
value: 0 }
address of reference count 0x55f59d230a20 value of reference count 1 from pointer 1
address of imrc: 0x7ffe89f057b8 address of value: 0x55f59d230a30 value RefCell {
value: 1 }
address of reference count 0x55f59d230a20 value of reference count 2 from pointer 2
```

A64 Linux output:

```
--- Shared Ownership ---
address of rc: 0xffffdd8c5208 address of value: 0xaf99fef8cb20 value 0
address of reference count 0xaf99fef8cb10 value of reference count 1 from pointer 1
address of rc2: 0xffffdd8c5368 address of value: 0xaf99fef8cb20 value 0
value of reference count 2 from pointer 2
foo: address of param: 0xffffdd8c4118 address of value: 0xaf99fef8cb20 value  0
foo: value of reference count 3 from pointer 3
value of reference count 2 from pointer 2
foo: address of param: 0xffffdd8c4118 address of value: 0xaf99fef8cb20 value  0
foo: value of reference count 2 from pointer 2
value of reference count 1 from pointer 1
foo: address of param: 0xffffdd8c4118 address of value: 0xaf99fef8cb20 value  0
foo: value of reference count 1 from pointer 1
address of imrc: 0xffffdd8c55a8 address of value: 0xaf99fef8caf0 value RefCell {
value: 0 }
address of reference count 0xaf99fef8cae0 value of reference count 1 from pointer 1
address of imrc: 0xffffdd8c55a8 address of value: 0xaf99fef8caf0 value RefCell {
value: 1 }
address of reference count 0xaf99fef8cae0 value of reference count 2 from pointer 2
```

Pinning

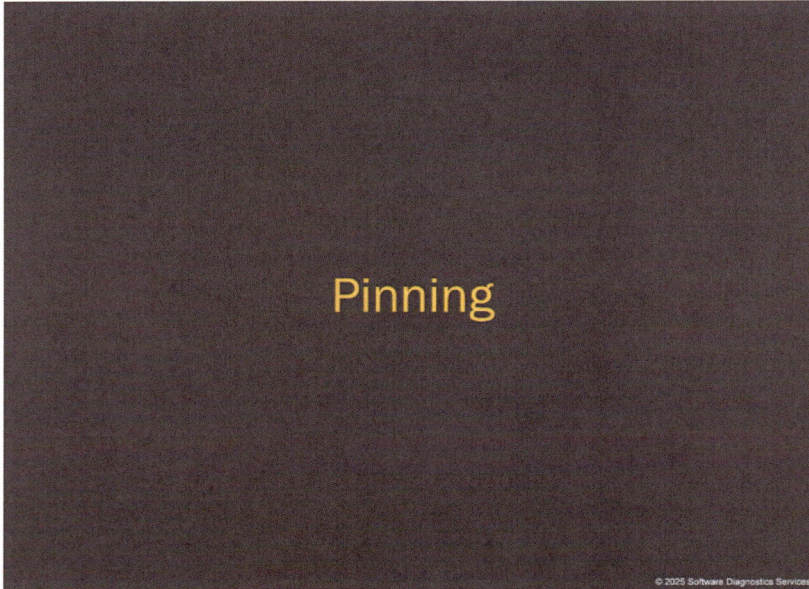

The `pinning` project can be found in the archive[19]. In the following slide descriptions, we only show relevant code snippets and their output on various platforms.

---

[19] https://www.patterndiagnostics.com/Training/MTRust/MTRust.zip

Use Cases

Rust works with values and may move them in complex scenarios. If structs contain pointers or references, these unanticipated moves may invalidate them. In this final part, we only look at the case of self-reference and see how struct value move may result in abnormal behavior. First, we see the problems with moving stack-based self-referencing structures. Next, we model such moves using heap-based boxed structs. Finally, we see how we can indicate to Rust that movement is forbidden.

```rust
println!("--- No Pinning for Stack ---");
{
    struct MyStruct {
        self_ptr: *const MyStruct,
    }

    impl MyStruct {
        fn new() -> Self {
            MyStruct {
                self_ptr: std::ptr::null(),
            }
        }

        fn println(&self) {
            println!("address of self: {self:p} value of self_ptr: {:p}",
self.self_ptr);
        }
    }

    let mut my_struct: MyStruct = MyStruct::new();
    my_struct.self_ptr = addr_of!(my_struct);
```

```
        println!("address of my_struct: {:?}",
            addr_of!(my_struct));

    my_struct.println();

    let my_struct2: MyStruct = my_struct;

    my_struct2.println();
}

println!("--- No Pinning for Box ---");
{
    struct MyStruct {
        self_ptr: *const MyStruct,
    }

    impl MyStruct {
        fn new() -> Box<Self> {
            let mut boxed: Box<MyStruct> =
                Box::new(MyStruct {
                    self_ptr: std::ptr::null(),
                });

            boxed.self_ptr =
                &*boxed as *const MyStruct;

            boxed
        }

        fn println(&self) {
            println!("address of self: {self:p} value of self_ptr: {:p}",
self.self_ptr);
        }
    }

    let my_struct: Box<MyStruct> = MyStruct::new();

    println!("address of my_struct: {:?}",
        addr_of!(my_struct));

    my_struct.println();
```

```rust
    // simulation of reallocation
    let my_struct2: Box<MyStruct> =
        Box::new(*my_struct);

    my_struct2.println();
}


println!("--- Pinning ---");
{
    use std::pin::Pin;
    use std::marker::PhantomPinned;

    struct MyStruct {
        self_ptr: *const MyStruct,
        _pin: PhantomPinned,
    }

    impl MyStruct {
        fn new() -> Pin<Box<Self>> {
            let mut boxed: Pin<Box<Self>> =
                Box::pin(MyStruct {
                    self_ptr: std::ptr::null(),
                    _pin: PhantomPinned,
                });

            let self_ptr: *const MyStruct =
                &*boxed as *const MyStruct;

            unsafe {
                let mut_ref: Pin<&mut Self> =
                    Pin::as_mut(&mut boxed);
                Pin::get_unchecked_mut(mut_ref).self_ptr = self_ptr;
            }

            boxed
        }

        fn println(&self) {
            println!("address of self: {self:p} value of self_ptr: {:p}",
self.self_ptr);
        }
    }
```

```rust
    let my_struct: Pin<Box<MyStruct>> =
        MyStruct::new();

    println!("address of my_struct: {:?}",
        addr_of!(my_struct));

    my_struct.println();

    // simulation of no reallocation
    let my_struct2: Pin<Box<MyStruct>> = my_struct;

    my_struct2.println();
}
```

Windows output:

```
--- No Pinning for Stack ---
address of my_struct: 0x5149cff680
address of self: 0x5149cff680 value of self_ptr: 0x5149cff680
address of self: 0x5149cff6d0 value of self_ptr: 0x5149cff680
--- No Pinning for Box ---
address of my_struct: 0x5149cff708
address of self: 0x167e6ccbea0 value of self_ptr: 0x167e6ccbea0
address of self: 0x167e6ccbec0 value of self_ptr: 0x167e6ccbea0
--- Pinning ---
address of my_struct: 0x5149cff790
address of self: 0x167e6ccbea0 value of self_ptr: 0x167e6ccbea0
address of self: 0x167e6ccbea0 value of self_ptr: 0x167e6ccbea0
```

x64 Linux output:

```
--- No Pinning for Stack ---
address of my_struct: 0x7ffe53ed3ca0
address of self: 0x7ffe53ed3ca0 value of self_ptr: 0x7ffe53ed3ca0
address of self: 0x7ffe53ed3cf0 value of self_ptr: 0x7ffe53ed3ca0
--- No Pinning for Box ---
address of my_struct: 0x7ffe53ed3d28
address of self: 0x561e96be49e0 value of self_ptr: 0x561e96be49e0
address of self: 0x561e96be4a00 value of self_ptr: 0x561e96be49e0
--- Pinning ---
address of my_struct: 0x7ffe53ed3db0
address of self: 0x561e96be49e0 value of self_ptr: 0x561e96be49e0
address of self: 0x561e96be49e0 value of self_ptr: 0x561e96be49e0
```

A64 Linux output:

```
--- No Pinning for Stack ---
address of my_struct: 0xffffc58b7258
address of self: 0xffffc58b7258 value of self_ptr: 0xffffc58b7258
address of self: 0xffffc58b72a8 value of self_ptr: 0xffffc58b7258
--- No Pinning for Box ---
address of my_struct: 0xffffc58b72e0
address of self: 0xaaab1dcbead0 value of self_ptr: 0xaaab1dcbead0
address of self: 0xaaab1dcbeaf0 value of self_ptr: 0xaaab1dcbead0
--- Pinning ---
address of my_struct: 0xffffc58b7368
address of self: 0xaaab1dcbead0 value of self_ptr: 0xaaab1dcbead0
address of self: 0xaaab1dcbead0 value of self_ptr: 0xaaab1dcbead0
```

Rust Books

Rust Books

- Programming Rust: Fast, Safe Systems Development, Revised 2nd Edition

- Rust for Rustaceans: Idiomatic Programming for Experienced Developers

- Rust Atomics and Locks: Low-Level Concurrency in Practice

- Code Like a Pro in Rust

- Asynchronous Programming in Rust: Learn asynchronous programming by building working examples of futures, green threads, and runtimes

- Effective Rust: 35 Specific Ways to Improve Your Rust Code

- Rust under the Hood: A deep dive into Rust internals and generated assembly

When preparing for this training, in addition to online and compiler documentation and help, I used the following books as a reference. The first one is highly recommended as it also contains memory implementation topics, albeit abstracted from OS differences.

www.ingramcontent.com/pod-product-compliance
Lightning Source LLC
Chambersburg PA
CBRC091940210326
41598CB00013B/871